Alexander Robb

The Gospel to the Africans

Alexander Robb

The Gospel to the Africans

ISBN/EAN: 9783743383630

Manufactured in Europe, USA, Canada, Australia, Japa

Cover: Foto ©ninafisch / pixelio.de

Manufactured and distributed by brebook publishing software (www.brebook.com)

Alexander Robb

The Gospel to the Africans

HE GOSPEL TO THE AFRICANS

A NARRATIVE OF THE LIFE AND LABOURS OF

THE REV. WILLIAM JAMESON

IN JAMAICA AND OLD CALABAR.

BY HIS SON-IN-LAW,

THE REV. ALEX. ROBB, A.M.,

MISSIONARY AT OLD CALABAR.

The Missionary School and Graves at Creek Town, Old Calabar.

SECOND EDITION.

EDINBURGH: ANDREW ELLIOT, PRINCES STREET.

LONDON: HAMILTON, ADAMS, & CO.

TO

THE ROSE STREET UNITED PRESBYTERIAN CHURCH

AND TO

THE GOSHEN MISSION CHURCH

THIS MEMORIAL

OF THE LIFE AND LABOURS OF THEIR

FIRST FOREIGN MISSIONARY AND PASTOR

IS INSCRIBED BY

THE AUTHOR.

PREFACE.

THE documents from which this Volume has been compiled, were read and arranged by the Reverend R. S. Scott, M.A., of Manchester, soon after Mr. Jameson's death, with the purpose of preparing a Memoir; but for reasons which it is unnecessary to state, this purpose was not carried into effect. Mr. Scott, however, wrote a succinct narrative of Mr. Jameson's Life and Labours, which appeared in the *Scottish Christian Journal*. From that narrative the Author of this Memoir has obtained valuable aid, which he begs thus gratefully to acknowledge.

These documents consist of Letters, Journals, and Reports, which were addressed to the Rose Street Missionary Society, and to the Secretary of the Mission Board of the United Presbyterian Church. Those addressed to the Rose Street Society were read at their meetings ; and interesting portions of them were printed in the Yearly Reports of the Rose Street Congregation. Large portions of those addressed to Dr. Somerville were given in various numbers of the *Missionary Record* for 1847 and 1848. To have introduced these into this Volume would have increased its size beyond what was thought proper ; and it was not needful, inasmuch as the *Record*, with its stores of interesting missionary information, is, or should be, in the hands of every family in the United Presbyterian Church. Many of the most characteristic and touching letters in the Memoir were obtained from private friends.

The Author has not considered it necessary to give the documents in full, but has exercised his best judgment in selecting what appeared to be at once interesting and useful.   Neither has he given those selections word for word.   Mr. Jameson, like many other missionaries, wrote amid labours of an engrossing kind, and therefore hastily, pouring out his thoughts and feelings with great rapidity.   A little liberty has, therefore, been taken with the selections; and, in a few cases, where two or more letters referred to the same subject, and one contained statements which were not found in another, these have been put together, making the narrative fuller.   Repetition has, as much as possible, been avoided, but some instances of this may have escaped notice.

This Memoir is a contribution to the story of Emancipation —that never-to-be-forgotten passage in the history of Great Britain.   Memoirs of West India missionaries are important, and invaluable in this connexion.   The faithful men who were missioned by the churches to evangelize the victims of avarice and oppression have a right to be heard.   Indeed, their evidence will one day be considered the only evidence that should be trusted.

The Portrait is considered to be a very good likeness. The Vignette, showing the mission burying-ground, and the wood-cuts, the first of which exhibits a splendid stretch of the Old Calabar river, as seen from Old Town, and the second, the scene from Creek Town Mission House, are very good representations of African scenery.   They have been made from sketches taken on the spot by Mrs. Robb.

ANNAN, *December* 2, 1861.

CONTENTS.

CHAPTER I.

CHAPTER VI.

CHAPTER VII.

CHAPTER VIII.

CHAPTER IX.

CHAPTER X.

MEMOIR OF REV. WILLIAM JAMESON.

CHAPTER I.

His birth—Ancestry—Father—Childhood's promise—Early sense of religion—
The schoolboy—The student, at the University; at the Divinity Hall—The city-
missionary—The probationer—Prefers missionary work—At Firth. Called to
Jamaica—Ordained—Married—The farewell soirée.

THE subject of this Memoir lived so loving and useful a life
that he was greatly missed when he died. He was missed in
every sphere through which his course led him : in Orkney,
in Jamaica, in Old Calabar, in the circle of his friends. In
each he was greatly loved and leaned on ; and severe was the
wrench that affection suffered when he was taken away.

The best improvement that survivors in the field of labour
and of conflict can make of the death of an honoured and
zealous servant of God, is to believe and work like him. William Jameson, being dead, yet speaketh to missionaries; to
those still living whom he taught publicly, and from house to
house ; and, not less, to all who may become acquainted with
his singularly affectionate, pious, and devoted character.

He was born at Methven, in Perthshire, on the 27th of
December, 1807. As he came of a godly race—of men honoured
in the history of the cause of God in Scotland—a few notices
of some of his ancestors will, we doubt not, interest the reader.
Margaret Pringle, his mother, was a daughter of the Rev. Dr.

Pringle of Perth and Jane Moncrieff, one of the children of the Rev. Alexander Moncrieff of Culfargie, minister of the parish of Abernethy. His father, the Rev. John Jameson of Methven, was the son of the Rev. William Jameson of Kilwinning and Mary Wilson, youngest daughter of the Rev. William Wilson, minister in Perth. He was thus a great-grandson, by the mother's side, of one, and, by the father's side, of another of the honoured fathers of the first Secession. The late Rev. Dr. John Brown of Edinburgh, whose name will be long fragrant in the Church of Jesus Christ, once said, in his own emphatic and kindly manner, to the only daughter of the subject of this Memoir: " Your father is in heaven, your grandfather is in heaven, your great-grandfathers are in heaven, and your great-great-grandfathers are in heaven ; see that you lose not your honourable inheritance."

In the published " Remains of the late Rev. John Jameson of Methven," there is a passage like the above. In a letter to his son Alexander, March 12th, 1830, referring to the Memoir of the Rev. William Wilson, A.M., by the Rev. Andrew Ferrier, and which had been newly published, he says : " It would do you good to have the Memoir by you, and to read in it daily, how one with whom you are so nearly connected, lived with God. He prayed much, and much for his children, and we who are his children's children, have come into his prayers. My dear A., when the Memoir is put into the bookseller's window, let some one who knows, have to point to you, with honourable respect, saying, ' And there goes one of his descendants, and, by the grace of God, not unlike him.' In Glasgow, your own grandfather preached Christ ; and your great-grandfather and his father were men of God, and witnesses for his cause. I did not know, before perusing this Memoir, that we were connected, by Mr. Wilson's mother, with Mr. James Guthrie, who suffered martyrdom, in the reign of Charles II., at the cross of Edinburgh. Our little family is compassed about with a cloud of witnesses."

The father of William Wilson was Gilbert Wilson, who possessed a small estate near East Kilbride, in Lanarkshire.

Being a zealous Presbyterian, he was persecuted during the reign of the second Charles. The authorities deprived him of his heritable property, and sold his moveables at the cross of Glasgow. Mearns Muir, an extensive moorland in that district, was his hiding-place for a whole winter. At length, he escaped to Holland, where he found an asylum, until he returned with the Prince of Orange in 1688. His estate was not restored to him ; but, as some compensation for his losses, he was, at length, appointed comptroller of the customs at Greenock. Such was William Wilson's father.

His mother, Isabella Ramsay, was the eldest daughter of Mr. Ramsay of Shielhill, a gentleman of property, near Kirrie-muir in Forfarshire. Mr. Ramsay was an Episcopalian, and a keen supporter of the Stuart dynasty. Miss Ramsay was Mrs. Guthrie's niece ; and while on a visit to her aunt, she became pious, and joined herself to the Presbyterians. Being disowned, in consequence, by her father, she found a shelter under Mr. Guthrie's roof, until her marriage with Gilbert Wilson. When her son William was prosecuting his studies for the ministry, her brother, who had succeeded to Shielhill, offered to leave it to her son, provided he would become an Episcopalian. This con-dition not being accepted, Shielhill was left to a younger sister and her heirs. Father, mother, and son, all thus suffered for con-science' sake ; and the last had a further tasting of the same cup when, along with Moncrieff of Culfargie, the Erskines, and others, he had to give up his living in the Church of Scotland, through the violence of a faithless and unchristian majority. They were animated with the spirit that had breathed in the martyrs and heroes of the Scottish Covenant.

The wife of William Wilson—one of the great-grandmothers of the subject of this memoir—was a lineal descendant of George Jamesone of Aberdeen, the " Vandyke of Scotland," " the first inhabitant of Great Britain, the works of whose brush could stand comparison with foreign painters."

The Rev. William Jameson of Kilwinning, when a preacher, in 1762, was appointed by the Secession Synod to proceed as a missionary to America ; but as the congregation of Kilwinning desired him for their minister, the Synod, at its next meeting, released him from his missionary appointment.

The memory of the Rev. Dr. Pringle is still fragrant in the city of Perth, where, for a period of sixty-two years, he was minister of the North Secession Church. He died in 1839, in the eighty-seventh year of his age, retaining his faculties fresh, and keeping up with a progressive generation to the last.

The Rev. John Jameson, father of the subject of this Memoir, was a man whom to know was to love and to esteem. In his Memoir of the late Dr. John Brown, Dr. Cairns speaks of Mr. Jameson as a "man of true genius, and the fragments of whose mind show an originality and brilliancy not often reached in the finished productions of others." The Rev. George Gilfillan also writes of him in terms of the most generous appreciation. He says that he "was a man of various moods, as many men of genius are ; but, unlike some of that class, he was, in all his moods, amiable." "Jameson was indeed a singular composite. He was in intellect and genius a man, in simplicity and unconsciousness a child, and in affection a woman." "Even more than a man of genius, he was a man of heart, and of a heart that had been cradled and cultivated in the school of many sorrows." Of his "letters," he says that they "are, in pathos, in beauty, and in originality, inferior to none in the language." And of his sermon on "True Fame," that "it told with prodigious power, and constitutes, next, perhaps, to a sermon on Elijah, by Dr. Ferrier, the best printed discourse by any one minister of the United Presbyterian Church. The introduction is musical as the liquid lapse of the Earn itself, and several other parts are highly energetic." And of the subject of this Memoir, "Jameson's beloved son, William," that he was his father's "picture in appearance and fac-simile in disposition."

Those are indeed blessed whom, in answer to the prayers of pious parents, God converts in early youth, and whom those parents are affectionately wise in training for nobly doing their life's work. Such parents as Mr. Jameson of Methven and his excellent wife, could not but exert a most benign influence on their children. In their case, grace has run in the line, and they have all chosen the God of their fathers for their own God, and been identified with the Saviour's public cause.

William Jameson was pious from his childhood. On the evening of the day on which he left Methven to sail for Jamaica, while the lessened circle sat together sorrowful at the departure of one so greatly beloved by them all, his good father said, " Well, my children, I got William from the Lord; from the hour of his birth I gave him to the Lord; and I never had cause to regret either the receiving or the giving."

The following incidents show the budding of an early piety which, at length, expanded into the fragrance and fruitfulness of maturity. He was about three years of age, when, one day, his father led him out of doors during a thunderstorm, to see what he would think of it. They soon heard a very loud peal; and William, grasping his father's hand in his, said, pointing upwards, " Stop, papa, stop! God is playing a tune on the clouds."

When he was about four years of age, a brother was born, who died in two weeks. He was named Adam. After the infant's death, his mother overheard William praying very earnestly, and weeping out, " Lord, I thank thee for Adam, though Adam is dead."

On another occasion, when he wanted money for some of his own purposes, his mother heard him in his little closet praying for coppers. The word struck her, and she asked him when he came out, why he used that word. Blushing deeply, he said, " Mother, money was too big a word for me. I wanted only pence." He was then about six years old.

When he was about twelve years old, one Saturday evening before the Lord's Supper, his sister Jane and he were sitting together. He spoke to her about the badness of her heart, and mourned that his own was so hard with respect to God and eternity. Among other things, he said, " This heart of mine is very cold and dead. I have been fighting to bring it under the influence of the Word of God; but to-night, that blessed word makes no more impression on it than a piece of

small cord would make on a lump of hard, thick, tarry rope."
Then, lifting up his tearful eyes to heaven, he implored the
Lord to have pity on his heart, to subdue it to himself, and to
fill it with love to Jesus Christ.

The following incident shows the existence, in the boy, of
the kind and generous disposition which made it a pleasure for
the man to spend, and toil, and suffer for others. When he
was at Methven school, on one occasion the master thought it
to be his duty to punish a few of the girls for being late.
One of these was the constant companion of the young Jame-
sons, and a relative of the family. When she was about, in
her turn, to "hold out" her hand, William started from his
seat, ran up to the master, and said, "Sir, do give me the
punishment, and let her off." The little girl for whom he so
kindly offered himself as a substitute, afterwards became his
wife, and the partner of his missionary labours till her early
death at Goshen.

After attending school at Methven, he was sent to the Perth
Academy, where he remained till July, 1823. He then returned to Methven, and spent a year under the eye of his
father, preparing for the University, which he entered in November, 1824, in his sixteenth year. During that period he
opened an evening class, at the desire of several young men
who wished to improve themselves in general and religious
knowledge, and in this work he spent two hours each night.
The meetings of this class were happy meetings, both for the
teacher and for the learners. Six or seven of these young men
became preachers or teachers, and filled important situations in
different parts of the country with credit and advantage. Mr.
Jameson studied four sessions at the University of Edinburgh,
punctual, conscientious, and diligent in his work, and with
characteristic ardour seeking such academical acquirements as
become a minister of the Word of God.

In 1828, he entered the Divinity Hall of the United Associate Synod, which was then under the care of Drs. Mitchell
and Dick. After his second session at the Divinity Hall, in
October, 1829, he became an agent of the Perth City Mission

till July, 1831, when the connexion ceased, as he and his friends thought it proper that, since the period approached when he would become a licentiate, his time should be wholly given to study.

In one of the reports of the Perth City Mission (March, 1831), the Committee say that they "have reason to bless God, that, while their other agent has been so frequently changed, Mr. Jameson has been permanent, and still continues the zealous and indefatigable agent of the Society. Of Mr. Jameson, as he is present, the Committee cannot speak with freedom, as delicacy forbids this. Yet the Committee will earnestly pray that he may be strengthened for, and preserved in, his many arduous duties; and that, while it pleases God to favour the Society with his valuable services, the consolations of the gospel may abound, more and more, to his own soul."

In 1832, the Committee reported that "it was with extreme regret that they parted with this gentleman. They feel justified in saying that his labours were abundantly characterized by a humble and devoted spirit, and they are justified in adding, nay, they would be culpable in withholding, their testimony to the success with which it has pleased God to crown those labours. They see, in his case, the fulfilment of the gracious promise of God—a promise which will be fulfilled in the experience of all his humble, persevering, devoted servants, if not in this, at all events, in another world: 'Them that honour me I will honour.'"

The missionary visited, for four hours daily, except on Saturdays; held three meetings weekly; and, on Fridays, visited the sick. Mr. Jameson's service was not mere task-work. It was conscientious; and was, obviously, a labour of love. It was the labour of one who was anxious to do good to souls, and to glorify his blessed Master. Two cases in which he was honoured to bring souls to the Saviour, are thus narrated in the *Missionary Record of the United Presbyterian Church*, for January, 1848 :—"An old woman was greatly opposed to his visits, and, at last, became so annoyed at his perseverance, that, one day, when she heard his foot on the stair, she threw a stool at him, and, in the act of turning round to get away, fell and hurt her knee. He raised her up, helped her into the house, and got a medical man to put her knee to rights. A bad swelling came on, which, in eighteen months, cut her off. He saw her every week, and, during that time, the poor woman came to herself, and was brought to the Saviour. She expressed, at almost every visit, her thankfulness that he had been led to her door, notwithstanding her anxiety to keep him away, and blessed the Lord for the accident which, though producing death to her body, had, she said, wrought life in her soul. The other case was that of a man who led a very bad life, and had, by his vicious habits, brought his family to want. Mr. Jameson was anxious to get hold of this man, but was for a long time unsuccessful, as he invariably bolted his door when he was aware that Mr. Jameson was near the house. One day, however, he noticed this man's door open, and, looking in, saw that he was laid upon his bed. His complaint was inflammation of the lungs. The man listened attentively to what he said to him, declared that he was sorry for the way he had treated him, and asked him to return soon. Mr. Jameson visited him frequently, conversed and prayed with him ; and his instructions were blessed. This man, who was formerly a terror to the neighbourhood, became meek as a lamb, and delighted to hear about Christ and his salvation. Being obliged to leave home for two weeks, Mr. Jameson hastened, the morning after his return, to this man's house. The door was standing open, the bed-curtains all thrown up, and the neighbours assembled in the room. He entered softly, and found him near his end. The people informed him that the dying man had longed greatly for his return, in order that he might tell him what the Lord had done for his soul. He waited to see the issue. In a few moments, the man opened his eyes, and looking up, as if he beheld his Saviour, sang audibly, ' Thou fairer art than sons of men ;' and immediately expired."

The interval between the sessions of 1831 and 1832 was

spent with his father at Methven. This must have been a season of profit and progress. Hallowed intercourse with such a parent, and continuous study in a quiet rural town, where there was comparatively little to distract attention and consume time, could not fail to enlarge and perfect his views of divine truth, and fit him for the work of the ministry. His father was peculiarly fond of studying the Hebrew Scriptures. A portion was read and pondered every morning; and he frequently came down into the family circle with a face radiating delight and satisfaction at the ever fresh and cheering views which he was obtaining of the Word of God—views which he used to say were conveyed to him by the ministry of angels. To enjoy daily the discourse of such a father was an inestimable boon to the student and to the future missionary.

In September, 1833, Mr. Jameson was licensed to preach the gospel, by the United Associate Presbytery of Perth, and placed upon the list of probationers. He continued doing the work of a probationer for upwards of two years.

During the period when he was a preacher, Mr. Jameson was sent to supply at Tunley, in the Lancashire Presbytery, and, while living there, he wrote to his aunt, Miss Mary Pringle, a letter of which the following is an extract :—

"I am working at Tunley with this encouragement, at least, that it is the work of God, and that his word does not return unto him void. The people are extremely ignorant, careless, and depraved. . . . A religious Scotchman who comes to such a part of the country as this, sacrifices much, whatever he may gain in a temporal point of view. . . . I love the classes ; a number of the pupils are making considerable progress. I preach twice at the chapel on Sabbath, and have commenced a preaching station in a small village, on my way home on the Sabbath evening. . . . My lodgings are very comfortable. I have a snug parlour and bed-room, with a most excellent feather-bed. To my breakfast, I have toast and coffee ; to my dinner, roast or boil ; but I am starved for want o' kail. My landlady makes a kind of soup she calls broth, but they are no kail. If I don't live well it is my own fault."

An incident which occurred to Mr. Jameson during the time when he was a probationer, is worthy of being mentioned. He was once benighted somewhere in the wilds of Galloway, while fulfilling one of his preaching appointments. The way was new, and he became apprehensive of danger from exposure. After wandering for some time, he observed a light which he followed till he found that it issued from a lonely house. He knocked at the door, and the mistress appeared. Mr. Jameson told his plight, and requested shelter. This she refused. Her husband was dying in a wild and wretched state of mind, and she had no accommodation for a stranger. But he told her that life was precious, that he had lost his way, that he wanted neither food nor bed, but he must be allowed to stay there by the fire, till day should break. He walked into the house and seated himself. There he heard the dying man groaning in the other apartment, and saw from his words how unfit he was to die. Mr. Jameson offered to speak and pray with him ; but the woman objected, saying that her husband would not hear a word about religion. But the stranger determined to take his own way. He prayed and conversed with the poor man, till he became calm and passed away. In the morning, the good woman would not allow him to go until he had broken his fast, saying that he had been a messenger of mercy to that house. Whether or not the dying man found Christ at the last hour of his godless life, we may know hereafter. But we know now, that that evening proved a new era in the history of the woman, who from that time became a true Christian.

Dr. Newlands, of Perth, in a letter written, November 17th, 1835, says :—" When I was last in company with Mr. Ellis of Saltcoats, I asked him, in the course of conversation, why Mr. William Jameson had not had appointments in the central districts of our church. Mr. Ellis replied that Mr. Jameson had always been appointed to the missionary districts, in compliance with his own special request, as affording scope for that species of labour which was most congenial to his mind. I have reason to believe that his mind has been turned to missionary service from the commencement of his studies, and that a call to any congregation in this country would interfere with plans of usefulness which have been ardently cherished." It is, however, said that one of the vacant churches in the denomination had resolved to call Mr. Jameson, and was deterred from doing so by learning that he was bent on foreign service, rather than on the pastoral work at home. His father, writing (January 29th, 1836), says :—" I know my son's intentions to be, and to have been, for a long time favourably turned to the West Indies." Missionary work, both at home and abroad, he specially liked. He desired rather to gather a little flock in some heathen wilderness into the fold of the Good Shepherd, than to be employed in tending a flock already gathered. He has been known to exchange an appointment to a vacant congregation, even when he had reason to believe that he was favourably regarded by it, for one at an obscure missionary station. And, therefore, he readily agreed to take charge of a station of this kind at Firth, a parish lying between Kirkwall and Stromness, a piece of outfield which the Presbytery of Orkney were trying to cultivate. The station was supported by the Secession Church in Kirkwall, under the pastoral care of Dr. Paterson. The Orkney Presbytery appointed Mr. Jameson to labour in this field for three months. At the end of that time, he had gained the hearts of the people ; and he agreed, at their request, made with the Presbytery's consent, to remain with them during the winter of 1835-36. When there was a prospect of Mr. Jameson's departure, and Firth was asked to give him up to Jamaica, Dr. Paterson wrote (March 2d, 1836) : " It is true, from my own strong desire, and from the universal desire of my congregation, to retain Mr. Jameson as our missionary, I shall comply with reluctance (with the request to give him up) ; but, in the circumstances of the case, I do not see what else I can do. I am happy to be able to say, that in getting him, I think your congregation will get an excellent and very devoted missionary. The people of our station are exceedingly attached to him, and I see that his leaving them will be a great stroke ; but I must admit that Jamaica has, in some respects, preferable claims."

Mr. Jameson so manifestly spent himself for the people among whom he served in the ministry of the gospel, that he soon came to be regarded as necessary to their happiness. "So completely did he succeed in gaining the affections and confidence of the people of Firth, that it is believed there was scarcely a dry eye in the district when his resolution to leave it was made known." If a few months of labour so endeared the young probationer to the people of that Orcadian parish, how strongly attached must his own Goshen flock have been, after an intercourse of nearly ten years !

Among Mr. Jameson's papers, there remains an address, delivered in connexion with the " Stromness Missionary Society," in the beginning of 1836. This address is written in a fluent and ardent style, and glows with great warmth of zeal in the enterprise of missions to the heathen. Taking a glance at the wretched condition of fallen man, and the divinely prepared remedy revealed in the gospel of Christ, he illustrates the suitableness and power of the latter in the hand of God, by a reference to the moral history of our own beloved land. He then surveys the regions of darkness—the moral wastes—which lie outside the pale of the Church of Jesus, where the devil holds unbounded sway over by far the largest part of mankind, by means of popish errors, Mohammedan delusions, and the idolatries of paganism. In looking at the work which has to be done, the Christian finds courage and hope nowhere but in our mighty God. " Desponding spirit ! lay aside thy doubts and fears. Lift thine eyes from these citadels of strength, with their towering battlements, and their numerous and well-disciplined forces, to Him who sits upon the white horse, on whose vesture, dipped in blood, and on whose thigh the name is written—' King of Kings, and Lord of Lords.' See what the gospel—the sharp two-edged sword that proceedeth out of his mouth—hath already done, and learn what it shall again do."

He then glances at several modern missionary spheres, as New Zealand, the Sandwich Islands, and the British West Indies. Not only had the labours of Christian missionaries been blessed among the bondsmen of our West Indian possessions, but it was to gospel influence, and to gospel power, that the recent glorious act of emancipation was due. In order that the whole world may be conquered to God, the divinely-appointed means must be used by the people of God. Is that man a genuine Christian who does not long to see the kingdom of Christ embrace all mankind, and who does not exert himself to help forward this glorious consummation? While some, as the messengers of the church and of the church's Lord, bear the " lamp of life" into the dark wastes of heathenism, the church, collectively and individually, dare not look on with indifference. " The hearts of Christians must not be shut by avarice, or their arms enervated by sloth. All their stores they must bring into the storehouse, ere God open the windows of heaven, and pour out millennial blessings upon the church and the world." Vigorous, humble co-operation in every way, conduct becoming the gospel, and united earnest prayer, are all required at the hands of the friends of Jesus, in order that they may fulfil their duty, and be entitled to the reward of faithful service. Gratitude requires this, and so does compassion for the wretched and helpless. " What, brethren! shall the Hindoo any longer be permitted to throw away his life under the ponderous wheel of Juggernath? Shall the tender infant still be plunged into Ganges, to appease an idol? Brethren, awake! Hear the voice of God! Let gratitude, and pity, and conscience arouse you to the help of the Lord against the mighty."

By this time, the battle of freedom against slavery had been fought and won. After a struggle of twenty years, in which Clarkson, and Wilberforce, and Pitt, and Burke, contended against the African slave-trade, the importation of fresh negroes into the colonies was declared illegal, in 1807. And on the 15th of May, 1823, a new struggle was begun, when, in the British House of Commons, Mr. Buxton rose up to move the resolution, " That the state of slavery is repugnant to the principles of the British Constitution, and of the Christian religion ; and that it ought to be gradually abolished throughout the British Colonies, with as much expedition as may be found consistent with a due regard to the wellbeing of the parties concerned." After a conflict of ten years, on the 28th of August, 1833, the bill for the total abolition of colonial slavery received the royal assent. The slaves were to be apprenticed for seven years to their former masters, and their masters were to be compensated by a gift of twenty million from the treasury of Britain. By this arrangement, seven hundred thousand of the children of Africa, who were held in bondage in the dominions of Great Britain, ceased to be slaves on the 1st of August, 1834. From that period, to the 1st of August, 1840, they were to serve their masters under the name of apprentices, and then they were to have the full liberty of British subjects. Not content with breaking the yoke of slavery, British Christians sought to provide for the education and religious instruction of the negroes. Missionaries had long laboured among them, amid reproach, and some of them were persecuted to the death. The record of these devoted servants of Christ, whether Moravians, or Wesleyans, or Episcopalians, or Independents, or Baptists, or Presbyterians, is on high. They have, and shall have, a greater reward than the trumpet-blast of human fame.

In the year 1835, the United Secession Church sent out the Rev. James Paterson and the Rev. William Niven as missionaries to Jamaica. " The congregation of Rose Street, Edinburgh, under the ministry of their much loved pastor, the Rev. John M'Gilchrist, in the awakening spirit of the day, embarked in the Christian enterprise of accompanying the maintenance of the gospel among themselves, with the activity of a mightier effort, to procure its extension also to others. They had a city mission, with its missionary ; and a Gaelic mission, with its Gaelic missionary, in Tiree, both maintained at their own proper charge. They resolved, also, to send out an ordained minister, as their own missionary, to Jamaica, with all expenses at their own proper charge."

They sought a man from the Lord, and were directed to Mr. Jameson, who was then at Firth. They received from those who knew him, the best accounts of his piety, steadiness, prudence, and zeal. " With regard to Mr. William Jameson," wrote Dr. Newlands of Perth, " only one opinion can be entertained by those who know him. He is a young man of good talents, and very decided piety ; and is more deeply imbued with missionary zeal than any of our preachers with whom it has been my lot to have personal intercourse. He is a person of the greatest prudence and amiability. I should consider any congregation or society which can secure the services of such an agent, eminently fortunate." November 11th, 1835, Dr. Young wrote :—" Mr. William Jameson is well known to me, and I hesitate not to say, that he is a young man of decided piety, steadiness, and prudence. His dispositions are peculiarly amiable and benevolent ; and he has long shown a strong desire for missionary usefulness. To all his relatives, however, he is very dear ; and the attachment of some of them is so strong, that it will operate as a painful difficulty in his way."

We shall not apologize for inserting here an extract from a letter written by Mr. Jameson of Methven, January 29th, 1836, when Mr. M'Gilchrist brought to his notice the desire of himself and his people to secure his son as their missionary to Jamaica :—" I confess to you that, although I know my son's intentions to be, and to have been, for a long time, favourably turned to the West India mission, yet your letter brought the matter so much nearer to the point, that it did awaken in my mind all the emotions to which you so delicately refer ; and it will not surprise you, when I own that the mingling of such emotions has made me tardy in acknowledging, on my part, the honour which your congregation has done him, in making the application which your letter bears. I sincerely thank you, dear sir, and the gentlemen of your missionary committee ; and I regard it as no ordinary tribute of esteem and respect to any of mine, to be so accounted of by those, who themselves are standing so nobly forward in the most noble of all benevolent enterprises. I have no idea what my son may resolve upon, in the event of your applying to him. I can as little say how I shall feel, if he judge it to be his duty to accept the mission. In a matter of such importance, I would leave that which concerneth me and mine to the higher and better ordering of our blessed and gracious Master ; and I humbly trust, that, in this matter, in which you and your congregation are so deeply and so honourably concerned, he who has sent his Shiloh, will send for your confidence and comfort, by the hand of him whom he will send."

The Lord seems always specially to prepare those servants whom he calls to any work of unusual difficulty or responsibility. Trains of thought are traversed ; feelings corresponding with the enterprise are aroused ; sympathies are awakened and cherished ; and thus, unconsciously, the servant of the Lord is made ready to sever the strongest ties, to say farewell to the dearest friends, to go out of the known and accustomed track, and to enter on new and formidable enterprises. The history of modern missions abounds with notable illustrations of this remark, as is seen in the many records of the lives of missionaries, which have so happily been made for the instruction and encouragement of the Church of the living God, ever anew summoned to carry forward the work which is to be gloriously consummated in the overthrow of the kingdom of the prince of darkness, and the complete establishment of the kingdom of God, in every corner of the earth.

The letter written in name of the Directors of the Congregational Missionary Society of Rose Street, Edinburgh, which intimated to Mr. Jameson their wish to send him as their missionary to Jamaica, did not find him unprepared, as appears from the following reply, dated Orkney, February 9th, 1836 :—

" I received your letter of the 3d, and hasten to return my warmest acknowledgments to you, and to your committee, for the confidence they repose in me, in offering to commit into my hands a trust of so great responsibility. I humbly pray that, if my Divine Master lead me to accept of it, he will give me grace to be faithful. Although the missionary field in Jamaica has been before my mind for some time past, as the subject of earnest thought and prayer, yet I have not been able to come to a decision as to the will of my Master regarding myself. It is my most anxious desire to know his will, and to have a heart to do it. I desire to look up to himself, saying,

' Speak, Lord, for thy servant heareth.' Before I come to any determination on a matter of so great importance, it is the wish of my father, and it is also my own, that I should see him and my other friends, at home; and their suggestions may lead me, by the guidance of unerring wisdom, to see the path of duty in the present case. I have laboured, for the last five months, as the missionary of the Kirkwall congregation. Your letter requires me to hasten home ; the interest of the station requires that I should not abruptly leave it. It will be my concern, looking at all the views of the case, with the help of my father, and under the guidance of the Spirit of God, to know that line of conduct which I ought to adopt."

Accordingly, Mr. Jameson left Firth (on the 20th of March, 1836), and, in eight days, addressed Mr. M'Gilchrist from Perth, before he had reached Methven, saying, that he became daily more satisfied that the path of duty was the one now set before him, in the providence of his Divine Master, and hoping that that Master would enable him to go forward joyfully.

After a month passed in prayerful consideration, and in consultation with attached relatives, he visited Edinburgh, and having met with the Directors of the Rose Street Congregational Missionary Association, and preached to the congregation, he was, at a general meeting of the Association, held on the 5th of May, unanimously and cordially elected as their foreign missionary agent. The call thus presented to him he at once accepted, and returned to Methven to prepare for being ordained.

On June 13th, 1836, he wrote to the same :—" My mind is more and more reconciled to what is before me ; the more I look, the more I am satisfied that I am in the path of duty. I am now better able to look at the matter with calmness, and though many difficulties appear, why should I be afraid when my Master has said, ' My grace is sufficient for thee ? ' I leave the land of my nativity, but seek a better country, even heaven ; afflictions and trials very possibly await me, but the Saviour lives, my shield and fortress, my comforter and deliverer, my portion, and my all. Without a grudge, yea, joyfully, I leave all, trusting that the gospel, in the hand of the

Holy Spirit, will prove joy to many to the land to which I go ; and what can I wish more ? The darkness and misery of Jamaica, and the recompense of reward move me. But, above all, the thought that he who was rich for our sakes became poor, moves me that no more I should live to myself, but to him who loved me, and who died for me."

At length the United Associate Presbytery of Edinburgh met in the midst of the congregation in their own church, on the evening of September 7th, to separate their missionary to the solemn and interesting work of benevolence and mercy by the laying on of their hands. "The Rev. James Watson, missionary from Jamaica, commenced the services with prayer ; the Rev. Mr. Cooper from Fala preached from 1 John v. 19 ; the Rev. Mr. M'Gilchrist offered the ordination prayer, and addressed the young missionary and the congregation ; and also in the name of the Rose Street Missionary Association, presented Mr. Jameson with an elegantly bound copy of the Bible, as containing the message which he was to proclaim, and the only instructions with which it was their wish to charge him. The Rev. Dr. Pringle of Perth, the venerable grandfather of the newly-ordained missionary, concluded the solemn and impressive services by prayer." [1]

Mr. Jameson, senior, says of the ordination, that "a scene more befitting the occasion, or more deeply interesting, has rarely been witnessed. Everything was in keeping. It was truly as if the Sun of righteousness had indeed broken forth on the princely willing people. Every eye looked, every ear listened, and every heart was gratified. The whole audience, and the house was filled to overflowing, hung on to the close of the service, with intense and unbroken interest."

On the day after his ordination, Mr. Jameson was united in marriage to Nicolis Mackersy, only daughter of the late William Mackersy, Esq. of Kinkell, in Perthshire, who also was a descendant of the Rev. William Wilson of Perth. As it is considered desirable that new missionaries should reach a tropical field of labour at the coolest and most salubrious season, their

<hr>

[1] Mr Scott's narrative.

departure was deferred for a time ; and thus Mr. Jameson had an opportunity of enlarging his acquaintance with the members of the Society, under whose care he was to go forth to the work of the Lord. " In the new and extraordinary circumstances into which the congregation was brought, in the almost universal interest throughout the congregation, the people could not rest satisfied with only acting together, and, in their devotional exercises, with merely looking at each other, in the understood confidence that they were of one heart and mind ; the craving of the common heart went out further, after a social meeting, in which they might break out in all the freedom of mutual conversation on the subject of their common enterprise. They threw themselves on the kindred feeling of the religious public in Edinburgh, and came together in a soirée, on the Monday after the ordination. That public, in fellow-feeling far beyond what the congregation had anticipated, responded to the proposal, and a great company attended."

The object of this missionary soirée was to bid the youthful missionary farewell and God-speed in his mission to Jamaica. " The joyousness which so blithely spread itself over the face of the whole company, the hum of the busy and cheerful conversation in which the words flew from heart to heart, left little room for conjecture that the disciples in Edinburgh, having come together in the very same spirit in which their brethren had done of old at Troas, entered, during their breaking of bread, also, into the same conversation, one with another. Did, at Troas, the conversation during the breaking of bread, assume its more elevated style, so common among the Hebrews, rising into set speeches ? Did Paul, as not a whit behind the very chief of missionaries, in such speeches sustain and take the lead in the conversation ? In the same manner in the Rose Street soirée, when the repast was finished, the easy and familiar talking of the evening to one another gave way also to the same loftier order of conversation. This part was sustained by Mr. M'Gilchrist, and by the Rev. Messrs. Cooper, Robson, and Alexander. Mr. M'Gilchrist gave a brief, luminous, and interesting narrative of the origin and progress of the Missionary

Association in his congregation, and its blessed results ;" and thus introduced the missionary in terms that flowed from the core of his genial soul, and which, eulogistic as they are, truthfully portray the subject of them, who was a man greatly beloved :—

"What may be called the more special duty I am this night expected to perform, is a singularly pleasing one. It is to introduce to this meeting my esteemed and beloved friend and brother, Mr. William Jameson, the ordained missionary of the congregation of Rose Street, to Jamaica. All of you, my friends, have repeatedly heard this gentlemen, with high satisfaction, from the pulpit. Many of you have met him, with no less pleasure, in private ; but I am confident it is with emotions of a higher and warmer satisfaction still, that you meet him, this evening, as one whom you have seen invested, at your call, with the holy office of the ministry, and who is about, as your agent, to leave his native shores to enter on the distant scene of his future labours. So now, as on a former evening, I would deem it improper to express in public, and in presence of my friend, the estimate I have formed of his character and worth. I am fully persuaded that such a liberty would wound and offend, rather than gratify him. Let me only say, that there is nothing I could desire in a foreign missionary which I do not find in him. His intelligence, his zeal, his prudence, his piety, his devotedness, and his genial and conciliatory manners, all combine to invest him with singular fitness for the work to which he is appointed. The better I have known him, the more I have loved him. I am not aware that any one, on so short an acquaintance, ever established himself so entirely in my consideration, or secured, by weight of excellence, felt and owned, so large a share of my affections; and the reason of this is found in my friend's character, of which simplicity and affection are the leading features. You don't require time to study him ; you are not left to apprehend anything at variance with your first impression, as in the case of artful and soft-hearted men. His character is like one of nature's untainted fountains,— however deep, in consequence of the translucent purity of its waters, you can look, in one glance, to the bottom, where nothing but shining sand and bright pebbles meet the eye. So it is with the character of friend. No mud of insincerity or of art conceals the bottom ; nor is its surface ruffled by the winds of temper ; you see him at once, as you always see him. There are no discoveries to be made, but such as are to his honour. With such an agent, under the guidance and blessing of Heaven, what expectations of happiness and success may we not entertain ? Sure am I, my friends, that, through the grace of God given him, the great ends of the compact will not fail of their accomplishment on his part. Let it be our care that there be nothing wanting on ours. I rejoice to think, my friends, that in sending Mr. Jameson to Jamaica, we have now the certain prospect (if both are spared) of sending, not one, but two missionaries, to that island. Our friend has been so wise and well directed as to secure, before leaving his native country, the incalculable advantages of a pious and accomplished companion for life ; and to a foreign missionary these advantages are indeed incalculable, whether we regard her as a woman or as a missionary. Nor are they less valuable to us. An intelligent and devoted female, standing in this sacred relation to the missionary, has a field of usefulness presented scarcely less extensive and important than his ; and such, by universal testimony, is Mrs. William Jameson. Surely we have to congratulate you on this happy consummation,—one so full of the promise of comfort to our missionary, and of more extensive usefulness in the great enterprise on which he is to enter.

"I cannot, my dear brother, bid you farewell on this public occasion, without assuring you, in my own name, and in the name of the people over whom it is my honour to preside, of the sincerity and warmth of that affection with which we in common regard you, and of the unlimited confidence we repose in you as our messenger, in Christ's name, to the heathen.

"I am fully aware that in the hour of discouragement and trial, of sadness and sorrow, the richest source of your comfort will be found in the sympathy and grace of your Divine

Master ; but, in such an hour, the thought may not be without its influence to soothe and sustain the fainting spirit, that you live in the esteem and affection of the people at whose instance and at whose charge you are serving the Redeemer in a distant land ; and that their fervent prayers, and fondest wishes, and ardent love follow you to the scene of your labours. Yes, you are in our hearts, my dear brother, if we cannot say to die and to live with you, at least, we can truly say to suffer and to rejoice with you; tenderly and intensely to sympathize with you in all your future experience, whatever be its character and complexion. And now I commend you to God, and the word of his grace, and to him who is able to keep you from falling, and to present you faultless before the throne of his glory, with exceeding joy."

The other speakers dwelt on the duty and necessity of Christian missions, the claims of the negroes, and the encouragements to increased missionary enterprise. Mr. Jameson, senior, signified how willingly he gave his son to God, to the work, and to the congregation. Mr. Fyfe, Convener of the Missionary Committee, addressed the missionary in name of the congregation, bidding him farewell, and praying him the countenance and aid of the God of their salvation. The missionary, in reply, claimed the unfeigned remembrance of their prayers ; and pressed upon them, above all, the sure and diligent attention to their own eternal salvation, as the best support from home which could reach him far abroad.

"It was now far in the evening. George Thompson, Esq., rose : for he had been earnestly solicited ; but such was the overwhelming interest of the scene, that a man, one of the master spirits of the age, seemed for a moment to hesitate, whether, from such an eminence of high excitement, it was lawful for him to proceed. He did proceed, and in that eloquence which has seldom, indeed, if ever, burst from the lips of man. The Spirit of God came down upon him. It was as if the veil which is hung between heaven and earth had been drawn aside for a little moment, to let out upon him, in the riches of a higher measure than is ordinarily allotted to the sons of the mighty, a stream, in its full flood of the vastness of thought ; of bold, and happy, and grand conceptions ; of ever-ready, ever-varying, and overpowering utterance. As the descending Spirit came down upon him, the impassioned language of the speaker rose, presenting to every eye the scene which, from such a meeting as this, opened on the view, and exhibiting the toil of years, and of many a struggle, to carry the strongholds of negro oppression, and remove the rubbish, now giving way to the loftier enterprise still of rearing in its place, on the very spot, the house of God, in all the simplicity, the truth, and the noble grandeur of the building of mercy. It was well-nigh midnight ; and as they hung on in breathless attention, as this bold, and interesting, and Christian philan-thropist continued his speech, the whole multitude looked one willing consent to cling to him, listening on to the break of day."[1]

" Other and more private meetings followed for prayer and conference on the work to which the Society and their agent were pledged ; and, on the 25th of October, the directors and collectors assembled, for the express purpose of commending Mr. and Mrs. Jameson to the divine guidance and protection, and of bidding them an affectionate and final farewell. In these meetings, Mr. Jameson confirmed the good opinion, and strengthened those friendly feelings with which the members of the association had, from the first, regarded him ; while the spirit of brotherly love, and of devotion to the cause of missions, which pervaded them, must have constrained him to thank God and take courage, and thus prepared him for going forth with greater cheerfulness and confidence, to proclaim that mes-sage of mercy and salvation with which he was put in trust."[2]

The devoted servants of the Redeemer in Rose Street Church, Edinburgh, have always acted thus by those missionaries whom they have sent out. They have ever sought to beget and cherish in them a spirit of confidence, and to send them on their way rejoicing.

The voluntary exiles, about to proceed on their distant

[1] Mr. Jameson, senior.   [2] Mr. Scott's narrative.

mission, had now before them a duty which is of all duties the most trying, and which is trying in proportion to the strength and tenderness of the affection that subsists between those who have to go and those who remain behind. They had to take leave of an attached circle at Methven, Airdrie, Perth, etc., who clung to them with ardent affection. It is natural that a parent should find it hard to part with a child who aspires to the work of preaching the Gospel to the heathen. But, surely, it is an offence of no ordinary magnitude in a Christian parent, resolutely to hinder one who is fitted in body, mind, and spirit, for that work ; and who, from being inclined, seems heaven-called, to carry the " lamp of life " to the dark places of the earth. We lately heard of a case which ought to warn parents whose affection blinds both their judgment and their conscience in this matter. A son was bent on being a missionary, but his parents persistently refused their consent. Mark the end ! That youth, once so full of promise, became a wanderer from God, and fell at once from religion and from virtue. Instead of leaving his native land, with the prayers and blessings of the Church of God, he left as a prodigal, and went no one knows whither ; and the child whom a mistaken affection refused to the honourable service of God, has gone, a miserable wreck, in the service of Satan.

This part of our narrative will best be wound up by a few sentences from a letter written by Mr. Jameson of Methven to Mrs. Mackersy, on the departure of his son and her daughter. It carries us back to the quiet manse at Methven, where so much that was good and amiable found a home ; and we weep in sympathy with the patriarch whose lover and friend had been put far from him, and whose eldest born was now departing for a distant land, leaving another big blank in the lessening household band.

" METHVEN, October 20th, 1836.

" Yesterday William and his spouse, Nicolis, left us to their *kail* with your old friend Mrs. Ritchie, on their way, for good and all, to Perth. . . . The morning of their departure was something like death ; although we were expecting it, and knew the hour as it drew on, yet there was still something to do ; but on it came—there was a hurry, a struggle, a tearing asunder ; off they went, and, in five minutes, we felt that they were gone. My little darling (Mrs. W. J.) behaved like a princess ; she adjusted everything. Her wondrous presence of mind never forsook her ; she was in no fluster ; she giggled not ; she smiled not ; pale as death, and silent as marble, she put her hand in mine, kissed me, and slipped away. God bless thee ! child of my heart, my daughter ! the fatness of the dew of heaven come down on thy sorrows and on thy joys ; the blessing of thy father and the house of thy fathers rest on thy lot, and be the crown of thy head !

"We had a soirée, too, in Perth ; and a feeling and interesting meeting in the school here with the congregation, on the occasion of their presenting William with a watch, as a memorial of their esteem. On Saturday, the elders and managers presented William with a psalm-book, as a companion to his Rose Street Bible. . . . I had little spirit for these things, and I was ofttimes angry with myself ; for, in the midst of the scenes of gladness, I could feel no kindred spirit in them. It was to my children ! my children ! my children ! that my heart ran and clung. I am, however, more and more satisfied that He who loved us, and gave himself for us, is claiming them for the work to which he hath called them ; and he knows that, without grudge or murmur, I frankly surrender them to himself and to his work of mercy. . . . I humbly trust that He will never forsake them ; and if, by their means, a single sinner be saved, a single soul be comforted ; nay, if but one word, a message of mercy, be carried across the Atlantic, to a single vessel of mercy, through their instrumentality, he is welcome to the messengers, and we are honoured, and more than paid, by the message given them to carry."

Thus did such a father give such a son to the work of God. With his whole heart, he surrendered him and his wife, whom he loved as a daughter, although his uncommon affectionateness of spirit made it a severe struggle, and cheerfully did he bid them God-speed.

CHAPTER II.

Leaves home—The voyage—First impressions of Jamaica—Country and people—
Wanted at Green Island—Duty calls to Goshen—Bagnold's Vale—Origin of Goshen
station—American Baptists—Dreams—Leaders—The new missionary in harness—
Death of his father.

HAVING said farewell to home and friends, Mr. and Mrs. Jameson proceeded to Greenock. The "Christian," in which their passage had been taken, was to sail on the 11th of November. But contrary winds detained her till the 22d, when the Rev. Mr. Sinclair, who had most hospitably entertained them, accompanied them to the ship. A letter of Mr. Jameson of Methven, November 25th, 1836, contains a reference to their departure. "William sailed on Thursday. God does all things well. By this delay, our missionaries had an opportunity, on Sabbath, of sitting down with their brethren in Greenock, and eating the Lord's Supper, ere they proceeded on their voyage,—a meal for forty days. If the wind has been with them, in the same direction as with us, they should, by this time, be getting on towards, or across the Bay of Biscay. Be this as it may, we know who sees them, and who hears us."

After being towed down the Clyde, they were forced, by a head wind, to take shelter in Rothesay Bay. "The next morning," writes Mr. Jameson, "we left the place of our retreat before a favourable breeze. On Friday, we found ourselves off the coast of Ireland. But now the wind turned completely against us, and we were, for several days, at the mercy of an unpropitious gale. On the following week, it veered round, once more, in our favour, and we had a speedy run to the Bay of Biscay. Again, the wind turned against us, and drove us back to the Irish coast, where we lay for a number of days, tossed without ceasing on the tempestuous deep ; till it pleased our heavenly Father to send a breeze which carried us on our way past the Azores, with St. Mary's full in view, into the region of the trade-winds."

The voyagers, however, were disappointed in their hopes of the smooth seas and favouring breezes of this region, so welcome after the anxieties and tossings and miseries of the Channel and the ill-famed Bay of Biscay. They met with head-winds and stormy waves, for some time, till about the 8th of January, 1837, when, at last, the trade-wind wafted them onwards to the sunny, smiling archipelago of the West—ever looked back to with affection and interest by those who have once had a home there. They passed " Deseada"—the desired—a small island off Guadaloupe, the first land seen after leaving the Western Isles. " It was, indeed," says Mr. Jameson, " an object of great desire ; we looked for it with much eagerness, and when we saw it, we gazed on it as a strange thing." Passing through the channel, between Antigua on the right hand, and Montserrat on the left, they would pass in view of the large rock Redondo—the round—which, when seen from a particular point, and especially in the dusk of the tropical evening, has so much the appearance of a large vessel in full sail, that, it is said, the captain of a Dutch man-of-war, cruising in those seas, fired several shots at it before discovering his mistake. On the 20th, the Blue Mountains of Jamaica rose to view. They saw, at length, the Queen of the Antilles, sitting there in all her mingled beauty, variety, and sublimity, one of the fairest spots on God's earth, though, for so many generations, polluted by an amount of moral vileness, of oppression, and of wrong, such as the great day of judgment alone can reveal. Mr. Jameson noted in his journal :—" In the morning, I rose about three o'clock, and on going on deck, the mate hailed me with the welcome tidings that the land to which we were bound was now in view. I looked, and, in the moonlight, saw before me the Blue Mountains. Oh, if ever I felt gratitude, it was then. Looking at these mountains, I was filled with wonder and awe ; every unholy feeling was chased away for a season ; I was elevated above the transient scene ; I thought of heaven, and wished that I was entering there, to look, and wonder, and praise.   The whole coast is exceedingly beautiful, diversified with verdant hills, and here and there a town, and here and there an estate, like a village at home for size."

They had prayers in the cabin every evening during the voyage, and Mr. Jameson preached on deck every Sabbath, when the weather permitted.   On the Sabbath evenings, he taught a class of seven or eight young persons.   While they were off San Domingo, an apprentice fell from the mast-head into the water, striking against the vessel as he fell.   " He was a very fine boy," writes Mr. Jameson, " one whose acquaintance with divine truth, and whose marked attention, while I was speaking, pleased and struck me much.   Alas ! his image is vividly before me, as he sat on his stool with his bonnet and his hands between his knees, his body reclining forward, and his fixed eye and interesting countenance resting on me, as I told them that we might not all meet together again ; that our next meeting might be at the judgment-seat of Christ ; that ere another Sabbath some of us might be in eternity.   The sad scene of to-day chides me for remissness. Oh, had I known that it would take place, with what earnestness would I have urged the Saviour upon them !   But may I learn from this ever to feel myself and my hearers on the brink of eternity ! "

Observe the exercises of a genuinely pious heart in these expressions, following a description of the calm and beautiful hour of setting sun and rising moon in the tropics.   " But, oh, how cloudy the mind !   How agitated with stormiest passions the soul !   No light is there, and no serenity.   Oh, wretch that I am, who shall deliver me from the body of this death ?   Thanks, eternal thanks to God, for the gift of his Son, who dispels the thickest darkness, and subdues all things to himself."   Reader, be not surprised.   The exercise is genuine ; the self-abasement is proper and warranted ; the consciousness of this sin and misery, while, along with it, there is a humble

but firm hope in God through Jesus Christ, betokens a not unhealthy spiritual state, and fits the servant of God for his work
whether at home or abroad.

On the 21st of January, 1837, the "Christian" anchored
at Montego Bay. On that day, Mr. Jameson wrote in his
journal :—"We have, at last, reached our long-wished for har-
bour. The passengers and the captain have gone ashore, and
we are left for a little to ourselves. We have just received a
letter from Mr. Paterson of New Broughton, expressing his regret at having to leave Montego Bay before our arrival, and
telling us how anxious they all were about us. This letter has
cheered us greatly. . . . Everything reminded us that we were
strangers. Our fellow-passengers were surrounded by friends,
who welcomed them home by their tears, and their smiles, and
their kind caresses ; but we felt that we were alone. Shield
of the stranger! We were happy in Thee. Doubtless, God
of our fathers ! thou art our Father. God is with us, and our
prayers, and the prayers of many on our behalf, lie before his
throne. Swarthy faces, strange-looking houses, the uncouth
dialect, cocoa-nut trees with their star-like clusters of waving
leaves, orange trees, mingled gold and green, and, above all, a
blazing sun, made us feel ourselves among new scenes and a
strange people. Not knowing any person in Montego Bay,
we remained on board all night. Next morning, Mr. Holmes,
a Scotchman, and editor of a widely circulated newspaper,[1]
came on board for us. He is a great friend and warm supporter of the Presbyterian missionaries. He gave us a hearty
welcome to Jamaica, and a pressing invitation to accompany
him to his house, and there remain till Mr. Waddell should
be sent for to take us to Cornwall. I need not say how thankful we were for the kind invitation ; how gladly we embraced
it ; how much of God's goodness we saw in it. When we felt
strange and lonely, He sent us this friend who cheered us by
his many kind attentions."

"*January 23d.*—Mr. Waddell arrived at an early hour, most
happy to see us, and expressed the fears which they had felt

[1] *The Cornwall Chronicle.*

regarding our safety. We reached Cornwall about seven P.M.
A number of negroes, who were waiting our arrival, flocked
around, and gave us a welcome. 'Good massa, we glad to see
you ; good massa.' After dinner there was a temperance meeting. Mr. Waddell apologized for the delay of an hour, caused
by his having to go to Montego Bay to bring the new minister.
They with one voice replied, 'Quite good, massa, we thankful
for the delay.' This was the first meeting of negroes I have
attended ; and I cannot describe my feelings, on seeing so many
sable countenances, bearing upon them the impress of the highest interest in what was going on. At the conclusion, all shook
hands with the strangers, repeating their former expressions of
kindness, their whole appearance testifying the sincerity of their
words."

"*January 24th.*—I examined the children, and was surprised
and delighted to find how accurately they answered the questions
put to them. Mrs. Jameson also examined them by herself,
and came in, also surprised and delighted with their progress.
The teacher is a young female, taught and trained for the work
by Mrs. Waddell. Mrs. Jameson noted one little girl, about four
years old, who read the New Testament with ease and fluency.
It is truly delightful to see them permitted to attend school;
and, more particularly, to see so much progress among persons
who have been declared, a thousand times over, to be as unfit
to learn as the brutes. Why should we not indulge the hope
that, ere long, under the benign influence of the Spirit of God,
through the feeble instrumentality of his servants, knowledge
shall bless this people, and holiness shall adorn them !"

"*January 31st.*—Took farewell of Mr. Waddell, and went to
visit Mr. Blyth at Hampden. Here everything goes on most
prosperously. The congregation is large ; and there are 200
at school. The teacher is Mr. Drummond, from Stirling, sent
out by the proprietor of Hampden.[1] He is well qualified for,
and most diligent in his work. His leisure time he spends
among the people, taking part with them in their prayer-meetings, and in every way striving to lead them forward. Had we

1 A. Stirling, Esq. of Keir.

many such persons, they would greatly strengthen our hands. Care should be taken to send men of approved piety and prudence; for truly, in this country, we may be said to be as a city set upon a hill, seen and watched by all."

"*Sabbath, February 5th.*—Preached, at Lucea, to 500 or 600 interesting people. They were longing much for the return of Mr. Watson, and were greatly delighted when I told them that he would be among them so soon. We commenced the work of the Sabbath at six A.M., and finished at five P.M. Some of the Green Island people were there to welcome me as the missionary sent out expressly for them. I was exceedingly grieved to find them so misinformed. I told them that I had not been appointed to occupy Green Island, or any other place; but was to follow the way marked out by my Divine Master. That this matter had been left to myself and to the Presbytery now formed in the country; that the claims of Green Island had been laid before me, together with those of Goshen; and that, after calm and prayerful consideration, and consultation with my brethren, I had come to the conclusion that Goshen was the sphere of labour to which I was called. The people were much disappointed, and clung to me as if they would not let me go. They crowded the vestry-room, entreating, and urging me; and followed me when I went to visit a sick person. I was moved; but duty evidently pointed me elsewhere; and I could not set aside the resolution so recently and solemnly formed. They resolved, ere I left them, to lay their case before the Church at home, and to make an appeal to the preachers. I encouraged them to do so, as it might, under God, be the means of deepening the Church's interest in the work of mercy in this land. When this appeal is published, let every one know that it comes, not from the missionaries wanting help, but from the people themselves, desiring the knowledge of Jesus Christ. It is the bleating of the flock for the green pastures and the life-giving streams of gospel ordinances. It is the cry of the poor and needy, the ardent desire of longing souls; and the servant of Jesus who shuts his heart against such an appeal, shows little of the spirit of his blessed Master."

"*Sabbath, February* 12*th.*—Preached to-day to a full and most attentive congregation at Hampden ; and addressed the Sabbath scholars, in number about 500."

"*Monday,* 13*th.*—We took leave of our kind friends at Hampden, and set out on our journey to Carron Hall, about 100 miles distant : our conveyance a gig, and our guide a black man, leading three horses for change, all being necessary on account of the wild and rugged nature of the roads, and the fatigue of travelling in a tropical climate. We passed the first night at the house of Mr. Naight, a fellow-passenger, who offered ground for a church and house, and every encouragement if I would settle on a property belonging to him in the mountains of St. Ann's, one of the most healthy and delightful parishes in Jamaica, where the people have no instructor. It is with sorrow that we turn from these calls.

"After a fatiguing journey, passing the night of the 14th at Drexhall, we reached Goshen at five P.M. on the 15th, where we met Mr. Simpson, who came to welcome us to our sphere of labour. The attorney, Mr. Geddes, was from home, but we saw him the following day, when he promised to do all he could to further the mission.

"On *Thursday,* the 16th, we reached Carron Hall, and received a joyous welcome from Mr. and Mrs. Cowan, and from all the people. One negro said that Mr. Paterson, when last here, had prayed much that God would send another labourer to this quarter, and God has heard his prayers. The labours of our brethren in this quarter are as abundant and successful as those in the west."

Turning from other fields, "white unto the harvest," with all the sorrow felt by the faithful servant of God, who has to say "No" to the call of souls hungering for the bread of life, Mr. Jameson chose to pitch his tent at Goshen. In the circumstances by which he was led thither he saw a manifest answer to all his own prayers and to those of his friends. Messrs. Simpson and Cowan had extended their labours to Goshen, often preaching there, and encouraging the people to pray and look for a servant of Jesus to come and live among them. The

time for favour had arrived, and the servant of the Lord came
in the spirit of his Master, and in the fulness of the blessing of
the gospel of Christ. True in his case were the words of the
prophet : " How beautiful upon the mountains are the feet of
him that bringeth good tidings !"

In 1837, the people were still apprentices on the properties
to which they had belonged before emancipation. Goshen had
as many as 500 apprentices, the most of whom were living in
the estate's village, half-way between the missionary's residence, Lucky Hill Pen, and the place of worship. Two other
estates, belonging to the same proprietors, lay on either side,
Goshen being in the midst ; and the three together covered a
surface as large as a Scotch parish. About twenty years
before Mr. Jameson went there, these Trinity estates, as they
were called, had together 1000 slaves. Besides these, there
were in Bagnold's Vale, through which flows the stream called
the Rio Neuvo, several properties with gangs of apprentices,
all within the missionary's reach. He calculated that there
were about 6000 or 7000 people in the whole district, "with
scarcely the means of salvation, so that gross darkness covered
the people, and they were sunk in brutish depravity." One of
the old proprietors of Goshen, Mr. Lang, who seems to have
been a superior man, had sought the spiritual good of his
slaves. He had fitted up a place of worship, and several
Episcopalian ministers in succession had held service there. He
also encouraged marriage among his people, and made a distinction between the married and those who lived only in concubinage, by seating them separately in the little chapel. But
the estates passed into other hands ; and an attorney who loved
the darkness rather than the light, demolished the chapel,
and forbade the assembling of the people for religious purposes.

Many years before the period referred to, several Baptists—
men of colour—went from America to Jamaica, and introduced
the gospel among the slaves in many parts of the island. One
of these, Moses Baker, laboured about Trelawny ; and another,
Mr. Gibb, laboured in St. Mary's and neighbouring parishes.
Mr. Jameson writes of them thus :—" They were, I believe,

sincere and zealous men ; but their knowledge of Christianity
was most imperfect, and their minds were filled with the most
absurd superstitions."   They held night meetings among the
slaves, instructed them according to their notions of truth, and
immersed those whom they approved.   Mr. Gibb extended his
labours to Goshen, where he had many followers.   The first
thing he did was to "set them off to pray."   He taught them
some words of prayer ; appointed influential slaves as his
leaders on the estates ; and told the people that if they saw
anything in their sleep, they must tell it to the leaders.   If
they dreamed, they had the spirit, and the leaders would say,
" Praise on, boy ; bright follower, you will soon be fittin' to
be baptized."   If the inquirer had no dream, he was told that
he was neglecting prayer.   Mr. Gibb said that they must seek
their dreams in the wilderness, that was, in the woods.   Many
did so.   They slept under the trees, night after night, sometimes for months, praying and waiting for the coveted dream.
One of Mr. Gibb's converts thus described the last " experience "
he had before he was immersed :—" I get under an orange
tree and draw my coat about me.   I fall down on my knees to
say my prayers.   I then look round me, this way and that
way.   Every ting was quiet.   My head begin to look quite
big, as big as my body.   My heart say 'patter, patter,' I
thought the devil come to me.   I rose and ran."   " Did the
devil run after you ?"   " I not know that.   I never look over
my shoulder till I get home, and shut the door."   He told his
" work " to the leader ; the leader reported it to Gibb ; and,
on the following Sabbath, the fortunate dreamer was baptized
in the White River.   Another once told the writer that he
slept and prayed in the bush three months, till, one night, he
dreamed that he was sitting under a tree with a loaded basket
at his feet, and that a white man came up and bade him lift
the basket and follow.   He followed till they came to a "sink
hole ;" and his guide told him to throw his basket into the
hole.   This dream was considered satisfactory.   The load was
his sins ; the white stranger was the Saviour ; and the throwing of his load into the hole indicated the pardon of his sins.

He was "fittin'," and was accordingly baptized. They kept fast on Monday, Wednesday, and Friday, on which days they ate nothing till four o'clock P.M. After four o'clock, when they left off work, they washed their faces, sucked an orange or other fruit, boiled coffee, roasted plantain, or prepared any other food they had, and went to the house of the leader to "broke picce." When they were eating, every one shut his eyes and pressed them hard, and if he then saw anything like fire, he rose up and told the leader. The leader would say, "Fight on, boy, you do well." After eating, they drank their tea or coffee out of white cups. At this meeting they sat up late ; and, on Saturdays, frequently till day-break on Sabbath morning.

Such were the puerilities and superstitions which were mixed up with the religion of heaven among the slaves in some parts of Jamaica. We may hope that some learned the truth as it is in Jesus, and were saved. But bad seed was sown, and it did not fail to bear much evil fruit. The leaders were nearly or quite as ignorant as the rest ; and they were sometimes as immoral as they had been before assuming the office. But, as they had great influence among the slaves, they were not favourable to any movement which would ignore or depose them. Mr. Jameson writes, at a later date, "There is the most abundant proof that the influence which the leaders exerted over the people was not unfrequently employed to effect the most abominable purposes. Seduction and avarice are sins too common in the history of Leaderism. Such is the fruit of a native agency imperfectly instructed. I might mention also some of the opinions circulated through this agency. That the Book (the Bible) is for Backra (white man), but God has given the dream to the negro, and it is a better guide than the Book for him. That John the Baptist is greater than Jesus Christ, for he baptized Christ. Hence, long after I came to Goshen, every such person whom I met, said that he belonged to John the Baptist's religion. Another frightful notion prevails, namely, that Jesus Christ had sin before he was baptized, but his sin was taken away by his baptism. Hence the very common opinion among the negroes that the 'dip,' as they themselves call it, is necessary to take away sin." Notions of an equally absurd kind, equally inexcusable, too, as existing in a country where the word of God was accessible, although few of the class referred to could read it, prevailed upon other important spiritual questions.

Missionaries had long laboured in Jamaica, but they were denied free access to the slaves on the estates, by the jealousy and enmity of the bulk of the planters. A few proprietors sought instruction for their slaves, and even helped to sustain the missionaries, but these were few in comparison with those who set their faces as flint against the slightest interference with the negroes. Some knowledge of divine things spread to places where no missionary lived, and a desire was felt for more. On Sabbaths, slaves used to steal away to church in their working clothes, carrying clean suits in their baskets to put on by the road, lest, if they set out dressed, they might be seen and hindered. Some walked or rode ten or twenty miles on Saturday night, and returned on Sabbath night, in time for the crack of the driver's whip which summoned them to work on Monday morning. Even before Mr. Jameson's arrival, there was a little knot of praying people on one of the Trinity estates, who used to hold their meetings at night. On these occasions, if there was any brother present from a place of greater spiritual privilege, his instructions were welcomed as a contribution to their little stock of Christian ideas. Their overseer did not like prayer work, and thought that he had a right to stop it. He felt as did a brother overseer, when Joseph Wilson, one of the present pillars of the church at Goshen, got married in a Christian way. The overseer himself was living in concubinage, and the marriage of Joseph sounded in his ears like a rebuke. Poor man ! he was very savage, and told Joseph that the slave should not go before the master ; and, he supposed, Joseph would now begin to pray too.

· The little meeting referred to was hateful to the overseer. He caused their meeting-house, which they had made themselves, to be pulled down. They restored it. He again caused it to be demolished. One of the praying people, who afterwards became a member of the church, was once flogged for keeping up the meeting ; and, on one occasion, the meeting was surprised by the relentless Busha and his bookkeepers, who locked up all present for the night.

With the exception of the little light which thus had reached the people of that district, all was darkness, ignorance, and superstition. The writer remembers the animated description given of their state by a female who had been brought to the knowledge of the Saviour, under Mr. Jameson's ministry :— " We were a wild people. Mr. Jameson found we wandering and stumbling among crags and gullies in the woods, blind, and with no man to care for we souls ; and he brought we into the light." His arrival was like life from the dead. His amiability, his kindness, his devotedness to the Lord's work among them, and the kindly interest which he took in their welfare, soon made way for him into every heart. It is refreshing to hear the few survivors of those times speak of them as with the fresh recollections of yesterday, while the tearful eye bears testimony to the sincerity and depth of the feelings which are thus aroused. They received the missionary as a gift from the Lord, and, to use the words of his venerable father, they had no cause to regret the receiving.

Lucky Hill Pen House, which the proprietors had granted to Mr. Jameson as a place of residence, was out of repair, and Mr. and Mrs. Jameson were therefore welcomed to make their abode, for a time, under the hospitable roof of Mr. and Mrs. Cowan, at Carron Hall. Seven months passed before the repairs were made, and great fatigue was thus caused in going to and fro ; while the missionary's labours among the people were interrupted by his having to live ten miles distant from them.

An extract from a letter to the late Mr. Bryden, who was then the Treasurer of the Rose Street Missionary Association, a man of genuinely missionary spirit, of date March 9th, 1837, will carry the reader, in spirit, to the opening scene of Mr. Jameson's labours.

" The field which I have chosen is very populous. I com-

menced my labours on Sabbath, the 26th of February. Mr.
Cowan accompanied me.   He preached in the forenoon, and I,
in the afternoon.   Our place of worship was a boiling-house,
which was put at our disposal by Mr. Geddes, the attorney.
It was the largest audience ever seen at that place.   Many had
to stand without at the doors and windows.   There were about
500 present.   Many came from Carron Hall, a distance of 14
or 15 miles, and a number of our own countrymen were with
us.   I told them that a congregation in the far distant land
from which I had come, were anxious that they should make a
right use of the liberty which Providence had now given them ;
and, also, that they should enjoy the more glorious freedom of
the children of God ; and, for this purpose, they had sent me
to preach among them the unsearchable riches of Christ.   For
this great and important end had I come, and, in carrying it
into effect, I was ready to spend and be spent.   As I spoke
they listened with much apparent earnestness and delight, and,
at the conclusion, they came around me saying, ' Thank you,
massa, good massa ; we soon be able to read good book, now
since minister come.'   One old man, when he heard that a
minister was come to labour at Goshen, left Mr. Simpson, who
had told him, and his neighbours, and, going to the side of the
field, in prayer returned thanks to God.   I hope God has heard
your prayers in my behalf, and opened a door of entrance : for
at present, at least, I seem to have come with the concurrence
not only of the negroes, but of the white population—the one
party desirous of being instructed ; the other, of affording them
instruction.

" Although such be the field in its present aspect, yet there
will be many difficulties to contend with, which we have not
begun fully to feel.   Hitherto our home has been with our
brethren, whose kindness has almost made us forget that we
are strangers in a strange land.   It is truly gratifying to see
how unwearied are their labours, and how great their success.
Their congregations and schools are flourishing ; and the confidence which the people repose in them is entire.   This arises
from their integrity, from their maintaining strict discipline,

and from demonstrating, by their whole procedure, that they have but one object at heart—the spiritual, temporal, and eternal welfare of their fellow-men. You have only to see what they have done, and are doing, to feel convinced that they have been misrepresented and calumniated. I speak advisedly, when I say that if anything is being done for the advancement of this people, they are doing it."

While sitting in the beautifully situated "great house" of Goshen, on the Sabbath evening, after the interesting services of the day, he writes in his journal :—"Sabbath evening is calm and serene. The vale below and the hills around covered with verdure, fields of cane waving in the breeze, and the scented gale from the groves of pimento, revive the spirits ; and the browsing of the herds on every side tells of plenty and of peace. All nature seems to enjoy the Sabbath. But man, the very creature for whom it was principally intended, knows not its rest, cares not for its enjoyment. Here is a group around the grindstone, sharpening their tools for to-morrow's work ; there, a number of persons around a pool, washing clothes ; while others are coming from their provision-grounds with baskets of fruit and provisions on their heads. How great the difference between this district and those others where missionaries have been labouring for some time ! O Lord ! give us also grace to labour, so that the wilderness and the solitary place shall be glad for them, and the desert shall rejoice and blossom as the rose."

On Saturday, March 4th, Mr. Jameson rode to Goshen, inviting all he met to come to the boiling-house on the following day. They seemed pleased to be invited ; and on Sabbath, the meeting was crowded. Having preached in the forenoon, he intimated that he would go over the same subject in the afternoon, and make it simple, so that all might understand it. The house was more crowded in the afternoon, when Mr. Jameson went over the forenoon's discourse, in the way of question and answer, and found that indeed there was much need for such an exercise.

"*Monday, 6th.*—Called at an estate on the way to Carron

Hall ; met the negroes in the middle of the day ; explained to them the object of my mission, and expressed the hope that, since I had come so far to tell them of Christ and mercy, they would come and hear what I had to say on this all-important subject.   Called at another estate, and was kindly received by the owner.   On my saying that I wanted to see the negroes, if it were convenient, to invite them to come to Goshen, he immediately called them to assemble at the door of his house, where I addressed them shortly.   I returned home with a heart full of gratitude to God for so many manifestations of his power and goodness.   In all the ways in which he was leading me, I saw him to be a prayer-hearing and a prayer-answering God.

" On my arrival, my joy was turned into grief, and my heart overwhelmed, by letters from home, announcing the death of my beloved father.   I would be silent, O Lord ! for this stroke is thine.   The God and Father of our Lord Jesus Christ hath done it ; therefore it is well.   It is well for the dead.   O that it may be well for his bereaved children, for the people who were his charge, and for the church of the living God !   How uncertain our time !   How evanescent the world's good !   O Lord ! we claim thee as our portion, and thy favour as our life.   From the willows we take our harp, and go forward still praising thee.   We rise from our sorrows to engage in thy work, with more singleness of heart, and with more unwearied activity ; that, at last, with our fathers, we may enter into the rest which God hath prepared for the faithful."

While the missionary voyagers were looking at their Deseada —the desired land—in the West, the ripened saint at Methven came in sight of his desired haven.   The " messenger of peace" entered the circle once more.   He came to call away the patriarch of the household and the pastor of the flock.   " There have indeed been cases in which good men have fallen asleep very gently, and smiled so sweetly in death's face, that the smile seemed to disarm the tyrant.   So did the great Chalmers ; so did the less known, but as good, and scarcely less gifted, Jameson of Methven.   These men died . in a moment, and with no apparent pain, and with a celestial expression on their faces."[1]

A letter addressed to his brothers and sisters, March 21st, 1838, shows a remarkable depth of piety and affection. As we gaze on the missionary far from the mourners at home, while he alternately prays, and weeps, and smiles through his tears, we see an instance of simple faith in, and cheerful submission to, God, which we should seek to copy, when the bitter cup is put to our lips.

"All the circumstances connected with this most heart-rending bereavement, even the most minute, we expect from you, and look for with the most intense anxiety every day. All that we know is, that on the 13th of January, our father came in from visiting the sick, went up to his room, and, at two o'clock, was found sleeping in Jesus. Oh, my dear sisters and brothers, Nicolis and I feel deeply with you all our common loss. The stroke is heavy, very heavy indeed ! We are like to sink under it. We are like those who dreamed, as if we had been suddenly awaked from a state of lethargy. Our father dead ! lying yonder in the lonely grave ! to see him no more, to hear him no more ; his pulpit empty, his study empty ! Oh, it is difficult to believe it ! I weep not for him. No, he is happy ; home to his Father's house ; entered into rest ; the work which his Father had given him to do being performed and accepted. He is now associated with the happy company around the throne ; with our dear mother ; with his fathers and our fathers ; and with all the spirits of the just made perfect ; with angels who, as he sometimes told me, suggested to him, in his happiest moments, those lofty thoughts, and new and interesting views of Scripture for which he was so remarkable. Above all, he is with Christ, in the presence of God, with whom he walked so closely, whom he served so cheerfully, and before whose throne he kneeled so frequently in this world below. He is removed from many evils which I fear are coming, and which might have proved too much for his fine feelings, and his high and sanctified spirit,—removed to a world free from them all, where

[1] Rev. George Gilfillan, *Alpha and Omega*, vol. i. p. 239.

there are joy and gladness without alloy, and where sorrow and sighing have for ever fled away. Weep for him ? Oh, no ! Dearest children, with myself, of our dear departed father, not at all. Our tears shall never flow from a heart fretful and repining against God for this heavy blow. No ; as our beloved father used to say, we shall subscribe this heart-rending dispensation, like the Psalmist, with ' Blessed God ;' though thou hast laid upon us a heavy hand, yet, O Lord, thou art our God after all; yea, after all this, and ten thousand times more, thou art in thyself, and in all that thou doest, most blessed. Neither shall our tears flow from a heart grudging our father the glories upon which he has entered ; nor shall they ever be shed as expressive of a desire that he should return to us. Ah, no ! we rather hail his glorified spirit ; we envy its perfect happiness ; we long to be partakers of its blessedness. But I weep, and how can I refrain ? for the strongest cord of my soul has been rent asunder in a moment, and without the least warning, so that the whole man bends, and is like to sink under the stroke. But, God of my father and his father, and my chosen God, I look to thee.

"But, my dear sisters, I weep for you. Our beloved father lived in your hearts. You anticipated, when I left you, many happy days with him. But, alas ! soon have all your hopes been dashed to the ground. Let me counsel you, oh let me entreat you, to bridle your grief. Sin not in your sorrow. Be still, and know that this is God, the God of our Lord and Saviour Jesus Christ, who spared not his own Son, but gave him up to death for us all. Such a God can do you no wrong. The blow is severe, but he will bear you up ; your hearts are torn, but he will heal them ; you feel forlorn and desolate, but he will be an inmate of your home—your God, your Father, your support, your counsellor, and your friend. Futurity is dark, and fills you with many fears, but the same God who has led our beloved father and our father's fathers, and who has led us until now, says, ' Fear not, for I am with you' (Is. xli. 10 ; xliii. 2). You have now a claim upon this gracious God which you never had before ; you are fatherless, and saith God ex-

pressly, ' He doth execute the judgment of the fatherless' (Deut.
x. 18).   'Thou art the helper of the fatherless' (Ps. x. 14).
' The judge of the fatherless' (Ps. x. 18).   'Leave thy fatherless children, I will preserve them alive' (Jer. xlix. 11).   And
truly we have all been left on the Lord.   You have the highest reason to expect the gracious fulfilment of these promises,
for ye are the children of his servant ; nay, of his servants for
many generations.   Hence, Ps. cii. 28."

CHAPTER III.

Mode and spirit of mission work—Pembroke Hall—Need of education – A prophetess—Visit to Kingston—Shed for meeting—The Missionary calumniated —The shed opened—Birth of first-born—Godless Europeans, missionaries of the devil—Liberated Africans—Take up house at Lucky Hill Pen—The Lord's table in a foreign land—Jamaica fog, and mortality among Europeans—Soul renewed—How far is the negro intellect inferior?—Scotch immigrants.

BEFORE proceeding with the interesting narrative of a ten years' missionary ministry, we shall give, in Mr. Jameson's words, a comprehensive view of the manner in which he and his brother missionaries sought to do their work.

"It is manifest that the first and great duty of the missionary of Jesus is to form a taste among the people for the pure and simple gospel. And this is to be done, not by attacking their favourite notions, or scattering anathemas against particular sins. Darkness is dispelled by the infusion of light, and error uprooted by the statement of simple truth. The cross of Christ rectifies all that is wrong in man's heart and life, sooner and better far than ten thousand times ten thousand arguments. How, then, do we proceed in forming and fostering a taste for the pure gospel? How? but as the Apostle of the Gentiles : 'I am determined to know nothing among you, but Jesus Christ and him crucified.' We bring before their minds the fact that they are 'children of wrath ;' that, through the love of God, every believer in Jesus Christ, the Redeemer, is saved; that the difficulty of believing in and obeying Jesus Christ arises from the wickedness of the heart ; that the spirit of God alone can rectify this ; and that holiness of life is the proof that he has done so, in any particular case. By our conduct we seek to show them that we believe what we preach, and that we earnestly desire their salvation. We strive to labour ' in season, out of season,' by preaching, by Sabbath and day schools, by visiting families and the sick, by keeping a strict watch over the conduct of our people, and by much prayer with and for them. Through the blessing of God, we have seen the happiest results follow such a course ; prejudices uprooted ; jealousies destroyed ; confidence restored ; soul-destroying systems scattered to the winds ; a taste for the simple gospel formed ; and a song of thanksgiving bursting from the hearts of a willing people to the God of salvation, for his loving-kindness and tender mercy."

The era of emancipation is a memorable one. Such imperial munificence in Christian Britain ! such a proof of the reality and the vigour of her piety to God, and of her love to man ! such munificence to the despised negro ! and such generous consideration of those who were, many of them perhaps unwillingly, in the position of slaveholders !—a name of evil sound, of which an honest man of free British birth, and of Christian name, must surely feel ashamed !

Depend upon it, there was a memorable work of grace, too, among the emancipated themselves. God saved the sons of Israel from Egypt, that he might give them his own laws and oracles. And while he gave civil freedom to nearly a million of the children of Africa, he also moved his people to send them the glorious gospel, that they might become free citizens, not merely of imperial Britain, but of the kingdom of heaven. The missionary went to his work. Both the veterans who had toiled amid reproach, before emancipation, and those who, at that time, entered the field, shared in the elevating influences of the time. And while Britain, impelled by high, and holy, and generous motives, paid the costly ransom-price, the ministers of Christ were constrained to proclaim, widely and unweariedly, his unsearchable riches. There can be no doubt that it was a harvest time of immortal souls—a kind of first fruits of Ethiopia. And be it so, that many who afterwards fell away were received into the churches. What wonder was there in that ? And what was such chaff to the precious wheat which was, most undeniably, then gathered into the garner of the Lord ?

While we record, with admiration, the simple, fervent, and unostentatious piety of the subject of this memoir, his hearty devotion, and oneness of purpose and of effort, it is not to compare him invidiously with other missionaries. God forbid ! The history of that period has yet to be written. But were it written,—were a correct picture painted of that scene when the representatives of Ethiopia stretched out their hands, unmanacled, to God, there would be seen, mingling in the very foreground, a band of as devoted missionary brethren as ever were sent by the Church into any heathen field. Many of them are now praising on high, and praising louder as souls pass from our West Indian churches into the church of the first-born in heaven. Some of them, unfit to labour more, under the sun of the tropics, have bid the sunny isle farewell, and are now serving or suffering at home ; and others are still where they best like to be—living and preaching Jesus in their old accustomed spheres.

We have accompanied Mr. Jameson on his way to Carron Hall, after his second Sabbath's work at Goshen. We have seen him rejoicing in the encouragement which the Lord was giving him. We see him riding up Hazard Hill, or by Windsor Castle, from Bagnold's Vale to Carron Hall, his and his partner's present home. There is time to look back and praise, to look forward and pray. We then enter with him into the chamber of mourning and of tears, which flow afresh, as busy memory recalls the scenes of childhood, youth, and opening manhood, in each of which mingles the form of an honoured and beloved parent. Only those who have passed that way can know the sorrows and the joys, the regrets and the pleasures of a Christian pilgrim at such a part of his road. We now see him getting meat out of this eater, and sweetness out of this strong. Heaven has been brought near ; the spirit-world has been vividly realized, and the missionary comes forth to his work with a new devotion.

On Saturday, March 11th, Mr. Jameson went to Goshen,

and stopped by the way at the house of a proprietor, John Jeffrey, Esq. of Salisbury, examined his apprentices, and was happy to find that, through the care and diligence of Mrs. Jeffrey, a number of the young people were learning to read. This gentleman was most anxious to have a church and school-house built, and offered £50 to aid in the work.

On Sabbath, the 12th, the boiling-house of Goshen was again crowded with a willing and interested audience. Those who came at the hour for classes were examined ; but very few indeed could read intelligently. A psalm was read and sung, but their voices had not been accustomed to sing the praises of their Maker. He then made them repeat a verse or two of Scripture, and catechised them thereon. 'Line upon line, and precept upon precept,' was the missionary's motto from that time forward.

"*Monday*, 13*th*.—Called at Pembroke Hall, an estate not before noticed. The overseer stated that the attorney[1] wished me to come every second Sabbath, and preach at the estate, and that he was most willing to aid my plans. I said I should most gladly come on the afternoon of every second Sabbath, but not the whole day. For the ultimate success of the mission, it was necessary to have regular service at some one place, and Goshen had been chosen. Pembroke Hall is also a place of much importance. It is about five miles from Goshen, and embraces a great portion of Bagnold's Vale."

"*Sabbath*, 2*d April*.—After the usual morning's and fore-noon's services at Goshen, I went, in the afternoon, to Pembroke Hall. The meeting was crowded, and as attentive and interested as formerly. At the close, about 300 remained, at my request, as I wished to know who could read. I asked those who could read to be so good as stand up. After a pause, the request was repeated. At last, one stood up and said, 'Massa, me the only one who can read !' I was much affected at the thought. Alas! gross darkness covers the people. Arise! O Sun of Righteousness, arise ! and, with the brightness of thy

---

[1] The overseer—in Anglo-Ethiopic, "obusha," contracted "busha,"—has charge of the estate, and is accountable to the attorney, who is the agent of the absent proprietor.

light, chase this long and dreary night for ever away ! This man said that he was trying to teach some others to read. At my request to see his pupils, about forty or fifty came forward, old grey-headed men and children, some with their spelling-books, and one with a Testament. I was much pleased to see the progress which some of them had made."

"*Sabbath,* 16*th.*—Exchanged with Mr. Simpson. The congregation at Port Maria is numerous, and the Sabbath-school is large. The church is plain and commodious. I attended a private meeting of the members, when I had an opportunity of entering freely into conversation with them. Here there is much fruit of the labours of Mr. Simpson, and of his predecessor, Mr. Chamberlain.[1] One lady of colour told me that she had long lived in the sinful ways of the country, but God, through the labours of these devoted servants, had found her out. In the afternoon, I addressed the prisoners in the workhouse. At the close, I told them that I had lately come from Scotland ; that the people there were very sorry when freedom was thus abused, and very happy when a good use was made of it. The negroes are always delighted to hear of the interest taken in them by people at home. At the conclusion, a prisoner came with his book, and begged a lesson. He is an interesting person, always carries his book in his pocket, and, at resting-time, may be seen sitting apart from the gang, with his chain round his neck and his book in his hand. His sentence is perpetual imprisonment ; but, I hope, in this changed state of things, it will be mitigated."

"*Friday,* 21*st.*—On my way between Port Maria and Goshen, I visited Mile End, a station formed by Mr. Simpson. Here I found a good number of interesting people, thirty or forty children taught by a coloured female, and a number of persons under training for church membership. As they are twenty

---

[1] The Rev. J. Chamberlain was sent to Jamaica by the Scottish Missionary Society. He commenced his labours at Port Maria, and, by his genial and kindly manners, gained the affections of all classes. He laboured with much zeal and success, beginning a cause which has been carried on, with equal zeal and success, by his successor, the Rev. John Simpson. Mr. Chamberlain died of fever, in the prime of life, after a few years of faithful service.

miles from Port Maria, and only six from Goshen, Mr. Simpson has put them into my hands. On my way to Goshen, numbers of people left their provision grounds, and came towards me. One brought in his hand a star apple and gave me.

"'Well,' I said, 'you seem to know me.'

"'Yes,' they replied, 'we know Massa very well. We see you every Sunday at Goshen.'

"'Do you attend every Sunday?'

"'Yes, Massa, every Sunday.'

"'Well, I am delighted to hear that. I have come from a far country to tell you of Christ, and happy am I that you come to hear what I have got to say. Do you come in the morning, to the class?'

"'Yes, Massa, we want to be able to read God's Word.'

"I said that I was sorry not to know them better; but that, when our house was repaired, I should live near them, and be able to teach them to better purpose.

"'Yes, my good Massa, this is what we want very much; we be very glad to come and get lessons and prayers.'

"'Well, now, I hope you will come always, and give up your sins, and pray to God to give you an interest in Jesus Christ, that your souls may be saved.'"

"*Sabbath* 23d.—Preached at Goshen and Pembroke Hall, to crowded meetings. After the forenoon's service, a man came forward and said:—

"'Sir, I think you said that we ought not to pray to John the Baptist. I want your opinion on this subject.'

"'My opinion, then, is that you ought not. You might as well pray to me. John the Baptist was but a man, and we must pray to none but God. In God you have all you need and can desire. John the Baptist can neither hear nor help you; but God is ever with you. He knows your heart, and is able to satisfy your desires.'

"This seemed to satisfy him; he thanked me, and went his way. These opinions and practices are the nurslings of ignorance—the offspring of exceedingly crude views of the gospel, which increasing light will utterly destroy."

"*Sabbath, May 7th.*—Exchanged with Mr. Cowan. Preached at Carron Hall to a large and attentive audience. The place of worship contains about 700, is crowded every Sabbath, and many have to stand around the doors. Besides Sabbath-schools and evening meetings, there is a day-school taught by Mrs. Cowan, with about seventy pupils. Some are learning geography, grammar, history, and arithmetic; and, as I have examined them frequently, I can bear testimony to the excellent understanding which many of them display, and the proficiency which they have attained.

"Our own missionaries, for of them only am I as yet able to speak, are in labours most abundant, both 'in season and out of season.' They are high in the affections of the people, and they enjoy the confidence of many in authority on the estates. One overseer told me that Mr. Simpson had done more for his negroes than all the magistrates in the island could have done. 'On coming to the estate,' he said, 'I found the negroes in a state of insubordination; work they would not, even for money. I asked Mr. Simpson to speak to them, which he did. The people, at once, laid aside their hostility, went to their work, and, from that day to this, I have had no further trouble with them.' An attorney has often told me how strikingly the superior training given by the Scotch missionaries appeared at the late rebellion.[1] Whole districts were in flames, but not one estate on which these missionaries laboured was burned. Nay, these estates proved barriers to the advancing tide of destruction."

[1] On the 15th of April, 1831, Mr. Fowell Buxton made one of his telling attacks on colonial slavery, in which he showed that while under freedom a negro population increased, under slavery it decreased at a rapid rate. In twenty-three years, the negro population in the West Indies had diminished by 100,000. The Government thought it was time to adopt stronger measures with the planters than mere recommendations to better the condition of their slaves. The planters took fire. In Jamaica they behaved and talked like madmen; and the result of their public speeches and private talk was that the slaves became convinced that the king was going to give them "the free," and that their masters were to keep it from them. They conspired to stop work from Christmas 1831, unless they were paid for their labour. This was a bad beginning, and had a worse ending. Scenes of violence followed; sugar-works were burned to ashes; martial law was proclaimed; and blood was shed

On May 16th, Mr. Jameson wrote, " On the Sabbath morning I am engaged with a class from nine till ten, teaching to read, when there are present fifty or sixty, young and old. From ten till eleven, I have another class for reading the Scriptures, when from 200 to 300 are present. From eleven till one, I preach and have a service, like one at home, with this exception, that I am the chief musician as well as the chief speaker. In the afternoon, I go over the same ground as in the forenoon, adapting the thoughts and language ,more to the negroes. This is necessary, as, in the forenoon, I find it of importance to address my discourse to the whites present, if, by any means, I may gain them also. It is, indeed, delightful to see the interest which the people take in the work, and their satisfaction at having a minister of their own. . ' Massa, we very glad you come ; very glad we get minister ; now we get good.' At first, their minds, unaccustomed to analyse, would not work ; but now, as you proceed, drawing illustrations from their own manners, you see the eye brightening, the swarthy countenance beaming satisfaction at understanding what minister says, and the head nodding assent. It also strikes a European much to see so many black faces in a worshipping assembly. It fills the soul with emotion to see attention and deepest interest looking out of the countenance, and portrayed in the different attitudes and motions of the people. Truly, it is Ethiopia stretching out her hands to God. In the school, you have a sight no less interesting. The grey-headed negro, bending with age, and exhausted with toil, coming with his spelling-book and testament, to beg a lesson. In the same class you have the boy of nine, the youth in the prime of life, and the old man with spectacles under his hoary eyebrows, all looking on the sacred page with deepest interest, all setting their faces to the lesson, determined not to be baffled with its difficulties, now reading, now spelling, still persevering. They are not content with reading the lesson ; they desire to go over it again and again, and still they are not satisfied ; they will not stop till Massa, as they say, give them the understanding of the lesson. A few nights ago, a young man came to the house begging for a lesson. Mrs. Jameson heard him read, and, as it was late, she thought that he would wish to get home, as he had far to go. She rose from the table. He looked at her, and said, ‘ Please, Missis, give me the understanding of my lesson ;’ and he stayed another half-hour for that purpose. Might *we* not learn a lesson from this !”

And thus did Mr. Jameson urge on the attention of friends how necessary it was that teachers should be sent to divide the work with the missionaries in the field.

“It is cheering to see so many of the negroes so deeply anxious to rise above the brutishness which sinks their race. It points to the future, and tells us that we shall yet see greater things than these.

“Teachers are much needed and desired. Children, freed by the Abolition Act, are running wild ; there are few to care for them, and fewer still to train them. Unless they be speedily trained to work, and educated, their manhood bodes ill to the country. Many proprietors and attorneys are anxious to aid in the instruction of the people. The Island Government has called the attention of the House of Assembly to this ; and the Home Government has given a grant of money to forward it. Thus, God is opening up the field ; and everything is in its order. He missioned the ministers of reconciliation first, who prepared the field for education, and weathered the storm which in consequence arose. Now, the storm is changed into a calm. It is found that education is as necessary for the negro, for the master, and for the country, as ignorance and the whip were thought necessary before ; and, consequently, the cry from all corners of the land is education, schools, teachers. In different parts of the island, schools have been erected by the Mico Institution,[1] and by the Government grant. In other parts, as among ourselves, the missionary himself teaches, or

---

[1] A Lady Mico died in 1710, leaving a sum of money to her daughter, on a certain condition. The condition was violated, and the money went, according to the will, to ransom Christian slaves in Barbary. In 1827, it had accumulated to £110,000. There being then no Christian slaves in Barbary, this money was invested to be employed in educating the negroes. The Mico charity now maintains a normal school, in which natives are trained for the work of teaching.

employs a teacher ; and in those places which are too far from school, if a negro be found who can read, he is employed, during his leisure time, to teach the others. Thankful we are for these beginnings, small though they be. They create an ardent longing, and give rise to many an earnest prayer that the Lord of the harvest would send out a band of prudent and devoted men to this work. At the importance and variety of the duties we have to perform, and at the difficulties we have to encounter, we sometimes feel appalled. But why this ? Our strength lies not in man, in the might of his arm, in the strength of his intellect, in his prudence, or his piety. No. O God, our sufficiency is of thee !"

Writing on this same subject (December 15th, 1837), Mr. Jameson says, " Every day people are bringing their children to live, they say, with Massa, and serve him, that he may teach them ; but prudence requires that we refuse these offers, else our family would soon be large enough. In the forenoon, Mrs. Jameson is occupied in teaching the free children who come to the house, and in the evening, both of us are employed in teaching the apprentices, who come, after the labours of the day, from the estates around. On three days of the week, I ride out to visit the estates at a distance. I first meet with the free children, and then with the apprentices, during their hours for resting."

Looking at the extent of the work, which exceeded the powers of one labourer, Mr. Jameson earnestly entreated that one labourer more might be sent to bear part of their burden, and to share in their joys. " I rejoice," he says, " that I can apply for this assistance to the Church to which I have the happiness to belong, which my great-grandfathers were instrumental in founding, where both my grandfathers have laboured, and amidst the labours of which my father died ; and I earnestly hope that I shall not apply in vain."

On his arrival, Mr. Jameson was led to expect liberal assistance from the attorney of the Trinity estates, as Messrs. Davidson, Barkly, and Company, the proprietors, had the furtherance of his mission, and the welfare of their apprentices much at heart. But circumstances hindered the giving of immediate help. The house that had been assigned him as a residence was being slowly repaired; and it was very difficult to obtain the labour necessary to erect a shed at a spot half-way between Goshen and Pembroke Hall, at which both congregations might conveniently meet together. At length, he was forced to take this matter entirely into his own hands.

He writes, " We are left entirely to ourselves. It is better that the Church of God should do her own work, and that she should be aided by those only who are her own. In this way she will preserve her independence. The Church forgets her dignity when she becomes a beggar at the doors of the wealthy, when the love of God and holiness dwell not within."

But the people for whose use and benefit the shed was to be made, were unwilling to aid him. They remembered that the chapel which Mr. Lang had fitted up for them, had been destroyed. At length, by paying them for their work at the ordinary rates, and stimulating them by his own example, Mr. Jameson succeeded. At first, some of the people were disposed to regard him as only an agent of the planters, whose influence would be against the interests of freedom. But this delusion was soon dispelled by his conduct among them; and they came to see in him a servant of the Most High God, who showed unto them the way of salvation, and not a servant of their masters to bring them and their children into new subjection.

At length, finding it beyond his strength to do his work at Goshen, and then, after a ride of six miles, to go through the same work at Pembroke Hall, Mr. Jameson resolved to take these places on alternate Sabbaths.

Sabbath, May 21st, was, therefore, spent at Pembroke Hall. " Two hours in the morning, and in the interval, I heard the children read, and catechized them. There were sixty children. At the close of the afternoon's service, resumed the classes. In the evening, the apprentices at Salisbury, where I spent the night, came to lessons and to family worship."

" *Monday, 22d.*—Called at an estate where the negroes were in a state of insubordination. A young woman there had set up for a preacher. She said that she had been in heaven, and seen Jesus Christ; that he had told her that the people were free in 1832, and should not work for Massa; and that she was commanded to preach, because the people did not understand 'backra preachers.' The people, therefore, had refused to work, and the magistrate had sent some of them to the workhouse; and advised the overseer to get me to speak to them. On hearing this, I promised to go the night following at seven o'clock."

" *Tuesday, 23d.*—Went, according to agreement, to visit the people on the estate referred to. The house was quite full. The prophetess, as she called herself, was there. As I began, she came forward into the middle of the floor, and cried out for her guava switches, that she might flog either me, or the people, or both. I stopped, and told her to sit down, and be quiet. As she still persisted in making a noise, I said I should have to put her to the door, but would prefer that she should sit quietly and hear. She then took her seat, and remained quiet till all was over. I told the people that I came there, to-night, intending not to take the least notice of this person, for her conduct was so extravagant, and her pretensions so absurd, that to notice her at all was making too much of her. But, as she had thrust herself in my way, I would describe her character from the Bible. I told them that her pretensions were false; that what she taught was false; that her conduct then, and before, showed her to be one of those deceivers who turn men from Christ, disturb the peace of his Church, and uphold the kingdom of darkness. The people listened eagerly, and with apparent satisfaction. Such cases, I am sorry to say, are not uncommon. The knowledge of the people is scanty, their intellect is weak and clouded, and their passions are strong, so that they become an easy prey to the wicked pretender who has a little more cunning than themselves."

In connexion with this case, Mr. Jameson expresses his views, which he ever held very strongly, and of evils caused by imperfectly instructed teachers and guides among the black people.

Speaking of the leaders appointed by the American Baptists,

and of their successors, he says, " Persons, whose knowledge is exceedingly imperfect, set themselves up as leaders, explain the Scriptures, preach to the people, and sit in judgment upon, and certify their fitness for baptism, and for admission to the full fellowship of the Church. In consequence, these leaders frequently form a very erroneous estimate of their own capacities ; and, aspiring to a higher position, they leave the church to which, at first, they belonged, and, carrying their people along with them, form congregations of their own. Many congregations in this and other parts of the island have been thus formed ; and, I fear, it is an evil which will grow. We long for the day when persons of African race shall be preachers of the gospel. May that day soon come ! But we also desire that such preachers may be enlightened and well qualified, in every respect."

In the second week of June, Mr. Jameson went to Kingston, the commercial capital, passing through Spanish Town, the political capital of Jamaica. This was a journey of forty miles on horseback. He enjoyed the grand and beautiful scenery on the way from the north to the south side of the island. From the mountains where Carron Hall stands, the traveller descends into St. Thomas in the Vale, which is a hollow, being, in fact, a basin with several outlets to the south. Through one of these —the Bog Walk, a magnificent pass of about seven miles long —lies the road to Spanish Town. The Rio Cobre, Copper River, flows through it, and the road winds along the edge of the stream.

The next entry shows that the damp which fell on the missionary's spirit, through the backwardness of those who ought to have helped him, was clearing off. The people had come to a better mind. The Lord had answered the prayers of his servants.

" *Sabbath, June* 18*th.*—Preached at Goshen. The boiling-house was full, as usual. There were fifty or sixty young people, eager to read their lessons. Heard some in the morning, some during the interval, and some in the afternoon. ' Massa,' said some, ' we much need of you. We hope you stay with we.

We went to the church yesterday, and put on all the thatch we could get ; and if you get more we will put it on.'   One expressed his anxiety that I should come to his neighbourhood at night, to read and pray with them.   A young man asked me to christen his child.   I told him that I could not do so without first ascertaining the knowledge and piety of the parent. Another, who had given me his name to proclaim for marriage, came to tell me that, as I did not belong to the holy Catholic Church, I could not marry him ' good.'   The holy Catholic Church I found, on inquiry, to be the Established Church. I explained to the people how matters stood.   True, I did not belong to the Established Church.   But that Church is no more the holy Catholic Church than mine is.   The holy Catholic Church is the whole Church of Jesus Christ, and all belong to it who preach the doctrines of Christ, and in whose hearts these doctrines exercise a purifying influence.   I do not *read* a prayer when I marry, but I *say* a prayer.   I do not marry you out of the prayer-book, but bring the Bible and show you marriage as contained in it.   Now, will any of you say that my marrying is less holy, because I do not read a prayer, and because I do not use a prayer-book, but pray as the Holy Spirit dictates, and marry you from the Bible ?   ' No, Massa,' they replied.   By this time, the poor man came weeping, saying that he wished me to marry him ; that he had every confidence in me ; and he and his wife were to place themselves under my ministry."

" *Sabbath, July 2d.*—Had an opportunity of observing the Lord's Supper, at Carron Hall, for the first time in this distant land.   104 persons sat down at the feast of mercy.   The whole were at one table, and the services were conducted as at home.   Altogether, the scene was most impressive and cheering. Truly, Ethiopia *is* stretching out her hands to God.   Some of the members of Port Maria church were present, and one of them handed me a collection which the congregation there had made to aid in erecting the church at Goshen."

" On *Friday, July 7th,* went to Goshen, and hired a number of people to gather cane tops to thatch the shed.   At six A.M. on Saturday, there were thirty-four people in the field. By twelve o'clock, all the tops in the field were carried to the place. As they had refused to work before, I felt it necessary to show, by paying them for their labour, that the Church of Christ has resources within itself; and that to gain its object it will spare no expense, and be baffled by no opposition. Having sent them the message of reconciliation, it will also give them a house in which to proclaim it. There has been a great outcry because of the wasteful expenditure of money in Jamaica. But those who have to face the heavy and ever recurring expenses connected with an infant church, in a foreign and expensive land, and who know that these expenses must be met, or their credit will fail, and their usefulness be destroyed, know that this expenditure, though great, is not wasteful."

"*Sabbath, 9th.*—Preached at Goshen. The day was wet, with thunder and lightning. An earthquake shook the earth and our hearts. At the end a man came saying, ' Massa, me very hungry for provision.' I thought that his provision ground had failed, and proceeded to make some remarks, when he corrected me, saying that he had been hungry for the Word of God."

On July 17th, Mr. Jameson wrote to Mr. M'Gilchrist :—

"The church is a shed 50 feet by 35. Posts driven into the ground, in all the roughness of nature, support a roof of materials equally rude, and this is thickly thatched with cane tops. All we desire is a house in which to worship God, without exposure to sun, or wind, or rain. We look to God for this, and we believe that He will provide.

"The Port Maria congregation gave me a collection. Carron Hall has promised me another ; and with money thus raised, we have got the roof nearly thatched.

"Our own house is not yet repaired ; and our things are lying here and there, as they were packed in Edinburgh. I am chiefly grieved, because I cannot follow any regular system of work. We have to sing of great mercy, too, for our health is good ; and the attention of Mr. and Mrs. Cowan, and of Mr. Simpson, is unremitting. Their kindness has laid us under lasting obligations. The interest of the people is as great as ever; and managers and proprietors of estates solicit my labours. Should we ever be compelled to abandon Goshen, of which I have no fear, I know that other places, equally advantageous, will be offered."

"*Saturday, 22d.*—About eighty people were working at the shed. At twelve o'clock, I paid them for their half day's work. I then spoke about a report which had reached me this morning, that I want to teach their children in order that they may, by this means, be bound to the estate. I felt hurt that they should fancy I came to wreathe the yoke of bondage around the necks of their children. It was false. Had I been hindered from teaching them, except on these terms, I would not have come, and my friends would not have sent me. It was but just to their master to say that he had neither proposed, nor, so far as I know, thought of such terms. Those who spread these stories against me were the enemies of their children, and wished to keep them from that instruction which, most of all, they needed for freedom, and for death and eternity. We have, sometimes, much to bear from the suspicions of the negroes. They are exceedingly jealous of their liberty, and our enemies are ever active in fanning their suspicions to our hurt."

"*Sabbath, 23d.*—It is a great matter of thankfulness that all the reports against us fail to injure our Sabbath meetings. The classes and the audiences were as numerous as ever I have seen them. Two men told me of their desire that I should marry them. They had perfect confidence in my marrying. So that there is reason to hope that the objections made to my lawful authority to perform the marriage ceremony, mentioned in a former page, instead of having injured us, have done us good."

"*Saturday, 29th.*—We have this day finished the thatching of the church. The people exerted themselves to the utmost, and were not a little satisfied when the last handful was put on. They continued at work the whole day, for which I paid them at the common rate."

"*Sabbath, 30th.*—I preached vacant our old church, the boiling-house, and intimated that, on the following Sabbath, we should meet in our own church ; and desired the people to bring seats with them."

"*Sabbath, August 6th.*—At an early hour, the people began to assemble. It was cheering to see bands coming from every quarter, some carrying chairs, some stools, and some benches, wending their way to the house which we had erected for the worship of the God of Israel. This eased the pain of former discouragements ; it far more than made up for former difficulties. It proved to us that the Lord was on our side, and would still be with us, till we should have performed all the work which he had appointed for us. At nine o'clock, we began the classes ; at ten, the house was full ; at eleven, crowded. I preached from Matt. xviii. 20 : 'Where two or three are," etc., and showed them the two grand points of difference between the assemblies of God's people and those of the world ; that the former met in Christ's name, and for his service, and that Christ himself is in the midst of them. That, therefore, the glory of such assemblies consists not in the presence of wealth and rank, or in the magnificence of the building, but in the excellence of the work, the spirituality of those engaged in it, and, above all, in the gracious presence of Jesus Christ. They listened with much seeming interest and delight, and, I trust, with profit. In the middle of the day I arranged the readers into different classes, for the sake of order and comfort. I took down the names of 120 persons who promised to attend the classes regularly. At the close of the afternoon's service, the people came forward and expressed themselves highly satisfied with their church, and said, 'Massa, just one thing more now : to have you down from Carron Hall in the midst of us.'"

An interesting little incident happened on that occasion. A humming bird flew into the open shed, when Mr. Jameson was leading in prayer, and, after fluttering about his head, as it flutters while sucking honey from the flower, it perched upon his crown. The people saw it, and were pleased ; for they thought it was a favourable omen. The people of Africa, like the Romans, are wont, at this day, to take omens from the flight of birds.

Arrangements were made for boarding the shed all round, and for seating it. On the 2d of September he writes, " Five P.M. The people all home ; the church seated, and the sittings calculated to contain from 450 to 500 people." None but a missionary who has had to go through the labour and effort needed to procure shelter for his family, and a roof under which to carry on his work among the people, can fully sympathize with Mr. Jameson, as he lingers in this unadorned shed, and looks around on the rough structure. This is the best he can get. If it were infinitely finer, it would not be too good for its purpose. But its appearance does not hinder it from being the meeting-place of the Lord of salvation with this people, in the dawn of the day of the gospel upon them.

" *Thursday, September 9th.*—Mrs. Jameson confined. Sad night ! All other anxieties and fears were for the time forgotten in my concern about the safety of her who had become my companion in this land of strangers and of many difficulties. I cried unto Thee, O Lord ; I said, Thou art my refuge and my portion in the land of the living. Her sorrows terminated in the birth of a dead boy. I feel thankful that the Lord, while He has taken to himself our first-born, has spared the mother. The Lord permitted him not to abide with us. He took his soul to himself, and gave us the body to lay in the grave. He is buried beside Mr. Cowan's first-born, under the shade of a bamboo tree."

The following extract expresses the missionary's feelings about the hindrances that are put in the way of the gospel among a heathen people, by the want of religion, and the positive wickedness of Europeans. A man must either be a true man—a genuinely godly man—in the presence of heathenism, or he is all but certain to be decidedly bad. A morality which springs merely from a regard for appearances, or for the public opinion of a country like Scotland, but which is not the outcoming of a regenerated heart, soon withers and dies amid the

moral miasma of heathenism.   How many promising youths
have become vile, and been lost to all good, on leaving religious
circles, to push their fortunes in foreign lands !   Their morality
not being rooted in godliness of heart, is speedily sapped and
swept away ; from bad they grow to worse ; in the lowest
depth they find a lower deep, till they are hardened into shame-
lessness, and frequently die the death of the wicked."

" *September* 19*th*.—The simple gospel is scorned and
nauseated by Scotchmen, and the sons of Scotch ministers are
foremost in the band.   Alas ! we have much reason to blush
for our countrymen.   With one exception they have forsaken
us.   At first, they professed to stand by us, but they love the
world with its unholy pleasures too much to love the gospel
too.   They do not openly oppose me, but by their coldness to
all that is good, by their disrespect to all that God has appointed for man's salvation, and by the impurity of their lives,
they show what spirit they are of."

" *Saturday, September* 23*d*.—Visited a sick person, at the
request of her husband—the first since I came to the country.
These visits to the negro houses need to be made with caution.
The day of man's claiming property in his fellow-man is fast
drawing to a close.   In the meantime, we must diligently use
the opportunities we have of sowing the seed of eternal life,
which, blessed be God, are now many, and are daily increasing."

Writing to Mr. M'Gilchrist, September 26th, 1837, he says,
"Some negroes were lately placed under my care, who were
taken in a slave-ship by H.M.S. ' Racer.'   500 of them were
brought to Jamaica ; and the Governor distributed them among
the different estates, as apprentices, on condition that they
should be clothed, fed, and educated, and, at the end of five
years, receive £10, to enable them to follow any pursuit they
might desire.   The proprietor of Salisbury, Mr. Jeffrey, received
thirty, all young people.   They were fresh and good-looking,
and some of the boys decidedly interesting and smart.   It is
only four weeks since they came, and one of the boys knows
most of the letters, through the attention and perseverance of
Mrs. Jeffrey.   Mr. J. ranks them before the house every night,

and teaches them the names of the different parts of the body, which amuses them much. Their great delights, at present, are their clothes, of which they received two changes, and their food. A few nights ago, one of the boys stole a hen from the coop, plucked it, and was proceeding to eat it, when the theft was discovered. Next morning, Mr. J. called the boy to the door, and showed him his error. In a few minutes, all his fellows surrounded him. They tied a piece of cloth on his head, and then, dancing around him, singing the songs of their country, with switches in their hands, every one, as he passed, struck him with his switch, until Mr. Jeffrey had to interfere. The dead fowl was tied on his back, and he was sent to work. In the evening, the poor boy underwent the same treatment from his countrymen, and was to have the fowl tied to his back in the morning, but he devoured it during the night."

In the same letter, Mr. Jameson refers to certain exaggerated accounts of the emancipated, on the one hand, and of the masters, on the other. The former were depicted in too favourable a light; and the latter were too much blackened. The friends of the negro were not always wise in their defence of him, any more than his enemies were fair in their attacks. The latter set forward only the bad ones as the sample; and the former, sometimes, set forward only the good ones. A medium representation, both of the people and of the planters, would have been truer, and, therefore, more expedient. There were well-behaved and industrious negroes, as well as lazy, good-for-nothing fellows; and there were kind and righteous masters, as well as harsh and oppressive ones. "The statement that all the planters are brutes and barbarians, is a very extravagant one." To represent Jamaica as evangelized, and the negroes as all pious and patient, was equally extravagant. This misrepresentation was calculated to do mischief in several ways. It encouraged the churches at home, in some cases, to abandon the infant communities before they were able to stand alone; and it stirred up the enemies of emancipation and of missions to depreciate and slander the good that, by the grace of God, had really been accomplished. We must bear a little with the extravagances of both sides ; and the friends of missions will do well to learn, from the case of Jamaica, neither to form exaggerated notions of the good which they do, nor to expect too much in a short period.   There are laws of progress in the kingdom of God plainly laid down in the word of God.   The growth of a minute seed into a spreading and umbrageous tree, the leavening of a large mass by the silent and gradual influence of a little leaven, are figures of the history of that kingdom, given us by the Lord himself.

Fiat justitia ruat cœlum, do and speak according to justice and truth, whatever may be the consequences.   No good is ever done to a good cause by extravagance of statement on the part of its promoters, or by painting their opponents blacker than they really are.   Neither is that style of praise at all judicious in which so many are apt to indulge, either on their own account, or on account of others.   Obedience to our Lord's law of love, as explained by Paul, would prevent much bitter feeling between individual Christians and bodies of Christians : " without preferring one before another, doing nothing by partiality."   " Let nothing be done through strife or vain-glory ; but, in lowliness of mind, let each esteem other better than themselves.   Let us not be desirous of vain-glory, provoking one another, envying one another."

In sending home his journal, containing these notices of engagements and labours during nine months, Mr. Jameson concludes thus :—" We have certainly experienced some difficulties in this distant land, but these are few and light when compared with those experienced by our brethren before us ; they are insignificant when compared with the mercies we have enjoyed ; they are far fewer and lighter than might have been expected. They have taught us to confide in God rather than man.   When we sing of judgment, we would, in a higher note still, sing of mercy."

At length (20th October) the missionary and his partner took possession of their house—Lucky Hill Pen—a small residence about three miles from the place of worship.   It stands quiet and cheerful, amid rich evergreen pastures, where hundreds of cattle feed, and has been a pleasant home to Mr. Jameson's successors. The people began to gather round them, in the evenings, to learn to read the word of God. The lessons being heard, religious instruction was given to those who thus assembled. " While I write," says Mr. Jameson, " my wife is in an adjoining room with twenty of these learners. The answer just given by one of the children to a question, amuses me much. The question was, ' Where is God ?' the answer, ' All about.' This was his idea of God's omnipresence."

Having been laid down with fever for two weeks, and unable to officiate on the Lord's day, he records :—

" *November 5th.*—Preached to a large and attentive audience. Many of them came, they said, uncertain whether or not there would be service ; but they were so wearied, or hungry, as they expressed themselves, that they were willing to run the risk."

The people were now as willing, as they had formerly been backward, to aid in preparing a roof under which to worship God. The Goshen carpenters waited on Mr. Jameson, and asked to be allowed to finish the boarding of the church in their own time.

" *Sabbath, November 12th.*—After service, I intimated to the people that, as I had not had an opportunity of ascertaining who were my own people, and who not, I intended to open a class for persons who wished to be instructed with a view to become members, and that they must come and converse with me privately before I put down their names."

During the week many came ; and the missionary was greatly cheered with finding so much interest and earnestness, although their knowledge was scanty and imperfect. As many couples were living according to a fashion, alas ! too common still, that of " beastly concubinage," it was made a rule that none such should be admitted, unless they consented to marry. Many of these couples, therefore, complied with the divine law, and were married accordingly.

Mr. Jameson also began to visit from house to house, and

was much encouraged by the tokens of an awakening interest and anxiety among the people.   One sick person told him that her husband had long since died, and she wished to be married to the Lord Jesus Christ.   " Met a man who told me that he and his wife could not agree, and that he belonged to John the Baptist's religion.   I told him that there was no such religion, and that he had no peace in his family, because he was not yet acquainted with the religion of Jesus Christ.   If he prayed to Jesus every day, and submitted his heart to Christ, he would enjoy peace in his family, and peace in his heart, for then he would have peace with God."

On the 10th of December, Mr. Jameson says :—" Spent a happy day at Port Maria, with my brother, Mr. Simpson, and his flock, in observing the Lord's Supper.   After the forenoon's service, Mr. Simpson ordained three elders, and in the afternoon, the disciples gathered around the table of the Lord.   It is delightful in any circumstances to sit down at that table, more especially with the interesting children of Ethiopia.   The solemn stillness which pervaded the church when the disciples were partaking of the emblems of the Lord's broken body and shed blood, was, every now and then, interrupted by the sighs and sobs of the melting heart.   On the Monday, we held the first meeting of session ever held in Port Maria, and I can truly say that I was surprised and delighted at the sound judgment and manly deportment of the members in the different cases which were brought before them."

On December 21st, Mr. Jameson visited a part of his district where he had not formerly been, and was delighted to find himself welcomed by a great number of interested and steady friends. It is a joyous thing when the husbandman alights upon a spot which the Lord of the vineyard has been secretly cultivating through his feeble instrumentality.   This is casting precious seed upon the waters, and finding it when and where it was least expected.

A meeting was held, on Christmas day, for the purpose of explaining and enforcing the advantages of education.   " Instead of preaching a sermon on education, I made the people judges, and called up before them all those who had made application for Testaments. I examined them on the book they had read, and then asked them to read a verse in the Testament, and left it to the meeting to decide who were worthy to receive a Testament. Out of fourteen applicants eight were considered worthy ; the rest were advised to persevere at their books. I then presented each of the teachers with a Bible, and addressed them on the advantages of education."

" *Sabbath, December* 31*st*.—We made our first collection—£3, 12s. sterling—much more than I expected."

" *January* 1*st*, 1838.—To-day I went, according to appointment, to visit the estate of R— H—. On my arrival, I found the people rioting and dancing in the great house. I thought, what is the use of talking so much about moral instruction, and of expressing so great a desire for the visit of the minister, when the people are thus encouraged to trample under foot the one, and trifle with the appointment of the other ? I told one to say to the people that the minister had kept his word, that he was sorry to find them thus employed, and that it would have been much better had they been reading their books, and spending the first day of the year with God."

" *January* 12*th*.—During the last week, we have been busily preparing for our journey to the Presbytery,—feeding our horses, mending our saddles, bridles, and portmanteaus, and resting and strengthening ourselves. A journey of 80 miles, in a coach and four, along a smooth turnpike, is nothing compared with a journey of the same length here, where one has to jog on horseback, over precipitous mountain tracks, and by paths which the torrent has torn up, and, in a great measure, swept away."

" *January* 31*st*.—Since my last entry in the journal, I have experienced much of the Lord's kindness, in the long and tiresome journey. In our way, we passed through a great variety of scenery, which delighted the eye and beguiled the weariness of the ride,—the stupendous precipice, the rocky mountain, the endless evergreen forest, the green vale, the extensive coffee plantation, and the refreshing green of the rich cane-field. At our various halting-places, we met with much kindness ; and we were, in different quarters, requested to return and preach the gospel of peace.   At length, we arrived at New Broughton, and received a joyous welcome from our friends, Mr. and Mrs. Paterson, and had a happy meeting with the brethren.   After remaining six days together, we separated, refreshed by our mutual intercourse. In labours, our brother Mr. Paterson is most abundant, and the fruit of them appears to be no less so.   In his school and in his congregation the Lord seems to be blessing him."

"*March* 1*st*.—Preached at Goshen negro village, in the house of one of my people.   I spoke to the audience about the thief on the cross, and all appeared to be deeply interested.   After speaking for nearly an hour, I told them that I must now conclude, when a number of voices cried : ' Go on, Massa, we no tired yet.'   Having spoken for some considerable time longer, and examined them upon what I had said, nine o'clock came, when I was obliged to move.   They seemed reluctant to part.   ' Good-night, Massa ; give my howd'ye to Mrs.,' sounded from every corner as I left the house. Found Mrs. Jameson in the midst of the evening class, waiting my return to have family worship.

" Have just heard that Mr. O——, a curate, has been attacking me in every quarter where my influence extends, throwing doubts into the minds of the people about my power to dispense the sacraments, to marry, etc.   I take no notice of him or his attacks, unless my opinion is asked.

" It is a pity that individuals, instead of busying themselves with that work in which they profess to be engaged, turn their shafts against those whom they ought to regard as brethren and fellow-labourers.   The Church has long slumbered in this country, and she is moving now because she is moved by an external force ; and, with characteristic self-complacency, she is loud in her own praise, both as to what she has done, is now doing, and is able to do.

" One expects no enemies in Jamaica, but the prince of darkness.   Least of all does one expect to meet with foes among those who have left their country professedly with the same object as one's-self. These things, however, do not move me, otherwise than, I hope, they humble me, and train me to the Christian exercise of blessing those that curse us, and praying for those who despitefully use us."

Returning late from an evening meeting, he writes :—" I have often heard of a Jamaica fog, but never was in the midst of one before. The moon was full and bright, the air cold, and the fog, an endless cloud, dense and piercing. This is one of the causes of Jamaica mortality. Europeans leave their carousals in a heated state, and dash into the fog ; perspiration is suddenly checked, fever ensues, and in a short time, death."

Mr. Jameson did not know, while he was riding home that evening, under the pale moon, and through the snow-white fog, that one soul in the meeting had been savingly impressed. She was a person who, from age and weakness, had not been able to attend the meetings at Goshen boiling-house. She was one of the few who used to meet for prayer, and were persecuted by the overseer, as has been already stated. Some years before this, she felt a strong desire to be able to read. By begging a little help from any one who knew letters, she, at length, mastered the art. In his visits to Goshen, Mr. Simpson found her out, and gave her a New Testament. Being unfit for labour, Mother Winter took charge of the children while their mothers were in the field. To keep them out of mischief, she began to teach them. This angered the overseer, and he took her before the magistrate, saying that she was an idler. The wisdom of the British Parliament had provided a stipendiary magistrate in each parish, whose business it was to see that the provisions of the Act of Emancipation were not infringed. These magistrates, when not, as in some cases it is alleged they were, partial to the employers, were efficient protectors of the negroes. The people in St. Mary's say, " Had it not been for Massa Walsh, we no been live to see the free." This gentleman, Henry Walsh, Esq., has been uniformly the friend of the black people, and his protection was needed by many apprentices in the parish of St. Mary's. Mother Winter's case could be decided only by Mr. Walsh. On hearing it, he said that she was obviously unfit for field-work, and what better could she do than teach the children? Mother Winter, who had come into the presence of the magistrate, as she tells, trembling and praying, had her mouth thus filled with a song of deliverance.

Mother Winter used to tell the writer that before Mr. Jameson came, she feared God, but did not fully know the Saviour. On that evening, he spoke on the rich man and Lazarus, and the word came with power. From that time, she became a new creature, and began to live in a new world; and still she holds on the tenor of her Christian way, a very happy, humble, and faithful disciple. She is living in a green old age, respected by all, in the hope of going home to the happy land, and there meeting Father Jameson, of whose ministry she was one of the first fruits, and whose joy and crown she, with many more, will doubtless be.

The following letter is to his sisters, on their leaving their Methven home :—

"I am just recovering from a slight attack of fever. Much reason have I to bless God for his gentleness towards me in my sicknesses. Oh, may they be sanctified! O that they would make me live less for myself, and more for Christ, and work for me an exceeding and eternal weight of glory! Nicolis enjoys good health; and this is an unspeakable blessing to me. Her anxiety about me is extreme, and her care of me the most unwearied.

"Your account of leaving Methven—our home from childhood—interested and affected us much. It was a time the most trying, but the Lord stood by you, and now you will look back and sing the song of mercy. When Nicolis and I left you, many said that we were going from ease and comfort, to enter on a thorny path. In some respects it may have been so; but yours, as well as the path of many friends at home, has been so too. Afflictions and trials are confined to no one country or situation, but are common to all. Nay, wherever there are heirs of glory, there must also be the purifying furnace ; wherever the children of God are, there must also be the rod.

"In Perth you will find scope for usefulness. In the lanes and back-lying districts there are many poor and destitute, living in darkness and ignorance ; but you will find, too, many a willing ear and grateful heart. Many bed-ridden patients will esteem you, and be comforted by the word which comforted you in your affliction, and whose affection and gratitude will be expressed by tears. I wish you could find out some of my old people, and tell me about them. Imitate Dorcas, or rather, I should say, Christ himself, who went about continually doing good."

Sugar estates, in slavery time, had each a *picaniny* gang— the boys and girls, who were sent to work under a female driver. The Act of Emancipation provided that these children should be allowed to attend school. But many planters disliked this, and disliked also Mr. Jameson's energetic efforts to educate. He had to complain of certain malicious reports which had been spread against him in connexion with this. Facts were the best answer which he could give. He resolved to make the school useful, and that would shut the mouth of slander. The school throve, as schools always thrive, under lively, hearty, and kindly management. Goshen school became what Mr. Jameson wanted it to be, "a centre of light to the district." We have heard one of the old members, on a meeting day, rise up and declare that almost all, even in other churches around, who could read their Bibles, owed it to Goshen school.

"We have children of every colour, white, brown, and black. I have been trying to discover the boasted superiority of intellect of the white ; but I confess I cannot find it. Every day's observation convinces me that there is not the thousandth part of a hair's breadth between the untutored negro and the untutored Scotchman ; that the one is as dull and stupid as the other ; and the black child is as apt to learn, and is as often at the head of his class as the white child."

Surely the opinion of those who have taught the white and

the black, and have taught them together, is worth something in the question still agitated as to the capacities of the whites and negroes respectively. Missionary testimony alone is trustworthy in a question of this kind. It is not fair, and it is not philosophical, to slight the evidence of fact and of experience. Negro children have, undeniably, a fair average capacity to receive an ordinary English education. Many missionaries know this by experience. The writer of this has taught the school at Goshen, in the absence of the teacher, and therefore knows that there is not a greater amount of stolidity in a Jamaica school than in a Scotch parish school. This much we say in justice to the negroes. It is ungenerous in men of British race to scorn them, as some seem to pride themselves in doing. The British race is the foremost in the world, and what land is like our own island home? But we lower ourselves when we unjustly disparage others.

The following passage describes a visit which Mr. Jameson paid to Middlesex, a place among the mountains, six or eight miles from Goshen. At that place a number of people were living, who had emigrated from Scotland. An attempt was made at that time to allure European labourers to Jamaica; and many from Ireland and Scotland went out with high expectations which were doomed to be disappointed. White men from Britain cannot work under the sun of the tropics. They are not adapted to endure the rays of a vertical sun, as the negroes and other natives of the tropics are, by the colour of their skins and by the thickness of their crania. This European immigration proved a complete and miserable failure; and it entailed fearful suffering on those who had been deluded by parties guilty of culpable rashness, or of something deserving a far more dishonourable name. Many of the immigrants died, a few returned to Britain, and scarcely a vestige now remains of this other instance of colonial folly.

Mr. Jameson writes (April, 1838) :—"I found them all busy in their provision grounds. Some of them are old men and women bordering on sixty; one man is almost seventy. There is a number of stout young men and women, and a good many are children. I asked all the people to meet me in the room where the business of the township is transacted. Forty people soon gathered, and we spent an hour in devotion. I cannot describe the feelings which almost overpowered me, when I saw so many of my own countrymen before me, and thought, every moment, that I was addressing them in a foreign land, 5000 miles from the country of our birth. I read Psalm cxxi. An old man came forward, with his Bible in his hand, and a Highland bonnet under his arm, and struck up 'Bangor.' We sung, but our harps were sometimes, for a moment, on the willows. While we sung, I frankly confess, we wept. We all seemed to feel that we were singing the Lord's song in a foreign land. I read Psalm xxv., and prayed. While I was addressing them, the manager, a native of the country, came in. I was exhorting them to attend to the instruction of their children, and to give them lessons, as far as they were able, in reading and writing. He seemed to think that I was exacting too much from them, and that they had other things to do. I explained to him that every Scotchman was bound to teach his own children, as far as he was able. After a meeting which I will not soon forget, I returned home, and they to their grounds."

CHAPTER IV.

Emancipation—Feelings of the Emancipated—Sir Lionel Smith's tour of the Island—The 1st of August, 1838—Missionary Influence, salutary—Defence of Anglo-Ethiopia—Mr. Jameson an educator—Wages difficulty—New Church needed —Examination of Catechumens—Mr. Moir arrives—Rent difficulty—Opposition— Birth of a Daughter—Conflicting views of Emancipation.

THE day of freedom at length dawned upon all the slaves who were under the sceptre of Britain. It had been enacted that non-praedial slaves—those who were house servants— should become free on the 1st of August, 1838, while the praedial, or field-working slaves should remain apprentices till the 1st of August, 1840. The apprenticeship was only a miti- gated, if, indeed, a mitigated slavery. And notwithstanding that stipendiary magistrates had been appointed to see the Act of Emancipation carried out, the apprentices were exposed to great wrong and oppression. Many persons in charge of estates seemed, like Satan, to be in great wrath because their time was short, and the nearer that the time approached, the fiercer burned the flame of their fury. It vexed them, as it vexed the Egyptians before them, to see their bondmen going free, and they pursued the fugitives with threats and violence. Still was the soul of humanity wrung by the sight of bleeding backs, mangled and torn with the lash. And these sufferers were not malefactors who were flogged for their crimes, but, sometimes, Christian men and women, whose offence was that they had lost time, or otherwise broken the regulations of a code which was inconsistent with the rights of freemen. For however the like of Thomas Carlyle, in one of his cross moods, may declare himself in favour of the whip for the backs of lazy Africans, there is a more excellent way ; and, so long as a man infringes on none of the rights of his neighbours, it must be a crime to treat him as a criminal. Undeniable evidence that the apprentices were suffering much harsh and unrighteous usage, stirred up in Britain a desire to bring the apprenticeship to an end at once. A motion to that effect was made in the House of Commons, on the 30th of March, 1838, but was lost by a majority of sixty-four. In May, however, another motion to the same effect was carried by a majority of three.

But the Legislature of Jamaica wisely resolved to take up the matter themselves. Mr. Jameson was in Spanish Town when the question was discussed in the House of Assembly. " All professed to detest slavery from their very souls, but loudly wailed for the injury which would be inflicted on them by emancipation. All professed ardent attachment to their Queen and country, but cursed the interference that forced the negroes from their grasp. They professed a desire to see the negro as free as themselves, but were very unwilling to untie the cords with which he was bound. The voice of Britain, however, was not to be misunderstood. The bill passed, and the nursling of ages, of money, and of blood, expired, and that in the house of its friends, and deprived of existence by their hands. With God all things are possible, and all things easy. He speaks and it is done."

The following is an interesting account of the abolition of the apprenticeship by the Island Legislature.

"*June 25th*, 1838.—The last link of slavery's chain is broken for ever. Saturday eight-days, the last and fatal stroke was given. Four weeks ago, the Governor received a despatch from home, intimating that the Government's new bill was to arrive by the following packet. His Excellency forthwith summoned the House of Assembly. The House met, and resolved to anticipate the expected bill, by enacting that the apprenticeship should cease, and unrestricted freedom should be the order of things, from the 1st of August. The measure was carried without a dissenting voice. The Assembly's bill was amended by the Council. These amendments the House rejected with scorn, declaring that their Honours ought to take their bill, and be thankful. That since they had submitted to sacrifice two whole years of the apprenticeship, their bill was entitled to better treatment. In the meantime, Lord Glenelg's bill arrived; and, to the no small annoyance of the Honourable House, it was immediately proclaimed by order of the Governor, and forthwith became law. There was now no time to fight about amendments. The opposing parties met in conference, when matters were adjusted; and on the 16th day of June, the bill was passed. The House was prorogued, and the members returned to their homes to make preparations for the approaching event.

" I need not say that this event has filled the land with joy and praise. The Lord has done far more for us than we expected. In our sequestered spot we were sitting quietly, making up our minds to receive, with gratitude to God, this new bill which Government was sending out. On Sabbath, I brought before them the Governor's letter, and told the people what improvements had been made in the Apprenticeship Act, and exhorted them to faithfulness. Next Sabbath, a letter reached me with the tidings that the apprenticeship was doomed, and that universal freedom was to be enjoyed from the 1st of August. Many believed not for joy. We stopped our usual work, and spent some time in offering to the Giver of all good thanksgiving and praise. It was in truth the figure clothed in reality— the bringing to the captive the unexpected message of freedom. Some days afterwards, I asked one of my people what arrangements they were making for the 1st of August. 'Indeed, Massa, we have not yet begun to think of making arrangements, we are so glad.'

" Last night, I had a meeting with those of my people who live on a neighbouring estate, to examine into a case of moral delinquency, of which I had just heard. It appeared that their master had taken possession of the property, that he gave a dance to his people on Saturday last, and kept it up till four o'clock on Sabbath morning. Such things are very grievous. Some were there for whom I had a high esteem, who have been my steadiest people, and who were most eager in their pursuit after knowledge. They told me that they did not know the impropriety of their conduct, or rather, as it afterwards appeared, had not the boldness to resist the wishes of their young master. I assure you we have much need of your prayers, and your special prayers for this, that the Lord would keep those whom he is gathering into his infant church here, from falling again into the pollutions of the world. Numerous and strong are the temptations which encompass the flock. In every way, the devil tempts them. Pray for us that we may have grace to stand."

"On my return from Spanish Town," writes Mr. Jameson, "I found all happy at the prospect of freedom ; but some doubted. One poor old man thought the news too good to be true. Massa would not part with him so easily. The paper, as he calls it, put this matter beyond a doubt. A notice was handed to him, intimating that, on the 1st of August, his apprenticeship expires, and that, three months after that date, he shall peaceably retire from the estate, if he cannot agree to remain, and work for the wages offered. This notice was given to all the people on the estates ; and many came to have it read and to get the 'understanding of it.' I told them not to fear the paper. It was the badge of their coming freedom. They would no longer be the property of their masters. But if they gave up working on the estates, they must also give up their houses and grounds. Some thought that, when the Queen gave them the 'free,' she also gave them their provision grounds. I told them that they were no longer to be as the horses and cattle—the property of the estates— to be bought and sold with the soil ; but were to be free men, to work for wages, and out of these wages to pay rent and educate their children. They thought that, as they had built the houses, and brought in the provision grounds from the bush, they had the best right to them ; I told them that the time during which they had already held their houses paid them for their labour in rearing them, and that the yearly produce of their grounds repaid them for the labour of cultivating them. Your masters gave you these grounds, because you were slaves or apprentices. But now you are to be neither slaves nor apprentices ; you are to work for wages ; and, therefore, you must pay rent."

The Governor, Sir Lionel Smith, sailed round the island during the month of July, to meet with the apprentices, and give them his best advice, with the view of preparing them for the duties of their new position. Ministers of the gospel were invited to co-operate with His Excellency in this important work. And there never was a time when their advice and influence were more required ; and they never had it more in their power to benefit the country. Physical restraints were nearly at an end ; corporal punishment had all but ceased ; the strength of the former system was gone ; and nothing remained but moral impulse. Every minister visited the people in their houses, or met them at appointed times, exhorting them to diligence and good conduct, showing them in what spirit they should enter on their new situation, and how faithfully they should try to discharge their new duties.

Messrs. Cowan, Simpson, and Jameson waited on Sir Lionel at Port Maria, and presented an address, which was well received. Apprentices came from all parts of St. Mary's to see and hear the Governor. His words were much to the point, and every one was highly gratified.

On returning home, Mr. Jameson was distressed to learn that the people were deserting their work on all hands, and he went round the district to show them the way of rectitude. Some had formed wrong and extravagant notions, from mistaking the Governor's speech, and they were elated by the near approach of the 1st of August. Mr. Jameson assured them that this folly of theirs was opening the mouths of their enemies, and shutting the mouths of their friends. They were apprentices till the 1st of August, and must work till then. Even then, it would be for their interest not to desert their work, but to be diligent and laborious, that they might receive wages, that the country might be prosperous, and that the great measure which secured their freedom might be crowned with success.

At last the day of freedom came ; and the way in which the

people spent it was greatly to their own praise ; for it won for them the golden opinions of all their friends, gratified and delighted, beyond measure, those who had fought their battle, and gave a manifest proof of the good effects of the glorious gospel of the blessed God. The 1st day of August, 1838, is a day much to be remembered by the freed-men of the West Indies, and by all generations of their children, as the day that saw slavery go down, with its whips, and stocks, and hand-cuffs, and tread-mills, "to the vile dust from which it sprung."

Mr. Jameson gave graphic and touching narratives of the 1st of August at Goshen, in his journal and letters.

"The sun went down, on the 31st of July, amid joy and singing. The people continued at their labour to the last. Now it had ceased ; and one after another came to the missionary's residence till the school-house was filled, while numbers of children marched round it, singing hymns of praise to God for sending minister among them, the old people following them and joining in the song. I went down, and found the multitude very happy indeed. 'Minister,' they said, 'we thought this day would never come. We cannot believe that on to-morrow we shall be free. Thank God ! We never can thank God enough. We want to sit all night, thanking God, if you, minister, think it proper.'

"'Oh no, my friends, it is not proper to sit all night, for you will be tired out long before morning, and unfit for the exercises of that joyful day that is to burst on you to-morrow. As for myself, I cannot do so, for I am exhausted.'

"Some wished to pass the night with us. I said that those who came from a distance should remain, but those who lived near had better go home. They asked me if it would be proper to fast all night. I replied that it was good to cherish the spirit of fasting at all times ; but, considering the heavy work in which they had been engaged all day, and what was before them to-morrow, I advised them to go to their beds, get a sound sleep, take a hearty breakfast in the morning, and come to church : for they could not worship God while their heads were sleepy and their stomachs hungry. As for myself, I was going to bed at once, for I had been toiling since five o'clock in the morning, and was very tired. To-morrow, I intended to eat an additional yam, to drink an additional cup of coffee, and to take an additional spoonful of sugar to it, because these things were no more to be produced by the labour of slaves, but by the industry of freemen. I told them, also, that the children of Israel did not fast the night before they left Egypt, but every family ate a whole lamb. With these things they were more than satisfied ; and, after prayer and singing, we parted for the night.

"At dawn, while the morning star was yet bright, the falling of the chain of the gate awakened me from my slumber. I arose, and hastening to the school-house, heard the well-known voice of an old negro, singing, ' Hark, the glad sound, the Saviour comes !' In a little, a few more arrived, moving through the thick fog which the rays of the rising sun had not yet dispelled. At break of day, our family were called together, to raise our happy hearts in humble acknowledgments to our Father in heaven. I had arranged with my people, the Sabbath before, that, at five o'clock, every family in the church should meet around the family altar to praise God for his goodness. By seven o'clock, the school-room was crowded. Every countenance beamed with joy. The old negro seemed to have got back the vivacity of youth. ' Massa,' said one old, feeble man, and my hand got a shake which well-nigh squeezed the blood out of my fingers, ' Massa, we never thought we see this day. We bless God for let we see this day. We were put in a ship, crushed and trampled down, carried away from our country and people, and brought here ; but, Massa, we forget and forgive all, for the joy of this day.' One who had already shaken my hand twice, came, a third time, saying, ' Massa, we cannot get too much shaking.' Hundreds were in and around the school while religious services were conducted. I married fourteen couples, some young, some old.

"After getting refreshment, the people ranked themselves, and walked to the church, three miles distant. We followed as soon as possible. When we came in sight of the church, a dense mass of human beings burst upon our view. The church was literally packed, and there were two or three times as many without. I wished them all joy. Sung a part of the 103d Psalm, and addressed them from the words, ' I will deliver thee, and thou shalt glorify me,' and also from Rom. xiii. 12-14. I showed them that God had wrought this deliverance for them, and was now saying to them, 'Glorify me.' But the work of emancipation was far from complete ; they saw the first day of a career, which I trusted would be a glorious one, ending in their rising into full light and liberty. They must forsake whatever would hinder their progress ; they must cease from the abominations of former days, from riot, and drunkenness, and chambering, and wantonness, strife and envying, from practices fit only for slaves, and which show men to be the slaves of the devil. They must carry with them all that can speed them onwards in the path of light and liberty ; they must cling to their bibles, their church and school, their minister and teacher, their Sabbaths, and, above all, their Saviour. We spent the day happily together, and parted full of comfort and of peace. In parting, I expressed the hope that they would end the day as they had begun it, with God ; so that the good impressions made by the services might not be disturbed by feasting and merriment. On returning home at five o'clock, I was glad to see my highest wish realized. All was order and peace ; and contentment seemed to have fixed her abode among the dwellings of the people.

" Next morning, a person said, ' Minister, your word yesterday be good, and have good effect ; I never see Goshen people so quiet.' All were happy, but there was no riot. Many were the visits made to us, and many the presents brought for transmission home. An old woman brought a pine-apple for the Queen. An old man wanted to learn to write, that he might send her a letter of thanks for sending the ' free.' "

The conduct of ministers of the gospel is very apt to be scrutinized with an unfriendly eye by those who cannot sympathize with their spiritual objects ; their proceedings are often grievously misrepresented, either through thoughtlessness or malice ; and their efforts to remove social evils, and to promote social righteousness, are often resented by parties who are thereby offended.   Yet it must be confessed that the influence exercised on a community by persons disinterested in their motives, pure in their aims, and prudent in their movements, is of the most beneficial kind.   The history of the Emancipation is a triumphant testimony to the truth of this remark. No one can doubt that it was chiefly through the efforts of pious missionaries that this great measure came into peaceful action in the West Indian possessions of Great Britain.   Freedom had, before this, visited the shores of a neighbouring island.   A Toussaint L'Ouverture—a son of Ethiopia, and a man of genius—had arisen and headed his kindred in winning liberty from the hated yoke.   But how different were the scenes that attended the emancipation of Hayti, from those witnessed in Jamaica, on the day of freedom !   In the British West Indies, freedom came, smiling and gracious, as the dawn of a Sabbath morn ; in Hayti, it came as the hurricane, and red ruin marked its path.   In the one, the banner of freedom was the white flag of peace ; in the other, the black flag of death. In the one, the day was ushered in with the song of praise and the voice of prayer ; in the other, with the trumpet of war, the shrieks of the dying, and the shouts of the once down-trodden slave, hewing with the bloody knife his way to freedom.   Beyond a doubt, it was God who caused this difference, by means of that blessed gospel which the missionaries preached to the slaves, and by means of the moral influence over them which they had obtained as the ambassadors of Christ.

Writing to the Directors of the Rose Street Missionary Association, about three months after this period, November 13th, 1838, Mr. Jameson thus truly, and with graceful modesty, gives his opinion on this matter :—

" In the late crisis, the minister of the gospel has been of essential service to the district in which he lived.   To him the people looked for advice, and made known all their difficulties. In those cases where he has imparted to them sound advice, and laid himself out to lead them with calmness and soberness,

the results have been peace, a general return to industry, cheerfulness at work, and a fair rate of wages.

"The great principle which has guided my brethren and
myself, has been that laid down by the apostle : 'Servants,
obey in all things your masters according to the flesh ; not with
eye-service, as men-pleasers ; but in singleness of heart, fearing
God.' 'Masters, give unto your servants that which is just and
equal ; knowing that ye also have a Master in heaven.' In
following this line of conduct, we have experienced many difficulties, and have been exposed to troubles. We have not passed
unscathed. At one time we were suspected by the people of a
desire to advance the interests of their masters rather than
theirs ; at another, we were accused by the masters of leaning
too much to the side of the people. My brethren and I looked
for righteousness, and wherever we found it, we steadily followed
it, without respect to party, rank, or colour.

"Up to the present moment, peace has prevailed on the
estates on which we labour. Mr. Blyth says in a letter, some
time ago, that his people were all at work, and conducting
themselves in a most exemplary manner. Mr. Waddell and
Mr. Paterson give the same account of their people. Of our
churches in St. Mary's I am glad to bear the same testimony.
In Goshen, my own district, I have been most happily disappointed, for the character of the people on this property led
me to expect very different things ; and it was the last that
I expected to see in a promising condition. It has, however,
been among the first to show an example of diligence in the
improved state of things. When I thus speak, I do not mean
to say that everything is well settled, that there is nothing to
lament, and nothing to rectify. I speak comparatively. Ere
things are fully settled, time, care, and diligence will be required, and especially the many and earnest prayers of the
people of God."

The following extracts are from the journal at this period :—

"An old woman, a house apprentice, was talking with me
about the 1st of August. I asked her whether she would remain on the property, or go away. She replied, 'Massa, we

heart well satisfied with you, and with the gospel which you preach, and we cannot leave you.'

" A house apprentice belonging to the congregation, was asked by his employer how much he would require a year for his services.   He did not know.   'For one thing, however, I am determined not to give up my Saturdays and Sabbaths.'

" 'You must give up your Sabbaths, for that is the day I need you most.'

" 'Well, Massa, rather than give up my Sabbaths, I will give up my place.'

" 'Why are you so anxious about the Sabbath ?'

" 'You white men who can read Bible, should know that better than I do.   Does not the Bible say, Remember the Sabbath-day to keep it holy ?'

" 'Oh, yes ; you go to church, I see.'

" 'Yes, Massa.'

" 'You are no better of that.   You are worse instead of better.'   This person came to ask my advice, and I counselled him to go on as he had begun."

Much has been spoken and written in the West Indies, in Great Britain, and in America, to the discredit of the emancipated people of Jamaica.   Many heartless calumnies have been spread to the injury of their reputation, and to the lessening of that sympathy which once in a full tide flowed through the soul of the piety of Great Britain, carrying in its bosom death to oppression and liberty to the slave.[1]   The truth, however, is, that the black people are just like other people.

---

[1] Of this we have an instance in a work of Anthony Trollope, who writes his travels somewhat as he writes his novels. He says that the provision grounds of the Jamaica negroes are "spots of land for which they either pay rent, or on which, as is quite as common, they have squatted without payment of any rent." Did Mr. Trollope not know that thousands of these spots are freeholds, and that they were purchased and paid for by negroes, who thus hold them in fee-simple? Or, knowing this fact, did he wilfully conceal it from the readers of his book, and thus, in effect, bear false witness against his neighbour? What confidence can be put in Mr. Trollope's opinions about the brains and the souls of the negroes, when he shows so much ignorance about the tenure on which they hold their lands? The man who found out that freeholders are either rent-payers or squatters, must be excused for saying that the negro " addicts himself to religion for the sake of appearances."

Their good and bad qualities, their virtues and their vices, are common to humanity. Depraved human nature is the same among them as elsewhere, and the same elsewhere as among them ; and so is sanctified human nature. The same appearances which present themselves in other lands which have civil liberty and an unfettered religion, also present them-selves among the freedmen of the West Indies, to an extent proportioned to the amount and duration of their civil and religious privileges. Anglo-Ethiopia is an infant people ; it needs time to grow ; it must be a child, a youth, before it can be a man. Guided by the light which the experience of other nations affords, this people ought to make more rapid progress than those which have had to feel, and force, and fight their way to honour, and liberty, and power. But all history teaches us that the rise of nations to intelligence, and virtue, and influence, is slow. " Rome was not built in a day." There is a long interval between the acorn which the tiny squirrel buries in the ground, and the gnarled oak that laughs at the blast. Are we to expect that a nation trained under slavery, shall, in one generation, free themselves from all the evils which slavery breeds and nurses ? Are they good for nothing because, trained unto evil, and destitute of aid and encouragement, except what the kindness of distant friends has afforded, they have not, in twenty-three years, shaken off all the vicious tendencies and habits which, common to man-kind, were fostered in them, to a fearful extent, by their pre-vious circumstances as slaves, and have not stood up adorned with the light of intelligence, the graces of social virtue, and the beauties of holiness ? Is this the law of national pro-gress ? What people, even in the most favourable circum-stances, ever made the progress which is demanded of this people, and the lack of which is thought by many to warrant their condemnation, and the condemnation of the beneficent measure which made them free ? In the course of this Memoir, testimonies in favour of the people of Jamaica will be given, in extracts from Mr. Jameson's letters and journal ; and we claim for him the confidence and the credit which are due to a witness of sound sense, quick observation, sincere piety, and unimpeachable veracity.

From the very beginning of his labours at Goshen, Mr. Jameson saw the necessity of education for the young, and, with the aid of his devoted partner, he laboured in this department of the work. Classes were formed for the young people, which, at first, met on the Sabbaths; and, occasionally, on other days, as was found convenient. In his earliest letters, Mr. Jameson dwelt on this pressing necessity, rendered all the more pressing, because emancipation had freed the children from compulsory labour, and they were running about in idleness. Convinced that the work would not be prosperous, perfect, or permanent, unless the young were taught, and that the people would not become intelligent Christians, would fail to profit to the full by the instructions of the pulpit, and would want one of the most precious means of grace, unless a Bible-reading and Bible-loving generation were raised up, he, like all other enlightened missionaries, exerted himself, even before he had any reason to expect assistance, in this department of the work.

"*August 6th.*—This week, there has been an extraordinary crowding to the school. Thirty-five scholars have been added to the list, some of them as old as myself. Novelty brings many; some desire to be permanent, and display anxiety to learn. If you could look in upon us, you would see benches round the room packed, and benches in the centre not less so, while many sit on the floor. Rude and ignorant though we considered them at first, and small though we considered their progress, yet, when brought into comparison with new comers, their superiority is great. I could not have imagined it.

"The peace and good-will which prevailed on the eventful 1st of August still continue. Up to this time there has been no sound of riot or revel. The house of God is crowded, and the voice of prayer and praise is often heard among our people. The people are anxious to begin work at once, but their masters are tardy in making arrangements with them; and those who have proposed arrangements, offer wages which the people refuse to accept. Both sides go to excess : the people, by expecting too much, and the masters, by offering too little. Work here is heavy, and the people, if underpaid, will get disheartened and cease to labour, and then the employers will lose more than if they had been more liberal in their offers.

"Death has been among you of late. Tender our sympathy to the bereaved families. Blessed are the dead who die in the Lord ; their sorrows are ended, their labours are closed, and their rest is glorious. O that we may live as on the brink of eternity ; then shall we serve the Lord better. Our good friend, Mr. Bryden, desires to know our hours of meeting on the Lord's day. We begin at nine o'clock in the morning, and conclude about four. We think much of you on the Lord's day, and feel much happiness in the thought that we are meeting together at the throne.

"As to the accordion which, I understand, has been talked about, and seriously objected to by some friends, I have to say that I do not intend to carry it to church. I would as soon take the bagpipes. I am fond of music, and desire to consecrate all that I have of the gift to the glory of God, but I never wish to see an instrument in the Lord's house as a substitute for my own voice."

A few weeks later, he wrote as follows :—" The balmy days of ease and cessation from labour must come to an end. The people say, ' We can't eat free.' They now come to us to know what they are to do. We say, ' Work for wages.'

" ' True, but what wages ought we to receive ?'

" ' That is a question which I cannot answer. Your masters only can answer it. I hope they will give you as much as they are able ; and this, I trust, will be as much as will make you comfortable. I advise, then, that you go at once to your masters, and tell them that you are willing to be employed, and ask them to state the terms on which they will employ you.'

" ' Well, minister, we have been to massa, as you told us, but he offers us only two *bits* (9d. sterling), with houses and grounds, medicine and medical attendance. Our wives must work, and our children above ten years of age. We must work ten hours a day, in rain and wind, as well as sunshine, and this for five days a week. We are anxious to work, but we must live by our work. We made four *bits* (1s. 6d. sterling) in the apprenticeship, and why give us less when we are free ?'

" ' Now, I will lay down a great principle which must guide you in settling this question. The master must not give you more than his property affords, else, in a short time, the estate would be in ruin, and you would be without employment and without wages. On the other hand, the master is bound to give you wages worthy of your work. You must not be too extravagant in your demands. You must yield a part on the one side, if your masters yield a part on the other.'

" The weather was delightful. The cane-fields were waving in luxuriance. The oxen were rejoicing in their freedom from the yoke, and too often, in their uncontrolled indulgence among the rich canes. The people were resting from their many years of toil ; and the masters were anxious that the resting should cease. Such was the state of things for the first two weeks. During the third week, the masters began to offer a *macaroni*, or 1s. sterling, a day, and the people began to move. Some, unwilling to return to work, went about stating that a law was coming from the Queen to fix the rate of wages, and that if any one went to work before the 1st of November, he would be imprisoned by the Governor, and that, for three months, they had their houses and grounds free of rent.

" ' At this juncture, the Governor desired the Attorney-General to publish his opinion as to the law on the subject ; and this was, that rent could be charged for every week since the 1st of August. Those who had been sitting at their ease had now to bestir themselves, to atone by their diligence for the past, and to keep themselves out of the hands of their masters. And now all is industry around us. Cheerfulness sits on every countenance, and peace and comfort reign. At sunrise you hear the cry of the wain-men driving the sugars to the wharf ; and on all the estates around you see large gangs of free labourers receiving a shilling a day."

Mr. Jameson had now to gird up his loins for a most important and necessary work, involving great anxiety of mind, and great pecuniary responsibility. A permanent and substantial place of worship was necessary, and also accommodation for the day-school. At home this is simply a question of money. If you have that, there are architects, and builders, and skilled craftsmen, ready to undertake the work. But abroad, the difficulties are great ; and from the want of efficient and industrious workmen, the expense of such undertakings is heavy. To this matter the following letter refers. The work being thus put into his hands, Mr. Jameson went about it in the spirit of faith in God, and persevered in it, until a plain but substantial and commodious building arose, beautiful for situation, surrounded with hallowed recollection, and destined, we trust, to be the centre of precious influences, and the birthplace of immortal souls for many, many generations.

"To the Directors of the Rose Street Missionary Society.

"Goshen, *August 25th*, 1838.

" My dear Friends and Brethren,—Your kind consideration of our circumstances was duly brought before us by your respected secretary. And now I return you our best thanks for so promptly sending us a fellow-labourer, to aid us in the work of the Lord in this distant part of the vineyard. We long for the arrival of our brother, Mr. Moir. The Lord control the winds, and bridle the waves, and bring his servant to his work in peace ; so shall our hearts be gladdened by his presence among us. The Lord bless him with long life and vigorous health, and make him an eminent blessing to us all. The Lord bless you for this renewed instance of kindness, and supply your wants out of his riches in glory, through Christ Jesus. And to Himself, the fountain of all mercy, be everlasting glory !

" Your kind request, to be informed of the sum which the enlargement of the present school-house, or the building of a new one, might cost, was also duly brought before me. I regret my delay in replying to this kind solicitation, but I desired to inquire further into the matter, that I might bring before you a scheme, which circumstances daily press upon my attention. This is the procuring a church as well as a school-house.

"1. On coming to Goshen, twelve months past last February, I preached a considerable time in the boiling-house. Finding that the temporary church, promised to be erected, was carried forward neither by the estates nor by the people, and after making application to the managers of the estates, and to the people, till I was ashamed, I found it necessary, for the honour of the cause with which I am identified, to take the responsibility of the work upon myself. In humble dependence upon Him whose I am and whom I serve, I began the work, and, with the aid of people from Carron Hall and Port Maria, a shed was finished, which shelters us from the sun and the rain. The cost of the whole amounted fully to £100 currency. It was my original intention to keep a daily school at the church; but difficulties occurring, which in present circumstances were unavoidable, my thoughts turned to some point nearer our dwelling. I applied to Goshen for an old pimento house in the immediate neighbourhood. I was told it was at my service, if I chose to be at the expense of fitting it up. This I did. The school continued to increase so rapidly, that I found it necessary to put a roof upon an old stable adjoining. Even still we are squeezed together, unable almost to move for want of room, and to breathe, from heat and confinement. This department of our work, from the causes now mentioned, we find exceedingly laborious and exhausting. The daily attendance averages from 100 and upwards. The accommodation is fitted for half this number, but, unwilling to put any away, we do the best we can. New ones are ever coming, but for want of room many stay away. Fever has seized numbers, the source of this malady having been the heat of the place. Such is our school.

"2. The church is similarly situated. The people are

packed together, and numbers are obliged to stand around the boards outside, so that the heat is excessive, and rendered more unbearable from the exclusion of the breeze by those standing outside. The roof, in many parts, has already begun to give way. It consists of sugar-cane tops, and cannot long resist the wasting influences of the climate. The posts which support the seats are sinking beyond their original level into the ground, and the boards are bending and creaking, so that the whole would require a thorough repair, costing upwards of £20. Similar repairs will be necessary every year, and the people are averse to lay out their money in this way. They would rather pay the interest and the capital of a debt contracted to erect a new and substantial house which would secure permanence to their present privileges, and the transmission of them to the children. Since the 1st of January, we have raised by collections in church £30, and by the end of the year I expect £20 more. The object of these collections is to pay the boards brought from town for the present church. When these are paid, we propose to begin monthly collections for a new church, and I have reason to believe that the people will contribute with tenfold cheerfulness.

" 3. The necessity for a church and school is so great, that were we to defer their erection till we raised the money, or were we to defer making application to home for aid till we raised the amount on the spot, a delay would be occasioned, which must prove detrimental to the cause, as well as to the health, if not the life, of the agents now employed, and of the friend and brother soon to join us. The voice of Providence is, ' Whatever thy hand finds to do, do it with all thy might.' I would be glad if I could point to our building fund as commenced and prospering. The time of my labour in this field has been short, and the expenses and debt which urgent circumstances have incurred, have contributed to prevent this. But the cause, I believe, has possession of the hearts of many of the people ; and I fear not, in a little time, and through the blessing of God, to be able to pay whatever sum may be intrusted to us.

"4. In applying thus formally to you, the Directors, I do it not expecting that, as a society, you will take up this matter. Your exertions are already wonderful ; and were I to ask you to do more, I would be going beyond the limits of propriety. I come before you now to solicit your best advice and co-operation, and to put into your hands certain facts, to be used in whatever way your prudence may dictate. I earnestly ask you to state without reserve your opinions, and your questions of every sort. I am stepping upon ground to which I am unaccustomed, but it is one to which duty calls, and where I may expect the direction and blessing of my Divine Master, and your service, co-operation, and prayers."

"*October 1st.*—This month is remarkable in the history of freedom for a counter declaration to that of the Attorney-General, given by two lawyers in town, that no rent can be charged till November. I do not enter into the merits of the question. But the declaration has done no good to any but the idle, and no good to them. Its effect has been injurious : for the people do not know whom or what to believe."

The following letter, being of a private nature, might be withheld, did it not breathe so rich a spirit of piety, tenderness, zeal, and fidelity. The expostulations addressed to his youngest brother, may be, doubtless are, equally applicable to other young men of piety and talent, and may be the means of drawing out such a one to the help of the Lord in some field of missionary enterprise,—perhaps in Ethiopia itself, on whose shores the standard of the gospel is now planted, and through whose moral and spiritual darkness the Sun of Righteousness is beginning to shine. May the Lord of the harvest send forth hundreds of such labourers to degraded and enslaved Africa.

"GOSHEN, *October 5th,* 1838.

"MY DEAR SISTERS,—You hung your harp upon the willows, or rather you took it down and sent us a song of lamentation. Dry up your tears, my sisters, your father lives and triumphs ; and, best of all, our father's God lives : and He has proved himself faithful who hath said, 'I will never leave you nor forsake you ;' for father and mother having left you, He has taken you up.

"The anniversary of our dear father's death brought with it many recollections which made the old wounds bleed afresh. I wonder not at this. But other thoughts, more consoling and animating, arise out of the same subject. A year in heaven ! How short to him who is surrounded with its glories and filled with its joys, although long and lonesome to friends left behind to mourn their loss ! Oh, how much has he learned in that time ! How much has his glory increased, and how much is it ever increasing ! A year, almost two years, since we parted ! How much nearer are we to the meeting-point ! Happy hour ! when death-divided friends shall meet to part no more.

"I am distressed at James's resolution to go to Manchester. I wish he had begun his career in Perth, and remained under the eye of his grandfather as long as he could enjoy his precious instruction and advice. My dear James, I thought you would join me in the ministry of the gospel. Your father desired this, but he ceased to urge it because of his tenderness to you. The training which he bestowed on your boyhood was intended to turn your heart to this holy and honourable work. He also prayed for this. I had means of knowing all this that you had not. I am glad to hear of your piety, and hope it is the gracious fruit of the Spirit of God. May he increase it aye more and more. But, James, I solemnly ask, Have you made your profession the subject of earnest and prayerful consideration ? Do you avoid the ministry because of the toil necessary in preparing for it, or because you will be ill repaid in money for your time and labour ? I cannot think this of you. You love Jesus Christ. Your heart is warmed by his love to sinners. Oh, then, why should you turn aside from the work of proclaiming this love to a perishing world ? You say that there is already plenty of preachers. Far from the truth. If your views be bounded by the British coast, and if you take as your pattern the hangers on for churches at home, there may be some truth in your statement. But when you regard the world as the field, and look at the small amount of agency employed for its conversion, the statement is absolutely ridiculous. Jamaica itself would employ the greater part of the unemployed. There may be plenty of bankers and manufacturers, but there is an incalculable want of the ministers of reconciliation. There is, at this moment, a pressing call for such in this country. The education which you have already received will secure you an extensive field of usefulness here ; and, under the inspection of the Presbytery, you can carry forward your studies, and be licensed and ordained in due time. As to your health, there is every prospect of its being much better here than in a mercantile house in Manchester. Your constitution is well fitted for this country ; and the pleasure of laying out your talents and your acquirements in bringing the children of Ethiopia to God, will be much greater than buying and selling for a master for even £500 a year. Think then, my dear brother, on these things."

James Kerr Jameson, to whom these sentences were specially addressed, was the youngest of the family. When only three weeks old, he was left motherless, and was an object of peculiar interest and solicitude to his affectionate father. The Rev. George Gilfillan says, " He grew up into a very promising and excellent young man. He became a banker, first in Manchester, and then in Hanley, where he was the principal founder of the Presbyterian Church, now under the charge of Mr. Martyn, and where, till his death, he continued a most efficient member. Mr. Martyn preached his funeral sermon. It delightfully attested the effects of Jameson's piety and prayers on his youngest child." A portion of Mr. Martyn's sermon is appended to the third edition of the " Remains of the late Rev. John Jameson." There are several touching references to James in that fragrant casket of " Remains," which has afforded sweet and genuine comfort to mourners in the hour of anguish.

An unknown friend having offered to the Rose Street Missionary Association the sum of £50 annually, for five years, either in support of their present missionary engagements, or in furtherance of some new scheme, the directors unanimously agreed to recommend that a catechist or teacher should be sent to assist Mr. Jameson, provided funds could be raised, in addition to former contributions, sufficient for the salary of such an agent. The recommendation was brought under the notice of the friends of the mission at the annual missionary social meeting ; and, in a short time, subscriptions were offered which were deemed sufficient. The proposed measure was, therefore, carried into effect, and from among five candidates Mr. David Moir was chosen. He arrived in Jamaica in October 1838.

Mr. Moir entered on his important work with the utmost zeal, and during the time he was Mr. Jameson's coadjutor, nobly seconded his efforts for the good of the people. The fruits of Mr. Moir's labours still live abundantly in that district. On the Sabbath after his arrival, Mr. Jameson invited the people to prepare a place beside the church, in which Mr. Moir might carry on his school. They cordially entered into the work. So hearty were they, that some came before the pulpit, and others stood up in different parts of the church, offering their services. The school had outgrown the accommodation, and a part of the scholars used to assemble under the spreading boughs of a neighbouring tree. On Saturday morning, old and young came out, when some dug holes for the posts, others went into the wood to cut and carry timbers, others gathered grass for thatch, and others prepared the rough timbers and fixed them. In a few Saturdays the shed was finished. " What reason," writes Mr. Jameson, " have we to thank God, and take courage ! At first the people would do nothing without wages ; now, they are happy in any way to help the cause of Christ among us."

Mr. Jameson, relieved of the school, was now able to devote himself to other work. He writes :—" I visit the estates to instruct those who are at work. Last week, I went to an estate, at the earnest request of the overseer. In teaching the children, I found that none of them could answer a single question. One boy from a neighbouring estate, under my care, repeated some of the things he had learned, and read a few verses in the New Testament. I said, ' Why does this boy read, and know so much, while all the rest are as ignorant as the mule ?'　They knew why, and looked at one another.　I went on to Pembroke Hall, and had a large meeting of old and young.　The people had just finished their work, and came to get a word from minister.　On the way, I met Mr. Cowan and a teacher who has come to begin operations in Bagnold's Vale, sent by the Mico Institute in Kingston.　The Lord is opening up streams in the desert.　Glory be to His name."

These efforts to teach the young were not pleasing to the planters.　They made a rule on some of the estates near, that all above ten years of age should pay rent, unless they did work ; and some were ordered off, because they preferred the school to the field.　At one place, Mr. Moir was interrupted by several whites, one of them being the overseer, who complained that the bigger boys and girls did nothing, and said, that unless the missionary got them to labour three days of the week, gratuitously, he would shut the school.　Addressing one of the boys, he said, " Sir, if ever I see you set your foot in the school again, or upon this estate, I will make you be taken to Port Maria jail."　Such interference was inconsistent with the freedom which these people now possessed.　They had a right, surely, to send their children to school, if they chose to do so, rather than to the field.　The missionaries were most anxious to be on friendly terms with the managers of the estates ; but they could not descend to be their tools.　The vexatious means which the latter adopted to coerce the people, only injured the properties. Had a more generous policy been tried, the people would have been bound to them ; but, instead of this, they were driven off, and now are, in great numbers, independent freeholders.

" *November*, 1838.—For some time I have been examining my people with a view to the ordinance of the Lord's Supper, and have been much pleased at the extent and accuracy of the knowledge which some have acquired.　I cannot speak with certainty as to the sanctified effect of this knowledge.　I hope, but that is all.　Some, of whom my opinion was most favourable, have disappointed me, and this makes me cautious.　Blessed be God ! that a minister's comfort depends not on sight, but on faith, not on seeing the fruits of his labours, but on believing the promise of him who cannot lie, that these labours shall not be in vain. Some have been cut off from the list for returning to the sinful ways of the country. One married man affords a melancholy example of a class, alas! too numerous. He was, for many years, in full communion with the church at Port Maria, high in profession, and in the confidence of both minister and people. I looked to him for efficient help in my labours, and he seemed most happy when aiding the cause of Christ. Some months ago, reports unfavourable to his character reached me. I was slow to believe them. At length, they came through a channel which rendered instant inquiry necessary. On examining into the state of his family, I found religion, on his part, much on the decline, his hours late, his habits irregular, and the company he kept the very reverse of what it ought to be, and of what it once was. The Session of Port Maria saw it dutiful to remove him from the midst of us. Recent events show the propriety of this step. The sin which before was secret, is now openly and unblushingly acknowledged. These things we must look for. There are ever some rocky ground hearers, who, in the time of temptation, fall away.

"A few evenings ago, I had a meeting in the house of one of my people. After we had concluded, the people seemed all very happy and delighted. One of them said to me :—'Minister, we are very happy when you come among us. We had no such thing as this before ; the people spent their evenings in dancing and riot, and their Sabbaths in walking about ; but now, all stay at home at night, attending to religion, and spend their Sabbaths in the church.'"

The following shows the kind of influence exercised by the missionary, and the results of that influence :—

"Last night, a man came to me with a paper. It was a charge for two weeks' rent, amounting to six shillings. 'Well, Richard, is this a just debt ? Whether would you have your house and grounds without rent, as a slave, or have them with rent as a free man ? Rent can be paid only in one of two ways,—either by money or by work. Now, have you paid it during the last two weeks, in work?' 'No, Minister, I was working out.' 'Well, then, the estate is just charging you that additional sixpence which you got by working out. The charge is just. You owe the debt, and Christ desires you not to get out of it in any dishonourable way. I advise you to go, to-morrow morning, and pay the money, and go to work and get your shilling a day. You will then have twenty pounds currency, with houses and grounds, and no rent to pay ; and, by the blessing of God, you will live in peace and comfort.' 'Minister, I will do as you bid me. I do not wish to go away. I once thought of going, but I cannot leave my church and you.' Our church and school have been blessed of God for securing the continuance of the people on their respective properties. Since the 1st of August, many have been restless. Dissatisfied with their present houses, they are going about in quest of what they consider better settlements. The estates on which I labour have been troubled, more or less, with this evil. But I believe that our church and school have tended materially to counteract this spirit, they being the centre of a powerful attraction, settling many in contentment, who would, otherwise, have been carried away with the current, drawing many to the neighbourhood who had left their former resi-dences, and bringing back others who, in the first excitement of freedom, had taken their departure from our midst. Many say, 'We love our church, we wish the education of our children, and we cannot leave you.' Some of those who returned said : 'We could have got work elsewhere, and been among our friends, but we want to be near minister.' One man said to me that he had gone to town to try how work would do there. 'I lived there three weeks, but returned, for I was anxious to be near my church.' An elderly woman said : 'I want to leave the estate, and indeed I would not care where I go, were it not that I cannot think of being far from you.' 'Minister,' they say, 'if you had not come among us, things would not have been so well on the 1st of August. The word you tell us makes our hearts soft, and we cannot think of doing wrong thing.' "

Jamaica has a church established by law. The Episcopalian section receives nearly £40,000 sterling annually, from the island revenues. There have been among the rectors and curates, some who obeyed and preached the gospel, and were not ashamed to co-operate with the servants of Jesus in the other sections. Others are Puseyites. One Sabbath, in November, 1838, Mr. Jameson had preached at Middlesex. On his way home, he met some persons, and asked them if they had been at church. They said they had been at father Whyte's at Halifax. "Who is father Whyte?" "A black brother, to whom Mr. O——, the curate, gave his books when he went away." "But do you think that the Sabbath will be as profitably spent at father Whyte's as at Lucky Hill church? Do you think that father Whyte is as able to instruct you as I am?" "No, Massa." "Then why do you spend your Sabbaths in the negro house, seeking instruction to guide you to happiness in time and in eternity, from one who is not qualified to instruct? I do not wish you to change your religion, if Church of England, or 'Church of Light,' as you call it, or if Baptist, or Methodist ; I do not wish you, unless you choose, to become Presbyterian. But I certainly desire that you should come to my church, except when your own ministers are with you."

"I am sorry to have to lay the blame of this pernicious system upon the minister rather than the people. During the time he was in this quarter, he busied himself in declaiming against me. When he left, he warned the people against joining my church. And to secure his object, he chose out a person on each property where his influence extended, and installed him as the spiritual guide of the people. If any of my people invite them to Lucky Hill church, they reply that they are forbidden to come. Such is the character of the zeal of some who ascribe divine efficacy to the touch of a bishop's fingers, who describe as hirelings those not thus touched, and who warn the people against us as fit only to give a little instruction which cannot convert. In their newspaper, the country is warned against those sectaries who come in shoals from the shores of Britain, who are a curse to the country, and ignorant of all literature, sacred and secular. The country is urged to resist them, and drive them from the island. This paper is the organ of the Established section, and is conducted by one of their parsons, who was missioned from his own country to preach peace and good-will. But facts which disprove these empty assertions, are as widely known as the assertions themselves. Their style of action is to be regretted, because of the injury which it inflicts on the Redeemer's cause : for it too often, and not unnaturally, happens that parsons' fighting is the planters' mirth."

Mr. Jameson was sometimes requested to administer the ordinance of baptism to the offspring of connexions unsanctioned by marriage. "Beastly concubinage" was, and still is, too much the order of the day in Jamaica, even among the upper classes. The following is a specimen. "Sir, through the grace of God, be kind enough to baptize this unfortunate illegitimate child, and oblige one who was brought up a Presbyterian." Shame on you, and on thousands like you ! A disgrace to their country are many Britons who go abroad to heathen lands or British colonies. While the capital and the commerce which pass through their hands, are a power in all places, yet their lives and lips too much testify against the blessed religion of God.

Writing to Mr. M'Gilchrist, on the 20th of November, 1838, Mr. Jameson says :—"I have now to sing of another mercy. The Lord never wearies in doing good to the unthankful and to the evil. He crowns us with his tender mercies, and is ever putting a new song in our mouth. On the 14th day of this month, Mrs. Jameson was safely delivered of a fine healthy daughter, and both are doing well."

He also alludes to the state of matters among the freed peasantry, defending them, and apologizing for them, in the peculiar circumstances in which they were placed. His remarks are just as well as generous. That so much should have been made of the unsteadiness of the newly free, merely showed that the supporters of slavery had neither conscience nor heart.

The same may be said of many in America, in Britain, and in the West Indies, at this day.

" I see by the papers that gloomy hints are abroad concerning the state of matters here, while the brighter accounts are kept out of view. The state of the question, as I understand it, is this : Since the 1st of August matters have not proceeded so smoothly as could have been desired ; but far more so than, from the nature of the case, could have been expected. Those who expected that the freed population would take their hoes and resume their toil, on the day of the week, or even in the month, when their chains were broken, expected what would be accounted extravagance in people at home, placed in like circumstances. How long is it after a coronation, a market, a Christmas, ere the tradesman settles down to his duties, or the school-boy to his lessons ? And why should the negro be expected to return to his drudgery, the moment he is a freeman ? Do we blame the school-boy because he does not return on the first day after his vacation ? or do we wonder at his buoyancy of spirit, when he rises on the first morning of his vacation, and finds himself free from his books, and at liberty to wander where he chooses ? Why should we blame the negro ? Why wonder at his buoyancy of spirit, when he rises on the first bright morning of freedom, and finds the whip laid aside for ever, the voice of the shell silent, and the chain which bound him broken ? Is it not natural that he should hasten to see his friends, who were sold in the days of slavery, and torn from him, to toil in some distant part of the island ? Let the negro alone. He will soon return to his old quarters, glad of rest, as the school-boy gladly seats himself on his old bench, after the vacation ends. The first excitements of freedom have passed, and the people are returning. They fondly cling to the estates on which they were born, and to the soil on which they spent their early days. The fact that they have exhausted their strength on this property, endears the spot. An old negro said to me, the other day : ' Massa, I have bought a little property, and I might go and live there, but my cocoa-nut tree is on Goshen, and I was born there. In my garden, my wife, my sons, and my daughters lie buried ; the sweat of my face has dropped on its earth ; I am getting old, and I cannot leave the spot where my strength is, and where all my joys and my sorrows have been.' The feeling of this old negro is the feeling of all. There is nothing on earth more distressing to the negro than to be driven from his birthplace, his friends, and his provision grounds."

At length, the missionary has the happy privilege of seeing some to whom he can give the right hand of fellowship. He has not been in haste to administer the ordinance of the Lord's Supper. But now he looks forward to it. In a letter to Mr. Bryden, December 4th, 1838, he says :—"I have not yet fixed the day when our first communion will be dispensed. Every day, I see greater need for caution ; for the Lord is showing me that those in whom I placed most confidence, are the very persons in whom I ought to have placed the least ; and thus I feel perplexed about the matter. The Lord will guide. Pray for us. Last Sabbath, I rebuked and suspended a number for dancing, who were coming forward to the Lord's Supper ; and some of them are among the most intelligent of my people. Early on Monday morning, a man came to the house telling me that some of the people had had a fight, arising from a dispute, after service on Sabbath. These had also been conversing with me, and seemed quiet, decent people. But the Lord is sifting us, and setting up marks to keep me right."

" *December*.—Mr. Moir's Sabbath-school advances prosperously. The new shed is full, yea, overflowing. Two hundred young people, whose regular instruction on the Sabbath I could not overtake before, are now classed, are learning, and following those who are more advanced. Were you to transport yourselves to Lucky Hill church, on Sabbath morning, at ten o'clock, and see 200 children busy with their reading lessons ; at eleven o'clock, and see them engaged with their questions and their different religious exercises ; and at twelve, and see them march in silence, and in order, from their school-shed to the church, your souls would magnify the Lord for all that he has enabled you to do for us here."

At this period, Mr. Jameson and Mr. Moir went, one day in

the week, to two estates in Bagnolds, to teach the children. There was also a daily school at Mile-End taught by a native of Jamaica. And so busy were all, that, at the end of 1838, there were about 370 children enjoying some amount of educational privilege. Those only who, by experience, know the fatigue of a long ride, and an hour or two of vigorous effort to instruct young people, and far more, old people who have grown up without early tuition, and all this under the enervating sky of the tropics, can fully appreciate the energy and zeal which such labours implied. The churches of all denominations have great cause to bless God for the valuable reapers—some of them still alive—whom they were honoured to send out to the white harvest of these earlier days of the mission. They were blessed with much success ; and, if one asks where the proof is, we answer, The numerous churches at various stages of intellectual and spiritual culture, which are to be found in Jamaica and other West Indian Islands. May these first fruits be followed by a yet more plenteous ingathering ! May the hopes excited by these earlier triumphs be realized an hundred-fold !

At Christmas, the school was examined. The white people present were surprised at the progress which had been made in so short a time. The black part of the audience seemed much delighted with the picaninies.

" During Christmas there is no work. People are hurrying to town to see and hear. Pigs are screaming in every quarter, under the knife of death ; and every one is determined to enjoy the ' free,' at Christmas-time. All is sobriety and order. I have seen no drunkenness."

" Certain musicians came to Bagnold's Vale, expecting the welcome reception of former times. At one property, they tuned their instruments, and began. Some gathered round to hear, but Mr. Moir made his appearance and they dispersed. In the evening, the performers renewed their attempt on the steps of the Busha's house. A Lucky Hill Presbyterian, imbued somewhat with the spirit of other days, came forward with a club, and knocked the end out of the drum, and silenced the fiddle with a blow. John, however, did not escape without a scar.   The musicians beat him lustily.   But he was comforted by knowing that he had suffered in a good cause."

At the end of nearly two years of labour, the following statistics were given :—Average attendance, 600 ; catechumens, 204 ; marriages, 42 ; adults reading in the Old Testament, 10 ; adults reading in the New, 50 ; children in Sabbath classes, 240.

CHAPTER V.

The Jamaica Academy—Anglo-Ethiopia, a lever to raise Africa—Goshen congregation formed—Wonderful deliverance—No partisan—The negroes on strike—Teaching the difference between mine and thine—Massa and the people at loggerheads—Church formed—Sets about building—Munificence of proprietors—Mr. Barkly—Light of the dwelling extinguished—Particulars of Mrs. Jameson's death—Verses by Mrs. Jameson—Mr. Barkly lays the foundation-stone of the new church—Bonham Spring—Touching retrospect.

New Year's-day, 1839, was spent in the church. Mr. Moir addressed the children ; and Mr. Jameson the married people, on the duties of husband and wife. A church and school building society was formed, and 194 persons became contributors.

The Jamaica Missionary Presbytery met at Port Maria, in January. It was a refreshing season to the brethren. At one of their sittings, they had the happiness of welcoming the Rev. Mr. Scott, a new missionary, who had just arrived. In a letter to Mr. M'Gilchrist, January 30th, 1839, we find an allusion to the academy for training natives of Jamaica for missionary service. The results of this institution have been very valuable. It has furnished most of our mission schools with efficient teachers, and some of these again have been trained for the higher office of the ministry of the gospel, by the Theological Tutor (Rev. Alexander Renton), with whom the liberality of the Church has also gifted her daughter in the West Indies. This academy, which, from its very commencement till now, has been conducted by Mr. Millar, with remarkable vigour and success, was begun at Bonham Spring, an out-station of Goshen, and, after a time, transferred to Montego Bay.

"The hearts of the Presbytery are set on an academy for

training young men for the ministry, with a view to Africa and the islands around us. I hope that Christians at home will aid us in the work. The desire and the determination of the Presbytery are to dispense, as little as possible, with any part of that course of preparation which is considered indispensable at home. We think that this course ought to be extended rather than shortened, and that what is necessary to enlarge, as well as simplify, the views of a home minister, is more necessary for a minister here. To say that a man of learning is requisite for the ministry at home, but that any kind of man will do for the poor ignorant negroes, is to say what is not true. A home preacher may throw out to an audience the crude views of an illiterate mind, without damage to any one but himself ; but to settle such a one here would be to risk immortal souls."

The academy was commenced with a view to both Jamaica and Africa. The brethren sought to attempt great things for God and for Ethiopia. They looked upon Ethiopia in the West as a means of reaching the heart of the great mother-land of the black-face. They wanted to regard Jamaica as a depot in which to find storming parties to assail the devil's strongholds in Africa. They thought of the churches of Christ throughout the world sending to them for men, and, at their call, men of Ethiopian race, well qualified and trustworthy, going forth to the work. The forlorn hope has, to a great extent, been formed of Europeans, who are seeking a lodgment and a base of operation on the shore of Africa. And who knows whether the anticipations under which the brethren sought to establish their academy, may not yet be realized ? Two of their objects have been accomplished : for the mission schools in Jamaica are taught, and well taught, by natives. Several natives trained in the island, have also been introduced into the ministry of the gospel. And who knows, but that at no distant day, labourers of the right kind may be chosen by the Lord from the Jamaica churches, to preach the unsearchable riches of Christ among the tribes of their father-land ! Surely ten millions of Africa's children are not in the West for nothing, or only to make sugar and rum, and to grow cotton. He who prepared Israel in the iron furnace, is doubtless preparing, in the West Indies and America, a powerful agency to act upon deeply degraded Africa. We, in our short-sightedness, are so impatient to see the fruit of our labours, that we lose patience with the unobserved, and frequently unobservable, majestic march of the plan of God. An impatient child, dissatisfied with the slow growth of his little garden plot, just as his young flowers are sprouting, pulls them up to see how they are growing, or leaves the whole to the weeds, and makes a garden in another spot. The foolish child loses much of his labour by such impatience. Even the growth of a flower or vegetable proceeds heedless of man's impetuosity. How much more the growth of the kingdom of God! Why do churches act over again the silly child, in the management of their mission gardens? Verily, were it not for the Great Husbandman above, the unreasoning haste with which, in some cases, infant churches are left to shift for themselves, would be the means of spoiling all. Such a mode of acting, to use Mr. Jameson's words, "is to take the ark from Moses, and leave the deliverer of Israel to perish in the helplessness of infancy; it is to deny Samson a mother's care, without which his gigantic strength cannot be nursed." Take care of the child: train him for his future work: teach him to look forward to it: and, when God's auspicious hour arrives, He will command his strength, and an inspiration from on high will move him to the enterprise of his mission. He will go forth to the help of the Lord against the mighty, and "Ethiopia shall soon stretch out her hands unto God." At the same time, we must pray to the Lord to raise up labourers in our little churches in Ethiopia herself. Could we get properly fitted men there, they would, in many respects, be the best of pioneers. But we must levy contributions from all quarters. The British missionary, with his broader training and his self-reliance, with his experience and his knowledge, must lead the van. The West Indies and America must give the cream of their Ethiopian talent, and piety, and self-devotion; and our infant churches in Africa must also contribute their share, however humble, and however scanty, to the great enterprise. There is room for all:

there is need for all. Standing on the edge of this dense jungle, this interminable and entangled continent of bush, we, the vanguard of the Lord's army of Ethiopia, wonder whether it shall ever become a field which the Lord hath blessed. When this desert shall rejoice and blossom as the rose,—when Ethiopia shall be seen sitting in the heavenly places of the church of Jesus, dispossessed, redeemed, washed, raising her dusky brow and swimming eyes to the Lord who has pitied her, and, with outstretched hands laying her tribute at his feet,— surely there will be heard in heaven hallelujahs as loud and rapturous as when it shall be said, " Lo ! these from the land of Sinim !"

Thus did Mr. Jameson first mention the mission to Africa, which has since become a fact :—" The people's hearts are turning towards Africa.   They are earnestly pressing us to send a missionary thither.   We all agree ; and, ere long, I hope our church here will apply for a missionary from home, or appoint one of our brethren, to go for us to the land of Ethiopia.   Our ambition is to send the first well-educated native missionary to that field of labour.

Two-and-twenty years have passed, and this aspiration remains still unrealized.   Yet it is gratifying that two educated and ordained natives of Jamaica have gone to Western Africa, in connexion with the Baptist mission.   One of these, the Rev. Joseph Merrick, died at Bimbia, much and justly regretted ; the other is the Rev. Mr. Pinnock, who went out in 1857.

At that meeting of Presbytery, it was agreed that the adherents of Goshen station should be formed into a congregation ; and Messrs. Blyth and Anderson being appointed to aid in that transaction, went with Mr. Jameson from the Presbytery, on their way home.   " On the fourth Sabbath of January, 1839, the relation of minister and people was solemnly declared by Mr. Blyth, in the manner usual among Presbyterians.   The ordinance of baptism was administered among us, for the first time.   My own child was the first offered to the Lord in our church.   This was its first outset from the house in which it was born, its first journey in this vale of tears, long enough for one so tender, and not without its dangers. When starting from the house, on the way to the church, the wheel of the gig, with which we had been favoured for the occasion, came into contact with the gate-post. The shafts were broken in two, and, in a moment, the vehicle was precipitated to the ground. Angels, the guardian spirits of the heirs of salvation, were in attendance. The mother and the tender babe escaped unhurt, and we brought the child, rescued from destruction, and gave her to the Lord, soul and body, for time and for eternity. It was a new situation for Mrs. Jameson and myself, but it was not the less interesting that it was our own child, in the midst of our own people—the people we were gathering to the Lord—and the public recognition of our own God, and our father's God, in a foreign land. It was a hallowed day ; many an arousing word, and many a comforting word were spoken ; it was the first sermon I had listened to in my own church, and the first Sabbath I enjoyed the satisfaction of being a hearer, since I came to Jamaica."

With all his zeal and energy, Mr. Jameson was distinguished for prudence and thoughtfulness. He was not easily carried away by appearances, but was alive to the real state of matters, and to what was for the true and permanent interests of the people. He lamented waywardness and want of principle among them, not less, perhaps more, than injustice and harshness among the planters ; and he impartially sought, on all proper occasions, to teach both parties the way of rectitude. On the 30th of January, he wrote to Mr. M'Gilchrist :—"I have tried to show you the working of freedom as it is ; its bright and its dark sides, that you may judge of matters for yourself, and that you may see the line of policy I have been led to pursue. I hope it will meet with your approbation. I wish to stand wholly out from parties, and to adhere to righteousness, and to lead my people in peace along its paths. I have been successful in this, in some good measure, although many times it has been a hard task. The more popular way would have been to identify myself wholly with the people, to support them in measures reasonable and unreasonable, just and unjust, through good and through bad report ; but I desire a conscience void of offence towards God and towards men."

In his journal he writes :—" This is the third week of cessation from labour, and the people appear disinclined to resume their work.   Upon inquiry, I find that they are waiting for a new law from the Queen, to the effect that they shall not work, in summer, for the same wages as in winter.   This strike is too general.   I have gone round the district, and showed to as many as I could meet, the impolicy and impropriety of this. I told them that they had not needed to stop working, in order that the 'free' should come.   Their working had rather helped it on.   If any other law, then, were coming, it would come not the less surely and speedily that they kept busy at their work. Besides, if they knew the difficulty which their friends had experienced in getting the rate of wages raised to what it was, they would not be anxious to disturb the question, so soon after its settlement."

" This week (the fourth), the people have, at last, taken our advice, and turned out to their work.   The country again assumes the appearance of life and activity.   The fields are again awake, and the face of society puts on a more promising aspect."

" Visiting a sick person, I saw a quantity of sugar-cane in a corner.   The daughter, a little girl, saw me fixing my eye on the cane, and shrunk back, squeezing her hand over her mouth, knowing that her mother was caught in a fault.

" ' Well, Mrs. ——, did this cane grow in your garden ? '

" ' No, minister.'

" ' How did you get it ?   Did you cut it ? '

" ' Oh, no, my minister, me just beg the wain-man as he was passing.'

" ' Who was the wain-man ? '

" ' Jock Whitter.'

" ' Well, I met Jock a few weeks ago, riding on a mule, and I asked him, " Jock, where have you been ? "   " I was at massa's," said Jock, " for money to pay the people, and I am riding home as fast as I can, lest somebody rob me in the dark."

"Very good, Jock," said I, "take as good care of the money as if it were your own." Now, Mrs. ——, if I had said to Jock, "Brother, give me a little of this money—a dollar or so," would I have done right ?'

" 'He! he! he! no, minister, no! that never do.' '

" 'If Jock had taken out a dollar and given me, would he have done right ?'

" 'No, minister, that very bad.'

" 'Well then, what difference would there have been, in God's sight, between my asking, and Jock's giving me, his master's money, and your asking, and Jock's giving you, his master's cane ? And ought not I to have returned the money ? And ought not you to return the cane ?'

"As I was standing with some persons, expostulating with them about the same thing, Mrs. ——'s daughter passed with the canes to restore them to the owner.

"The country, at the present moment, is the scene of interminable confusion. Nobody knows what is law, or not law. The local magistrates support the interests of the planters ; the stipendiary magistrates are on the side of the people. The contest assumes the appearance of a game at draughts, a struggle for mastery rather than righteousness. The Attorney-General says one thing ; some lawyers in town say another, and the opposite ; and authorities in England, the Attorney and Solicitor-General, disagree with the highest law authority in the island. Thus we are driven to silence from a respect to our character and office. It is high time that Britain demanded from some quarter a code of righteous laws for her emancipated colonies. The people are willing to work, and do work, but they and their masters are ever disputing, and there is no law to appeal to. What would be the state of society at home, if the question of rent and occupation were unsettled, and families were liable to be turned adrift on the world, at a week's notice, the doors locked, and the provision-grounds destroyed,—if wife and children were to be charged rent equally with the husband and the father,—if the child at school were charged rent, and were liable to be hindered from prosecuting his education, yea, to be driven 'from under the parental roof? Whilst this has been done in some quarters, I must say that it has not been general, in so far as I know; but the fact that it can be done shows in what confusion we are at present. Masters, too, are fully as much oppressed as the people. Their ripe canes are often not cut; their young canes are not cleaned; the cattle have been allowed to range at large in the luxuriant fields; future crops have not been planted; many work when they like, and sit down when they like. If ever Jamaica required the prayers of the Church, and the watchful eye of the Church, and of British philanthropy, and if ever prudence and discretion were needed to guide, it is at this moment."

: The gospel had now been preached for two years at Goshen, and among the surrounding properties, by this zealous labourer; and the word of God had not returned unto him void. The Lord had given the increase. Sinners had been brought to the Saviour. They had been carefully instructed, in order that their piety might rest on the foundation of a correct knowledge of the truth. Mr. Jameson had not hastily admitted any to the fellowship of the church, nor did he receive indiscriminately all who sought admission. After anxious and prayerful inquiry, thirty-two were selected from among the candidates. On Saturday, the 9th of March, 1839, these were received into the fellowship of the visible church of Jesus Christ; and Mr. Moir was ordained as an elder. Members of the church at Carron Hall were present, on the Sabbath; and upwards of 100 sat together at the table of the Lord. "It was," writes Mr. Jameson, "an interesting and solemn season—a season which will be remembered through eternity. 'Massa,' said one, 'we never thought to see such a day. We thought our children's children might see it, but not we.' Another said, 'We could sit there for ever.' Some who were detained by sickness, were grieved at being absent; but they said that it pleased God, and they were pleased."

The following (March 19th, 1839), gives an interesting account of the work at that period:—

" The school is succeeding far beyond my most sanguine

expectations. There are 246 on the list, and 200 attend daily. Our room at the Pen became far too small. Mr. Moir kept school under the shelter of a lofty tree, but this being inconvenient, we removed to the church, and since then the school has increased by dozens at a time. The people say they cannot get a picaniny (little child) to go a message for them ; they are all at school together. Some come a distance of seven miles, and return in the afternoon. Those who live farther away, bring their food with them, and sleep at the Pen, while some who cannot be accommodated, live with friends in the neighbourhood. Mr. Moir is everything we could wish.

" To hear their children read, sing hymns, repeat the catechisms, and say their prayers, is far beyond what the parents expected. When the father comes home from work, and the child from school, the latter must take his book and read, while the former listens as to an oracle. In various cases known to us, the child gathers the family together before going to bed, and is their mouth at the footstool of God. It is common in the congregation for the children to read and sing, and the father to pray."

It now became necessary to set about the building of a house of prayer, in good earnest. The saying of the Duke of Wellington, " If you want a thing well done, you must do it yourself," has special force in Jamaica, and, indeed, in all mission spheres. The building of such a house was not easy in the interior parts of Jamaica. The house proposed was calculated to cost £1200, but it was not finished for less than £2000. To find the money, to collect the materials, to hire the workmen, and then to superintend the work, were enough to fill one man's hands. But when he had also to oversee, and take part in, all the duties of Christian instruction, over a district two or three times as large as an ordinary Scotch parish, and to act as pastor of an infant church, we cannot but admire the energy of will, the perseverance in action, and the simplicity of faith which it was given him to exhibit.

The committee of the Rose Street Society, anxious to further the work, promised such assistance as was within their power, and also opened a correspondence with the proprietors of the Trinity estates, laying before them extracts from Mr. Jameson's letters, to inform them of what he was doing at Goshen and its neighbourhood. These gentlemen, while, being Episcopalians, they would have preferred a church in their own connexion, yet, in the most generous manner, agreed to aid Mr. Jameson's efforts. As Mr. Barkly—now Sir Henry Barkly, formerly Governor of Jamaica, now of Victoria—was then visiting the West Indies, they expressed their satisfaction that they would thus obtain correct information on the subject, and become acquainted with Mr. Jameson and his labours.

At length, Mr. Barkly arrived. He resided some time at Goshen, and gained golden opinions among the people, by his affability, and by the kindly interest which he took in their welfare, of which the survivors of those days still speak with obvious delight. Mr. Barkly conceived a high respect for Mr. Jameson's character, and a high opinion of his labours among the people ; and so favourable was his report, that, on his advice, twelve acres of Lucky Hill land were given in fee simple for the church and school, £300 sterling as a donation, and all the building material, as wood, stone, and lime, which the estates could furnish.

The Church and School Building Society, which had been formed, on the 1st of January, 1839, with 194 contributors, had swelled, before the end of that month, to 334, who gave from 3d. to 1s. monthly. Mr. Jeffrey of Salisbury contributed £60 sterling, and, under his superintendence, the people turned out and built a large lime-kiln. The foundation was dug, and preparations were made for the laying of the foundation-stone.

In the meantime, Mr. Jameson had to pass through one of those valleys of the shadow of death which lie in the path to heaven. He suffered one of the severest afflictions that can befall a missionary in a foreign land. His excellent and devoted wife was removed from his side, after three short years of happy union. She had, on the whole, been healthy ; and she had been most active in the work of the mission, seconding her husband's efforts, solacing his heart, cheering his home, and lightening all his labours. On the 21st of June, she was seized with fever, and on the 12th of July, she expired. We can sympathize with the afflicted husband in his fears and anxieties, during those three weeks of doubt and conflict ; and in his anguish, as his beloved partner is taken away from him, and he feels that now his strongest earthly tie is broken, and that henceforth his Master calls him to more devoted labour, and more earnest self-sacrifice.

Mrs. Jameson's father was the eldest son of the Rev. John Mackersy of Kinkell. He held the farm of Cultmalundie, near Methven, and was an elder and manager of the Secession Church at Methven, under the ministry of his uncle, the Rev. John Wilson, and of his cousin, the Rev. John Jameson.[1]

Mrs. Jameson's mother, Catherine Dempster, was a daughter of the Rev. Simon Dempster, Secession minister of Leslie, in Fifeshire. Mrs. Dempster's mother was a very godly woman. On one occasion, she said to her daughter : " I have got from the Lord the promise of you, and your seed, and your seed's seed." She thus expressed her inward conviction, which she regarded as a Divine monition, that God would answer her prayers for her posterity.

Mr. Mackersy of Cultmalundie died, leaving his children very young. He was a kind-hearted, good man. Mr. Jameson of Methven, writing to his widow, Mrs. Mackersy (August 29th, 1823), says :—" I was just thinking, as I walked into Perth, this afternoon, that as, on this day seventeen years, your husband and I rode in to bring out my bride, his conversation was more than usually elevated, and serious, and interesting—something akin to that going to Emmaus. I felt it wonderfully then ; what would I have given for it now !" Mr. Jameson was appointed trustee of the fatherless children, and as they lived at Methven, some time after their father's death, they were cared for by him, and instructed along with his own children. Living over again the scenes of his wife's death, on the anni-

---

[1] The Rev. John Mackersy, minister of the Secession Church at Kinkell, married Isabella Wilson, one of the daughters of Rev. William Wilson of Perth.

versary of that event—" a season charged with an accumulation of anxiety and anguish "—he writes to Mrs. Mackersy, " I beheld your children sitting at table with my own : it was, for a moment, like the shooting of a gleam of sunshine athwart a sky of clouds and gloominess. The thought that my friend and theirs was no more, to bid them welcome, came pressing on like the thick and murky cloud returning after the rain."

Mr. Jameson's only brother, John, became a solicitor in Airdrie, where he was much respected, and obtained the title of the " honest lawyer." A valuable gold watch was presented to him by the " liberal electors of Airdrie, in acknowledgment of his able services as their agent," at an election in 1842. He died in 1847, on the very day on which Mr. Jameson was taken with his death-illness in Old Calabar.

Mrs. Jameson was possessed of excellent abilities, and of varied accomplishments. She was thoroughly educated, very intelligent and humorous, and wielded a ready and graphic pen. She has left several oil paintings, one of them being a portrait of her grandfather, Mr. Mackersy of Kinkell, which show both taste and talent. Her portrait, painted by Sir John Watson Gordon, of Edinburgh, is now before me. It is one of those portraits which are obvious likenesses, and not mere pictures. There is nothing about it to attract attention, but the face, and it is such a face as one never tires looking at, and returns to gaze upon with ever new delight and love. It betokens the sweetness of disposition, the modesty, purity, and decision of character, and the wondrous self-possession for which the original was distinguished. Her diffidence made her indisposed to speak much about her religious experience ; but her piety was at once genuine and devoted. It was characterized by self-distrust ; and, no doubt, this arose from the integrity of a highly conscientious character. On one occasion, when some friends were engaged in earnest conversation about the attainableness of an assurance of personal safety, she expressed considerable dubiety ; and this is referred to in the following notices of her death-bed experience, when she said to her husband : " *Now* I know that all my sins are forgiven." Then, through the grace that is in Christ Jesus, the Holy Ghost gave her such a view of the Saviour as hers, and so enabled her to embrace him, that she felt his everlasting arms around her, felt that she was in his hands, and that, therefore, she could not perish, but should have everlasting life. She was indeed a woman of whom her husband could always justly be proud, and in whom his heart safely trusted.

. The following are instances of her presence of mind and courage. When she and her brother were little children, one day as they were playing together, his dress caught fire. No one was at hand to give assistance. Without any screaming or noise, she snatched off her own upper dress, and wrapped it round him. When she was travelling on the coach to Airdrie, on one occasion, the horses became unmanageable, and the driver told the passengers to mind themselves, if they could. Several gentlemen made their escape, by scrambling over the stern, and left Miss Mackersy to care for herself. She determined to keep her place, and the driver encouraged her to hold on. She did so, and clung with all her strength, till, at length, after a run of three miles, the horses slackened their speed.

After she was under engagement to go to Jamaica, she wrote to her future partner :—"If the Lord calls me, if He has need of me, I go cheerfully, and do count it greater honour than all the riches of this world. It has been my desire to renounce its vanities, and live separate from it. I have prayed God to deliver me from its temptations, when almost carried away by them. And if He is now granting my request, though giving me a pang with it, shall I grudge to leave all and follow him ? But I do not leave all, since you are with me, since you have given me your heart, the only one I ever could have cherished a thought of. Mine is yours ; and it is not the thought of a moment, but of many years of searching and trying. The earnestness of your youthful affection clung to me all my life ; and if, at any time, I have been thought of by others, then it has been most warmly remembered. This has often seemed strange to myself ; but, of late years, I have thought that surely God was leading me. If so, William, can

I not go with you to any land, to any people? Surely I can give you Ruth's answer. Although called to leave beloved friends, we have God with us; and shall He not unite us again where there is no separation, when this life, which is but a shadow, has passed away?"

Again :—"I should like much to be at your ordination, an event so deeply interesting. I should like to get into some corner where I could see you, and hear all. We may talk of it when solitary strangers in a far distant land, if you are spared. But, oh, my dearest William, I weep at the very thought of seeing you set apart, devoted, perhaps to death. This thought overwhelms me. It is the thorn in my flesh. It clouds every joy. I heard of a young man whose whole life and heart were devoted to missionary work, and who died some days after he landed. The ways of God are most mysterious. This fills me with fear, but I will try to trust in Him who has said, 'Cast thy burden on me.' Mr. Deans'[1] sermon was remarkable : for it was just at the time when I was in deepest perplexity. I came out of the church, that day, quite convinced that the words were spoken to me, and determined to leave my own heart and my foolish thoughts with God for direction."

Mrs. Jameson's labours among the people were much blessed, and we cannot help mourning that she was removed so soon. Writing about her, February 1st, 1838, Mr. Jameson says :—"Her labours among both young and old are unremitting, and eminently successful. She has gained the esteem and affection of all. No one will leave the house without seeing 'Missis,' and bidding her 'day day.' When they come, they always bring something to her ; and on the Sabbaths, when I am not at home, they flock to our house to get food, as they say, to their souls from Missis. At home, on Portobello sands, she was like the poet's gem in the cave of ocean, or like his flower, wasting its sweetness in the desert air. Here, she is laying out

---

[1] Rev. Geo. Deans of Portobello. On that occasion, Mr. Deans read the 24th chapter of Genesis ; and his remarks on the willingness of Rebekah to leave her home and kindred to share the lot of the man of God (verse 58), were what more particularly seemed to Miss Mackersy to be the voice, saying, This is the way, walk thou in it.

her time and talents in the noblest of enterprises—teaching Ethiopia to stretch out her hands unto God. And although she has left the ease and comfort of home, yet it is to beautify her own crown, by bringing a few more gems to beautify the crown of our Redeemer. . . . She is up in the morning, feeding her fowls, gathering their eggs, and superintending the children while they clean the house. During the day, she is in the midst of her pupils, teaching them to read, write, and sew."

The following extracts from her pen will convey some idea of the numerous and wearisome trials which our missionary sisters and partners have to endure in their self-denying service, especially in new fields of labour, before their heroic and persevering efforts have created helps for themselves :—

On March 12th, she wrote : — " Friends would not be offended at my never writing, if they knew how my time is taken up. All last summer we had the school. In the morning, we rode to the White River, and without this cooling bathe, I do not think I could have endured the heat. After school hours, I had always more to do than I could manage. . . . I assure you, there are no slumberers here. Before daylight, the bell is rung for all to rise. At half-past seven, the bell rings for worship. Then comes breakfast. Oh, what a multitude of trifling troubles we have in Jamaica ! Mr. Moir swallows his breakfast, and rides off, followed by all his train, and I am left to clear away as I can. The school is so popular, that none but the lame and the sick will stay to help me. I have often thought of you, when I had no servant at all, and wished that you could look across the Atlantic, and see me sitting at my threshold, watching the cooking operations outside—a fire erected near the door, the soup-pot on high, perhaps the beef in another under, a little black girl keeping up the fire, and anon running to the kitchen to turn the yam—me sitting in the shade, but the fire heat bursting in at the door, and the sun's rays coming through the very walls. I often wished Mrs. ——, who said that missionaries should not keep servants, had but one week of it. . . . The girls are very stupid about household matters, from being brought up like cattle. For instance, I told one the other day to lay down the carpet before the bed. She took a clean folded shirt of Mr. Jameson's, and began to lay it down."

Writing to Miss Jameson, March 20th, 1838 :—" Well done the Perth ladies ! Many thanks for their box. Truly you have done a good work to us. I made about £15 out of it, and this is the beginning of a fund for building church and school. I have been the seller, and have had my work, but I rejoiced in it. Some of our whites have tried to throw contempt upon me, by saying I was now keeping a store. I don't mind that ; I shall sell all I can, so that it forward our work."

Again, April 9th, 1838 :—" There is no doubt that the constitutions of the missionaries soon fail. As they have so much fatigue and exposure to the sun by day, and to the dews by night, they are liable to fevers, and then they are dosed with calomel till their stomachs become like a washed clout, as Mr. Cowan says of his. I think the ministers at home should exchange with their brethren here, and let them home to recruit. It would do good to both parties ; and, more especially, it would interest those at home in the poor perishing souls in this heathen land."

In a letter to Mrs. Mackersy (July 15th, 1839), Mr. Jameson narrates some of the circumstances of his beloved partner's death, and none can fail to see that the God of all comfort sustained his servant in his hour of woe.

" My beloved mother, I hope the Lord has heard, and will now answer, the prayer of many in this land, who love you because they dearly loved Nicolis who taught them, but whom the Lord, in his adorable but mysterious providence, has seen it good to take away. I hope that He has in his own way been preparing your mind for the heavy intelligence, and oh, I hope that, when this letter is put into your hand, you will experience the supporting and consoling influences of God's Holy Spirit."

' Having mentioned a few particulars of the commencement and progress of the malady, during which she was attended by three doctors, and that she had been removed to Salisbury, five miles from their residence, to try the effect of a change of air, he says :—" On Friday, the 12th, towards afternoon, she sunk, and at 7 P.M., she fell asleep in Jesus, without any symptom of pain or struggle. Not a finger or a joint moved, not a feature was distorted, but all the placidity of heaven rested on her countenance. At the moment of departure, a smile came upon her lips, and spread a melancholy sweetness over her pale countenance, yea, more than sweetness, a blithesomeness and an energy which I have not before seen. It seemed to indicate that our dearly beloved was in the happiest mood, that she had taken her flight, just as the glories of the eternal world burst upon her view, and that her last effort upon the earthly tabernacle which she was leaving behind, was the stamping upon the countenance this joyous smile, as a token to us that all our prayers were now answered, that our beloved had now passed the Jordan, that she was now on the shores of Immanuel's land, had got the first glimpse of its glories, and was refreshed after her cares and toils, with the first draught of its joys. It told me to weep for myself, but not for her ; that she was clothed upon with her house from heaven, while I was in a tabernacle, burdened and groaning.

" The day following, at 4 P.M., her body was laid in the grave, at Salisbury, beside her friend Mrs. Jeffrey, amidst a great assembly of those to whom she had first imparted the knowledge of Christ. Deep was the interest excited by this solemn event, and many the tears shed over her grave. Among no people could she have been more generally useful ; by none could the loss of dear Nicolis be more deeply felt or more sincerely lamented.

" During the whole period of her illness, Mr. Cowan was much with us, and contributed greatly to the comfort of my beloved wife. In the last week, Mr. Paterson arrived from Manchester, and came from Carron Hall to share in our affliction. Mr. Cowan and he were both with me on the sad day when the Lord called me to part with my sweetest earthly comfort ; they spoke and prayed with her ; they retired and prayed by themselves ; in this way the Lord made abundant provision for her spiritual benefit. On Saturday, Mr.

Simpson came from Port Maria to the funeral ; and he and Mr.
Paterson remained with me yesterday, which was the Sabbath.
The Lord sent these His servants to pour the consolations of
the gospel into my sad and desolate heart.

"Now, my dear mother, I know that your heart will be
very sad, that it will be overwhelmed, that the blow will be
heavy, heavy.   Oh, what can I say ?   I brought Nicolis to
the field on which she has fallen.   The Lord enabled me to
deliver my sweetest mercy into his hand, to give her back to
him who gave her to me.   But I feel sad when I think of
your sadness.   My poor heart feels doubly desolate when I
think of your desolation.   My dear mother, let me press on
your instant attention the last two verses of the 4th chapter
of second Corinthians, and the first part of the 5th.   Oh, let
me beseech you to look not at the things which are seen, but
at the things which are not seen.   Think, oh, think more of
the gain of our beloved Nicolis, than of our irreparable loss.
Think of the good which she effected among the children of
Ethiopia, and of the honourable position she holds among those
who have helped to fulfil the prophecy : 'Ethiopia shall soon
stretch out her hands unto God.'   The day of her activity has
been short.   It has, however, been all the time which God allotted to her ; every moment of it has been occupied.   She
trifled not ; many gems has she won to her crown, and to the
crown of her Redeemer, by coming here ; many more, than if
she had been the companion of your pilgrimage and the cheerer
of your solitary hours.   If sharp arrows pierce your soul, think
that the next time you see our beloved friend, you will envy
her exalted and honourable position, and you will say that she
has been wise, and that with those who esteemed her foolish,
has been and is the folly.

"The death-bed experience of Nicolis has been in full correspondence with her life, serene, and marked with the full
assurance of faith and hope.   Two weeks before her death,
she said : 'William, I think I am going to leave you.   My
time is come.   I desire to live only for your sake.   I feel at
leaving you alone in this sad country ; but the Lord will

take care of you, and comfort you. I fear I have sinned in being too anxious about baby, and about laying up for her education and for a time of sickness. I should have taken your advice, and cast myself and all my cares upon the Lord.' I spoke to her of Christ Jesus, and of the freeness, the fulness, and the sovereignty of forgiving mercy. She appeared much delighted and satisfied. She lay quiet some time, and then said : ' Oh, I have had a sweet meditation with the Saviour. *Now*, I know that all my sins are forgiven. *Now*, I know that all my backslidings are healed, and that I am accepted in the beloved.' And with emphasis she said : ' I desire to depart, and to be with Christ, which is far better. Tell me your lecture on the 23d Psalm. This I did, so far as I could recollect it. ' Ay,' she said, ' death is a gloomy vale, but Christ will lead me through. Now, I will tell you what I want you to do, my dear William. Send baby to Mrs. Cowan to take care of, and, if you find an opportunity, send her home to my mother.' "

" After some directions about gifts to be given to various parties, she added : ' Now, I have done with the world. O Lord, give me a quick, and, if it be Thy will, an easy passage.' After this, she got a respite of some days. She then said : ' William, the Lord has heard your prayers, and sent me relief.' This she said, I thought, with an air of regret. Her eye seemed to have been resting on heaven. She was much in meditation, and much in prayer. Sometimes she prayed audibly, and her petitions were expressed in short sentences, and clothed in pointed and powerful language ; and the intercourse which she enjoyed with Christ on these occasions, seemed to have quickened her desires for immortality.

" The night before she died, she slept none. She said to me : ' William, tell me some promises, some about pardon ; say to me the 23d Psalm. I am going to die, to pass through the gloomy vale. I think that the spirit of your father is not far away from me. The Lord will be with you, my dear William. Tell my mother that I die, not because I have come to Jamaica, but because I have come to the time appointed.'

Towards the last, the fever fell into her brain, so that the sweetness of our intercourse was now past.

"During her illness, I myself watched her, night and day. I gave her all her medicines. I trembled for, and wept over her. Prayer was made, everywhere, in meetings. throughout the congregation. The poor child of Ethiopia feared and prayed, and now mourns and weeps, and bids me keep good heart, for that the Lord will help me. And, my dear mother, they are praying for you. Oh, may the Lord sustain and comfort you ! . . . This moment your letter has come in. Alas ! a flood threatens to overwhelm me."

On the 16th of July, he wrote thus :—" My beloved aunts, the Lord has stunned me with the blow of his hand. He has taken my Nicolis from my sight. I feel the sadness of desolation and woe. My heart is overwhelmed. Lord, thy waves and thy billows go over me. I speak as an impatient one ; ascribe this to the infirmity of a heart that feels its loneliness, not to the blessed God whose arms support me. The Lord has done it, and what shall I say ? I bless him with my whole heart. I needed chastisement, and I am chastised. I desire to learn the depths of Thy holy law, O Lord."

The following contains a touching account of the removal of Mrs. Jameson to Salisbury :—

" Mrs. Jameson was now in the deep waters of affliction. The raging fever had baffled the skill of the physician, and mocked his most potent prescriptions. Change of air was our last hope. Young men were staying at the Pen overnight, to be ready to start with their afflicted friend, at the first appearance of returning day. There were a dozen of them together, and the first part of the night was spent in prayer. Their petitions were few, but much to the point ; their manner was simple, earnest, and affecting ; it was a solemn night—the last on which Mrs. Jameson was in her own house. The most of them were members of her Sabbath class. ' Massa Jesus, pity dear Missis ; give her comfort and heal her.' Another—' Pity our dear minister ; and, O Jesus ! take not away from him his dear wife.' Another prayed, ' O Jesus ! have pity upon poor baby, and take not away her dear mother.'

"Daylight was approaching, and the dear patient had now to be removed,—ah! never to return. The couch we had prepared was brought—a mattress laid upon a net made of cords, suspended between two bamboos. I carried the dear one in my arms, and laid her there. The bearers silently moved along through the dispelling darkness. She felt revived, but the fever continued. We reached the church, and found a company who had been waiting there from early morning, to carry her to Salisbury. They had spent the precious moments, amidst the thick darkness, in earnest prayer on behalf of their dying friend. Salisbury was reached at last. Mrs. Jameson felt refreshed and revived ; but this was of short duration. Fever returned with redoubled fury ; she sunk ; her spirit fled.

"This stroke, O Lord! is thine. All thy ways are faithfulness, and truth, and sure mercy. 'Massa,' said the people, 'keep good heart. It cannot be helped. We sorry for you. We never forget to pray for you. If you lose heart, what will become of us ? If the Bible do not give you good consolation, what can we expect ? You have often told us what blessed support the gospel gives to God's people in affliction. We now look for it in you.' 'Massa,' said an elderly woman, one of my people, and a good woman, 'I come to live with you, to serve you, and I can never leave you again.' From that day she became my servant ; and I find in her one who is faithful, and most anxious to please."

"One day at worship, we were singing the 30th Paraphrase. Jane, the servant now referred to, wept much, and, at the close, Miss Taylor came and said, 'Minister, there is something the matter with Jane. She seems very dull, and cries much.' I went and asked her, 'What is the matter with you, Jane ?' No answer. I asked her a second time. No answer. I said, 'Jane, are any of the children annoying you ?' 'No, Massa.' 'Anything pain you ?' 'Well, minister, I must just tell you. My heart is sore. I desire to know God ; but I am sorry I cannot know him. If I could know him, I would be happy.' I hope she is a child of divine mercy. She has made considerable progress in knowledge, since she came into the family ; and often at worship she is weeping. I may truly say she has left all for my sake. She has a little property of her own, and a house which she built upon it. This she has committed to the care of a cousin, that she may be with me."

Mr. Moir, who was a member of the happy little circle, thus refers to the death of Mrs. Jameson :—

" Her life was one of great activity. She seemed to be filled with the spirit of these words : ' Whatsoever thy hand findeth to do, do it with thy might,' etc. One evening about a week after she became sick, she conversed long with her husband, told him that she was dying, and gave him her last wishes. Her calmness and composure of mind surprised and delighted him ; and that night has been often remembered. One Sabbath, Mr. Jameson remained at home with her, and I supplied his place in the church. After the public services, there was a meeting for prayer on our friend's behalf. Those who led in prayer, poured out their souls in the language of the most experienced Christians. ' Though thou shouldst bray thy servant's wife in a mortar, heal her, and save her soul.' ' Flog the patient, but save her soul.' ' Bless thy hand-maid. Thou loan her to our minister. Heal her, Jesus, my best doctor ! and let not our minister hide face too much, and lose heart.' ' Anoint her from the very crown of the head, to the very sole of the foot.' ' Spare her for the little baby's sake.' On going home, I told her all that had passed. A holy calm came over her mind, a heavenly smile sat upon her countenance, and her words were, ' That is fine ; oh, that is sweet.'

" The deepest anxiety was shown by Mr. Jameson during the whole period of his wife's illness. He seldom left her. He often wandered between hope and fear. He often committed her to God : ' She is the Lord's, let him do with her as He pleases.' When she was about to leave him, he put her into the Lord's arms ; and when her spirit fled, he embraced the cold clay, pressed her chill lips with his, and heaved a deep sigh. Then turning to those around, he said, ' You know what to do with her. I know not. I leave her to you.' He retired to a room by himself, and, in a little, he came out, called together all who were about the house, and, in a most impressive manner, addressed them one by one."[1]

[1] How touching is the following incident! When Mr. Jameson had committed the remains of his beloved wife to the dust, and again reached his now empty home, he opened her private drawer, and saw lying before him the following stanzas, which, it is supposed, were written by Mrs. Jameson, in anticipation of her early death. There is a deep and tender pathos in the simple, though imperfect lines, in which she tries to comfort him, by leading his mind to the bright scenes into which the blow that saddened him had ushered her. It is not certain whether they are original or copied.

> " When I am dead, and silent lying,
>   Should you, in your hour of awe,
>   Gaze upon me, softly sighing,
>   Back the solemn curtain draw ;
>   But the frame of clay you'll see,
>   Oh, beloved, will not be me ;
>   I shall be with Christ, my treasure,
>   Drinking in eternal pleasure.
>
> " When I'm in the coffin shrouded,
>   Mantled in a winding-sheet,
>   All the springs of life beclouded,
>   In that peaceable retreat :
>   Stay the tear, to weep forbear,—
>   I, my friend, shall not be there ;
>   I shall be where Sharon's Rose,
>   Chief in beauty, fragrant blows.
>
> " When you see my eye fast closed,
>   And regret its quenched beam,—
>   Every fringy lash reposed
>   Where oft flowed the copious stream ;
>   Let no tear-drop fall from thine ;
>   Dear one ! it will not be mine,
>   Mine on Jesus will be dwelling,
>   All the sons of light excelling.
>
> " When my feet, devoid of motion,
>   Side by side inactive lie,
>   Should you think, with fond emotion,
>   ' Never more with me they'll stray.'
>   They will not be mine, beloved :
>   Mine, by love's impatience moved,
>   Will o'er heaven's bright pavement glide,
>   Till they reach Immanuel's side.
>
> " Should your mournful eye-beam linger,
>   Should your palm the surface press
>   Of my icy, marble finger,
>   Shrinking from its nothingness.

The following was written to Mrs. Mackersy (July 22d, 1839), a week after Mrs. Jameson's death, while the mourner's wound was still bleeding, although. the balm of heaven's consolation was soothing its anguish, and the fruits of righteousness were being rapidly matured in his smitten soul. This severe affliction was indeed the means of at once fitting the Lord's servant for a higher kind of service below, and of carrying him on a long stage in his preparation for his own too early removal. Never did the remembrance of his partner lose in vividness ; and Nicolis in heaven was always an attraction towards that everlasting home of believers :—

"My beloved Mother,—My last letter reached you, I hope, by last packet. I hasten to follow it up, by telling you much that is consoling to my sorrow-stricken heart, in hope that it will be no less soothing to yours. I watched my beloved Nicolis, from the first moment of her sickness, till she left me behind in this vale of tears. And, oh, my dear mother, if my mind is entirely satisfied about anything, it is that all is well with her, that she now is where she often expressed an earnest longing to be, and from which she desires not to return.

> Dearest friend, 'twill not be mine,
> Motionless in palm of thine,—
> Mine will then be sweetly playing,
> O'er a harp angelic straying.
>
> "When you mark my head reposing,
> Heedless, thoughtless, tearless still,
> Death's dark victory disclosing
> O'er the memory, heart and will ;
> As you trace care's furrowed line,
> Cross the brow, 'twill not be mine,—
> Mine will lean on Jesus' breast,
> Pillowed on eternal rest.
>
> "When the humid grave's receiving
> That cold casket, where to dwell,
> Oft my spirit, sadly grieving,
> Found it but a prison cell :
> I, my love, shall not be there,
> Clear escaped for ever, where
> I shall be with Christ, my Lover,
> Lord, Jehovah, Bridegroom, Brother."

Heaven was often the subject of her conversation, long before her illness. When we sat together, happy in each other's company, Nicolis would throw upon me that look which never failed to fill my eye and melt my heart—her dying look too, the last ere her sweet eye closed for ever—and as she looked, she used to say, ' How sweet and refreshing will heaven be ! No toil, no annoyance, no sorrow there ! Death is terrible, but it will soon be over ; and heaven will far more than make up for all crosses and for all losses.' Before retiring to rest, I frequently prayed with her ; she always put her hand in mine, and as we prayed she wept. Oh, these were very sweet and solemn moments. If ever I found my soul enlarged, and my bands untied, it was at these times, when we gave ourselves anew to God, and committed our babe into his hands, and when our spirits glanced across the ocean, and we laid at the foot of the throne our dear mother, our brothers and sisters, aunts, and aged grandfather, and all friends. Our union has been of short duration, but it has been exactly what our sovereign God appointed. And although short, yet it has been so full of sweetness and true happiness in the midst of much that was rugged and trying in our lot, that I feel the Lord has given me, in a narrow compass, what he has spread over the long lifetime of many others, yea, what many more are never able to attain. I blessed God, and will ever bless Him, for the precious gift which He gave me in Nicolis ; and it would be ill on my part were I not also to bless Him, when in infinite wisdom He has seen it right to take her away. The stroke is heavy, heavy. I feel solitary and sad. My heart is smitten and withered. But I would be dumb, because the Lord hath done this. The departure of my beloved Nicolis has made a blank in my heart and home, which nothing but God himself can fill up. He can do it ; and I trust He is doing it. I think I can say that His presence is sustaining and comforting my soul ; that He has brought me into the wilderness, but it is to show me more of his loving-kindness. Her seat is empty. With her looks, her words, and her watchful and tender care, I am no more blessed ; but when I think of her gain, how unspeakable ! of her escape from sin and suffering, and sorrow, and toil, of the fulness of joy that now fills her soul, of the exceeding and eternal weight of glory with which she is now arrayed and crowned, oh, it would be wrong in me to give way to that selfishness which would begrudge my love the full enjoyment of these glories, even for a moment, for the sake of the good which her presence on earth secured to myself. Oh no, my beloved Nicolis, you were happy on earth, but you are infinitely happier in heaven ! When present with me, you were absent from the Lord. Now, is your joy complete. In a little, I will follow you, sing with you, rejoice with you, and in company with you adore the Lamb for ever. Then, this sadness of heart shall have passed away, and these tears of bitterness been dried up, and death itself swallowed up in victory."

In the mission service of the Church there are ever occurring instances of disinterested Christian kindness. Does the mother die, leaving an infant in tender years ? Another sister never fails to take the motherless one into her bosom, and care for it as tenderly as if it were her own. Fellowship in Christ's service blends the mothers' hearts into one ; and nowhere may a dying mother be more certain of a warm nestling place for the object of her anxieties, than among a missionary sisterhood. Mrs. Jameson's daughter was only eight months old at her mother's death. But Mrs. Cowan sent for her sister's child, and tended her with all a mother's care, till Miss Jameson joined her widowed brother, in 1840. "Providence," wrote Mr. Jameson, "has shown much kindness in providing such a retreat for the dear motherless babe."

"To the Rose Street Juvenile Missionary Society.

" July 31st, 1839.

" MY DEAR YOUNG FRIENDS,—I intended writing you a long letter, but at present this is out of my power. I send you what will interest you far more—a sketch of our homely church, taken by Mrs. Jameson, a considerable time ago. Its colours are somewhat faded by having lain a year in this climate ; and Mrs. Jameson, discovering defects in its execution, wished to improve it, but was prevented by the pressure and increase of other engagements. It was intended, my dear young friends, for you ; and I feel bound to embrace this first opportunity of sending it, though I am loathe to part with it.

" As your eyes rest upon this little picture, think of her whose work it is. Think, oh, think, how early in life death laid his hand upon her, and seek, oh, seek yourselves to be ready ! Think of the glory with which she is now crowned, and be ye followers of her who, through faith and patience, now inherits the promises. Know that death waits not when he receives the commission. The king of terrors can neither be bribed nor driven back by violence. It is ours to wait his approach and be ready, and to have Jesus as the anchor of the soul : for ' blessed are the dead who die in the Lord.' Pray for me. I much need your constant and earnest prayers. For the present, farewell."

At length, everything was ready for laying the foundation-stone of the new church. That ceremony was performed by Henry Barkly, Esq., on Saturday, September 28th, 1839. Mr. Jameson writes :—

" We had an interesting day at the laying of the foundation-stone. The school was examined in the forenoon, and gave much satisfaction. Messrs. Barkly, Cowan, Paterson, and others, were present, and a great assemblage of people. I first spoke a few words to the people, and read the paper to be deposited in the stone, containing a short history of the station. Mr. Paterson prayed. After singing the 102d Psalm, verses 13-19, Mr. Barkly laid the stone. Mr. Cowan then prayed. Afterwards, Messrs. Barkly, Cowan, Paterson and Jeffrey addressed the people. The collection amounted to £48. Our people are increasing their subscriptions, and doing what they can in labour, with much cheerfulness. As yet, little more has been done than digging the foundation and laying the corner-stone. The plan proposed is somewhat as follows :—A building, 75 feet by 50 ; 12 feet being taken off the length for a vestry ; walls 20 feet high, to allow a gallery, if necessary.

The roof is to consist of three small roofs.   Mr. Moir is busy as usual.   The school is still numerous.   The children are getting a box ready with coffee, pimento, cocoa-nuts, etc., to send home."

Including the monthly contributions of the people, the sum of £600 was contributed in Jamaica the first year, and the rest Mr. Jameson hoped to raise by loan or donation from friends of the work in Scotland.

In 1839, several new openings had occurred, which Mr. Jameson and his valuable coadjutor, Mr. Moir, sought to improve to the utmost of their strength.   The school at Pembroke Hall was given up, as the children in that quarter could reach the school at the church, and as other more necessitous places seemed to claim attention.   Early in the year, Mr. Moir undertook to hold a prayer-meeting with the Scotch immigrants at Middlesex, every Thursday evening, to keep school, on Fridays and Saturdays, and, alternately with Mr. Jameson, to preach to them, every third Sabbath.   The people fitted up a house for Mr. Moir, and soon expressed a strong desire to have him stationed in their midst, promising to contribute as liberally to his support as their means allowed.   But it was resolved that, in the meantime, no change should take place.

" Education is now the order of the day among young and old.   From time to time, applications are made to us to extend our labours.   There is a fine field here, not only for negro schools, but also for boarding-schools to train the better class of browns and whites, especially the former—a class as degraded as, and more neglected than, the blacks.   For this purpose, a large and excellent house, healthily and beautifully situated, is offered to me.   The proprietor desires a well-qualified teacher from home.   In the meantime, I purpose going there, three days every week, to commence a negro school.   I have been induced to do so, because of the solicitations of the people, because it enables me to do something for a distant portion of the congregation, and because of the advantageous situation. I will begin operations in the hope of breaking up a field for some friend and fellow-labourer from home."

The place referred to in the above extract was Bonham Spring, a pimento estate, in the parish of St. Ann's, six miles from Goshen. Mr. Jameson thought that it would suit for the Missionary Academy, on which the Jamaica Presbytery had set their hearts ; and he brought the matter before the Synod's Committee for Foreign Missions, by whom Mr. Millar was sent to Bonham Spring, in 1841. He continued there till the Academy was removed to Montego Bay.

The following letter we are unwilling to abridge. It is exceedingly touching, and one cannot read it without profiting. Mr. Jameson had been from home, and on his return, his wounds bled afresh from a sense of his loss, and he immediately sat down to write.

"*November 1st*, 1839.—The third year of our connexion is about to expire. During this period, we have seen much of mercy and judgment. The Lord has wrought for us, and with us, and by us, both at home and abroad. He has severely chastened more than one of our number, not, however, too severely, or more severely than was necessary. No ! a living man ought not to complain. To be out of hell is a greater mercy than we deserve ; and to be crowned with loving-kindness and tender mercy, oh, joy unspeakable !

" In wandering over the past, the mind rests upon the happy and hallowed scenes we enjoyed, three Septembers agone. Ah me ! Some were there who are no more, whom the grave hides from our weeping eyes. What can we say ? Oh what ! but that the whole paths of the Lord are mercy and truth, that it is well with our dear departed friends, that such dispensations are for the good of God's people, that both in measure and kind, they are exactly answerable to the case in hand, that our beloved dead we shall see again in a better state, and that with them we shall enjoy holier and sweeter fellowship than ever. But they are away ! Our earthly intercourse with them has ceased ; their seat is empty ; we cannot pray for them ; we look for them, but cannot find them ; we talk to them, but receive no answer ; the vision is the object of our tenderest regards ; the waking thought is, ' all is well,' but still we must go to the grave to weep. How easily are our fondest hopes prostrated! How do men of the world befool themselves, when to gain the world they lose their souls! How do Christians miscalculate, when worldly interests and inclinations are allowed to interfere with the commands of the Saviour! Soon may these interests be overturned, and the disciple be obliged to confess, that, after all, it is the highest interest, as well as the first duty, to comply with the requirements of the blessed Lord. Had my beloved wife and myself been moved by the tears of friends, and had we been induced by their entreaties and arguments to abandon the great work to which we are called, oh, how many sparkling gems would her crown have wanted, and how foolish would I now look! I would have been a spectacle to men and angels—a convert to obedience, as the pettish school-boy submits to the laws of school, after having been soundly whipped. How blessed is it to be at our post, to suffer while doing our duty! When we look for comfort, then we find it. 'O Lord, this word of thine is my comfort in mine affliction, by it, in straits, I am revived.'

"I must now proceed to business matters.

"First, let me acknowledge with deep gratitude your letters and those of private friends; also those brought by Mr. J., and one from your secretary, which I found waiting me this afternoon. I thank you for your sympathy. I reached my home this afternoon, none to welcome me, none to embrace me; all was silence, the door was shut. I ventured in, and as I wandered from room to room, your letter caught my eye. I grasped it, opened it, and as I read it, my bursting heart got utterance and found relief. I thank you, and along with you the Session and managers, for the respect you showed my beloved wife in putting on the garb of mourning. I thank you for your interest in me and my. child. My warmest thanks to the ladies of the congregation for their letters and gifts to Mrs. Jameson in the box; also to the young people of the congregation, and to the Juvenile Missionary Society, for their gifts, and for the means of instruction which the school enjoys through their liberality.   Thank every friend who thinks of us, feels for us, prays for us, and who contributes in any way to the cause of the Redeemer among us.   May the Lord reward you all a thousand-fold !"

In 1847, referring to this season of sorrow, Mr. Jameson wrote :—" The resignation to His holy will which my blessed Master enabled me to show, when He, so unexpectedly, took to himself my beloved wife, and my continuance at the work to which He called me, I have reason to believe, from the testimony of many of the people, did more to recommend the gospel of Jesus to their opening minds, than any twenty sermons which I ever preached."

CHAPTER VI.

Incidents—The heavy tongue, but feeling heart—Scenes in the Session—Faithful discipline—Oppression and its results—The negro not a fool—Church building begun—Mr. Moir leaves—Mr. Jameson chosen Theological Tutor—Rejects polluted gifts—Arrival of Miss Jameson—Building struggles—Negro's account of the Fall of Adam—The Lord's Supper at Goshen—Letters of black people.

As work multiplied on his hands, and anxieties grew, Mr. Jameson was unable to keep a record of daily events. But, at the end of 1839, he threw together a number of statements and incidents, from which we make the following selections, without regard to the order of time. In speaking of his own want of memory for incident, he mentions a negro belonging to Eltham, one of the estates which he used to visit, who could tell the year, the month, the day, the hour, at which any particular circumstance connected with his own or his master's family occurred, during fifty years. He could also tell the weight of a bag of pimento or coffee, or anything which he could lift, with almost perfect accuracy.

The incidents and statements referred to are of two kinds : 1*st*, illustrative of the work of God in the souls of the people ; and 2*d*, referring to the state of matters on the estates, after freedom. Both classes are interesting, and may be regarded as specimens of what the experience of every missionary at that time could furnish in abundance.

"An overlooker of a gang on one of the estates was called by the overseer to identify a cloak which was found lying in the field, with some pieces of sugar-cane in its folds. He could not tell whose it was ; but, on taking it home, he discovered that it belonged to his own daughter. Next day, he brought her before the overseer, confessed with shame and tears that she was the culprit, and desired the overseer to put a particular brand upon her. The overseer said he would keep two days' pay from her, by way of fine ; but this would not satisfy her father. She had put him and his family to shame. They had now 'joined religion,' and were, every Sabbath, hearing of the evil of sin, and if his daughter acted thus, what could be expected of others ? What would the church think of him and his family, if this were allowed to pass unnoticed and unpunished ?

This was a kind of Roman virtue in a black man : for, in general, black people are very unwilling to reveal each other's faults. It would have been like the ordinary practice, if the overlooker had done his best to screen his daughter.

Mr. Jameson relates a praiseworthy instance of respect for the Sabbath-day :—

" One of our people was ordered to take a mule, and go to a distant part of the country. He was to start on Saturday, and would require to travel on the Sabbath. ' Busha,' said he, ' why do you always send me on Saturday, and make me travel on Sabbath ? If you send me out on Monday, I will go, but not on Saturday. Besides, I want to help in digging the foundation of our church, and if I am not there on Saturday, the minister, and the brothers and sisters will think that I don't care about the church.' Busha was angry, but the man held to his point. This man is very obedient and serviceable,—so much so that his kindness of heart exposes him to numerous applications of this sort.

" In conversing with my people, previous to the Lord's Supper, I have been pleased with the progress of many who had been admitted. After the last communion, I told the members that I would examine all, before another sacrament ; and, if I found any not making progress in knowledge and holiness, I would consider it my duty to keep them back. Some have grown much in knowledge, and others, of whom this could not be expected, appear to be growing in tenderness of heart, and in devotional feeling.

" I was examining an old African woman on experimental

religion.   Among other questions, I asked, ' Do you understand the gospel which I preach ?'   The poor Ethiopian, much moved by the question, said, ' Oh, me minister, me head tick, me tongue heavy, but,' pressing her hand upon her bosom, ' me heart feel.   Me poor Guinea woman, minister ; me no able for speak good ; but what you say come in here,' pointing to her ear, ' and strike me there,' pointing to her heart.   ' Understand you, minister !   How could all this change take place upon we hearts, and conduct, and families, if we not understand you ?'

" ' Well, what do you think of Christ ?'

" ' Oh, Massa, me love Jesus.   He died for me.   Me have nothing to think about but Jesus.   Me give myself for ever to Jesus.'

" It is delightful to see the progress of the gospel, not only in purifying the immoral atmosphere, but in bringing the ties of earthly brotherhood under subjection.   A member of the church brought his sister before the Session, for visiting suspicious houses, and for light and giddy conduct.   The Session advised him to take her to his own house, and look after her, which he has done.   One father complained that his daughter did not read to him so often as he liked, and that when asked to do it, she often took the book, in bad humour.   When the Session spoke to her, she wept, and promised amendment.

" Another brought his son, and said that the youth's folly was breaking his and the mother's heart.   He had been away for weeks, and they did not know where he was till last night, when his brother found him and brought him back, covered with rags and dirt.   The father could say little for weeping. The brother, who is a very excellent young man, after describing the humbling condition in which he found him, concluded with an appeal somewhat as follows :—' Oh, my brother ! you break your father's and your mother's heart.   You fill your whole family with shame.   You are destroying yourself.   You are putting to shame the whole church.   Listen to the Session.' He could not proceed any farther, but sat down and wept ; and it was some time before any of us could break the solemn silence, for we were overpowered.

" Thought I, these were the men who were kept in a degrading bondage by their mercenary task-masters, whose avarice and selfishness led them to hazard the assertion that, in mind and in heart, they are scarcely a degree above the brutes ! Let the barbarian of another hue look here. Let him learn what he has lost since he left his country, if, even there, he possessed aught of the high attainment of knowing what it is to feel, and what it is to love.

" Sometimes, strange scenes take place in the Session, which illustrate the character of the negro.

" A member was brought before us for rum-drinking, rude conduct, and improper language. He could not deny the charge. The elders, one by one, spoke to him in a most solemn manner. The man stood sullen and unmoved. I asked them what we should do with him ? They all agreed that as he had forfeited the confidence which the church reposed in her people, and had put her to shame, he should be cut off the list, and that this should be announced, on the following Sabbath. As I lifted the pen to erase the name, the man's patience gave way; he snatched up his hat and stick, and, quick as lightning, bolted out of the church, raging and roaring as if he had lost his senses.

" Next day, he came to the Pen, three miles, through a heavy rain, and said he could get no peace, but must come and confess himself to minister, and ask pardon. I told him it was not my pardon he had to ask, but God's, for he had sinned much against Him. He begged to be taken back again. I told him I could not take him back, for a long time, before I had proof that he had repented, and was living a new life. I prayed with him, and he went away.

" Francis Burton, a member of the Session, was called before his brethren, for quarrelling with his daughter-in-law. The girl was newly married to Burton's son ; and, like too many of the young negro women, was proud and full of tongue. She was evidently in fault, and had been abusing her father-in-law. The Session, however, thought he lacked patience, and lectured him on the duty of forbearance. They exceeded due bounds, and gave the old man more than he deserved.   The last elder arose to speak, but Burton could stand it no longer. He rose and ran.   An unmarried son, who was sitting beside him, followed and threw himself upon his father's neck, and wept, entreating him to return.   But feeling had mastered the old man, and he went away.   The son returned bathed in tears, and described how his father had been treated by this girl.   On being spoken to, she showed how proud was her heart, and unbearable her tongue.   These scenes arise from the irascibility of the people, and from the horror and disgrace which they feel at being called before the Session.   However painful, at the time, these things may be, they have always been followed with salutary effects."

As illustrative of the social state of the people, Mr. Jameson refers to the numerous family quarrels which had occurred in his congregation during the year.   The husband enforced submission on his wife, with his fists or his cane.   The wife used her tongue too hotly, and, in the height of passion, would take off the ring, trample it under foot, and throw it in the face of her angry lord.   The black man, patient in many respects, is not so with his brother, and least of all with his wife.

Rum, too, was producing incalculable mischief.   The opportunities of obtaining rum had been greatly multiplied, and many were plunging headlong into the vortex of intemperance. This led Mr. Jameson to counsel temperance or total abstinence. One after another came forward, resolving that, in the strength of " Massa Jesus," they would take no wine or spirits.   Some joined the total abstinence society ; others, afraid of attempting too much at once, joined the temperance movement.   These, feeling their own weakness, expressed their reliance on Jesus Christ for the help they needed, fearless of the taunts and jeers of the wicked.   The excuses of others for not giving up liquor were amusing.   One man did not know how he could take a dose of castor oil without a little rum.   With another, tea did not agree, and rum and water found the best substitute.   Another could not get wine, willing as he was to join the temperance.

" ' But,' said Mr. Jameson, ' do as I and others have done, give up wine too.'

" ' Oh, Massa, you want to kill we, to put we in we graves altogether.'

" ' Well, Jamie, you look very poorly ; have you been sick ?'

" ' I was in town, Massa, and bad water gave me sore belly.'

" ' Astonishing, Jamie, the town water never gave me sore belly. Now, tell me how much rum you drunk in town.'

" ' Not much, minister ; just a little among the bad water.'

" ' Now, Jamie, I know very well you were drunk every night. It is the filthy rum you swallowed, and not the bad water, that makes you look as if you had risen out of your grave. Give it up, Jamie, and that will save, not kill you.' "

The testimony of an eye-witness like Mr. Jameson, so conscientious and impartial, respecting the working out of the emancipation, must be regarded as peculiarly valuable, because it is correct and trustworthy. Those who had charge of Goshen estate seem to have acted in a violent manner to the people. The result was disastrous to the property. So completely were the people scattered, that the site of the negro village which, when Mr. Jameson went there, had a population of not less than 500, is now a solitary common.

The following cases are painful illustrations of reckless and unrighteous treatment inflicted by arbitrary power on parties who had not the means of resistance or of redress :—

" One of our people on Goshen estate, a very excellent man, and who has been steadfast in his profession, was admitted to the Lord's table at the first communion, which took place in the spring of 1839. On the Monday following, the overseer, on learning the circumstance, came to the field, and abused him in the vilest manner, opened and discharged the enmity of his heart by cursing and swearing, and calling him hypocrite, liar, scoundrel, etc. The follower of Jesus answered meekly : ' Busha, me wish to serve Christ ; me wish to do something good for myself now.' In talking to him about the matter, I said : ' Murray, you must lay your account with reproach for Christ, but be you steadfast.' ' Oh, yes, Massa, me know that ; me don't mind suffering for Jesus, for he suffered so much for me.'

" In a few weeks afterwards, he was turned out upon the world with his wife and children, homeless and destitute ; his provision grounds were spoiled, and the produce of them sold for the benefit of the estate, or eaten by its servants. On asking the reason, I was told that Murray was cunning, lazy, etc. I never could learn the particulars of his transgression. None of those who lived near him and worked under him, could lay anything to his charge ; and the general conclusion was, that he was too often with minister, and, for this fault, was turned adrift, and that he had once applied to the magistrate for protection against a wanton act of aggression on the part of one of the estate's managers, which step gave great offence. I cannot say how Murray acted in the field, but, as a professing Christian, he has been most exemplary all along ; and with tears and with much depression of spirits he used to tell me of the rudeness and unfaithfulness of those around him. He found an asylum on Salisbury. He and his family lived there during the summer of 1839.

" Robert Laing was the driver of the second gang. He became sick. The doctor saw him and prescribed for him. As medicines were furnished by the estate, he sent for the dose, and got it. Becoming worse, he sent again, when instead of the medicine, a rent account was sent him, amounting to six dollars, or 24s., for two weeks. I happened to call on him, that morning, and he showed me the paper. He wept, and said, ' Massa, I am not able to pay that rent. I am sick, and cannot work. And even were I well, how could I pay such a rent, when my wages are only 5s. a week ?' I remonstrated with the overseer ; and nothing for the present was done. A few weeks afterwards, as I was returning home, in the evening, a person called me. ' What is the matter ?' I asked. ' Robert Laing wants to see you.' On going to his house, I found it locked. When Robert came, he said, ' Oh, Massa, my house is taken from me, and my furniture is thrown out upon the road ; and my wife and I know not where to go, or what to do.' 'Who did so ?' 'Busha.' I turned my horse to go down to the house. The people said, 'You need not go, for he has left home.' Next morning, I went to the attorney, who lived fourteen miles distant, and got the sentence of ejectment recalled, and the house re-opened.

" Some weeks afterwards, I received a letter from the overseer, desiring me to interfere no more, but allow him to discharge what he considered his duty. I waited to see what this would be. A warrant of ejectment goes forth against Laing. The court[1] decides that the sentence shall be carried into effect on Monday, giving Laing Friday, Saturday, and Sabbath to prepare for the event. Against this decision, Henry Walsh, Esq., the stipendiary magistrate, protested in the most solemn manner, but a majority of the magistrates ruled against him. Laing came to tell me the decision of the court. He said : 'I will do what I can, on Friday and Saturday, but, on Sabbath, I will come to the church, and get some comfort there. I leave all with God.' On Monday, they were ejected ; their house was demolished ; their provision grounds spoiled ; and the defenceless family thrown on the world as vagabonds, to seek a home where they could best find it, and that among a number of estates whose managers have agreed not to employ a labourer from another estate, without a certificate from the overseer.

" Laing and his wife were sheltered by a neighbour. He was warned that if he persisted in affording them shelter, he would be ejected also. Grant, however, continued to admit them under his roof, although they dared not go there, except during the darkness of the night, when they would creep into the dwelling of their friend, to partake of that cheer and rest which it afforded. Before the morning star had ceased to shine, these children of hardship and sorrow had to rise and seek concealment. They had to separate, and sometimes did not see one another for several days together.

" The reasons assigned for this mode of treatment are such

---

[1] A court of local magistrates, consisting of planters or attorneys, or even overseers, who receive commission from the Governor of the Island.

as these :—" It is necessary to show the people what the law can do. Mild measures will spoil the labourers. Stringent measures are safest for the people and the country, and the only means of carrying on successfully the cultivation of the estates."

Mr. Jameson wrote to the attorney, on February 20th, 1839, protesting against the treatment which Laing had received.

" Ejectments, as I have now seen them, are a retribution fitted only for the worst of characters. Permit me, in the most earnest manner, to solicit your interference to put an end to such proceedings without delay.

" Ejectments are producing feelings in the minds of the people which will ultimately endanger the prosperity of the estate, which are unfavourable to yourself, and which, although pent up through terror, are yet ready to burst forth with terrible violence the moment that the proprietor (H. Barkly, Esq.), daily expected, sets his foot on Goshen.

" Again, I am disposed to say on behalf of Goshen, that the conduct of the people, since the 1st of August, has not merited such retribution.   They were among the very first, not only in the district, but in the country, to resume their labour, after the commencement of freedom, and from that time to the present moment, they have been among the few who keep the lead.   It is true that some things have not been as we could have wished. Those who were born, and have grown up as slaves, cannot, in a day, become true freemen.   At present, therefore, instead of alarming the people, and turning their joy into bitterness, it is our duty, for a season, to bear with the follies of what may be called the childhood of freedom ; and, with a discipline which the circumstances of the case, and which mercy require, to study to dispel everything utopian in the views of the people, and lead them to see more clearly what is their duty to God and to man. This object I keep steadily in view in all my labours ; and I feel that this severe system is taking my people from me, is raising their fears, disappointing their hopes, unmanning their energies, and setting them adrift upon the world, before that experiment be fairly tried, which, by the blessing of God, will in the end prove fully successful. These considerations I urge upon you from an unfeigned heart, from a desire to be faithful to God, and to a people who have placed themselves under my guidance, and from best wishes for yourself."

" Ejectments went on. In July, I received a letter from the attorney, praying me to interfere to stop the people from leaving the property, as forty were on the eve of moving, besides many who had gone, and many more who were preparing to go on the first opportunity. Only one or two belonging to the estate were in the field ; the whole work of cultivation was in the hands of strangers, and carried on at great expense."

Thus did Mr. Jameson endeavour to pursue an even course between the masters on the one hand, and the people on the other. He did not approve of rabid attacks on the former, but much regretted when they were made. He did not consider it to be his duty to discuss politics in public meetings with his people, but he endeavoured to correct what he saw to be wrong in their conduct. If the employers refused to listen to his expostulations on behalf of the oppressed, he knew that there was a self-rectifying principle in freedom that would soon write folly in their mad measures, and that in the most effectual manner. And so it came about in the case of Goshen. Mr. Barkly arrived in time to save his valuable property from the fate of a ruinate. The master came and reckoned with his servants. He delayed long enough to give the harsh mode a fair trial, long enough to show that a free population cannot be coerced by those to whom their hands are necessary. At his coming, the people flocked to state their grievances. Mr. Barkly declared he had never seen such an ebullition of pent-up feeling ; and he set himself to undo the mischief and injustice of the past. Amusing as well as exciting was the scene that was witnessed on that occasion, as it is narrated by individuals who were present. One old negro came up, and stared with mock surprise at Mr. Barkly's boots. He examined with feigned astonishment the trousers and coat which he wore. " High ! Massa Barkly have boot ! Massa wear good coat and trouser ! High

Massa G— tell we say, Massa Barkly no look boot, no have so so coat, s'pose it no be him give him."

All concerned in these measures were removed ; all the ejected were recalled, their houses were restored, and their wages increased, while a more equitable arrangement as to rent was proposed. The strangers working on the estate were paid off. Murray was reinstated in his former office, and a new house was erected for Laing and his family. "The work of the estate," wrote Mr. Jameson, "is now wholly carried on by the estate's people, they are cultivating their grounds with diligence, although they complain of scarcity, caused by the sad scenes of fast summer ; Goshen is now covered with rich cane fields ; the plough is daily at work ; sugar is being made; Goshen has thus surmounted past evils, and once more is happy and prosperous. All this proves that the perversity which has been so generally and loudly complained of, arises in part, and perhaps in good part, from the mistreatment, as well as from the disposition, of the people. Treat the black man with equity, and he will generally be found to make a grateful return, yea, he will be disposed to pass over those minute details which, were he scrupulous, he might urge in his own favour."

The following conversation between Mr. Jameson and a carpenter, who had been ejected from Goshen, and recalled by Mr. Barkly, is well told, and is exactly what one still carries on with the more intelligent of our West Indian peasantry. We may give it as a specimen of minister and man, and also of the position in which the freed people found themselves, in many cases after emancipation. It must be borne in mind, however, by those who would have correct views of the question between masters and people, in those days, that what was true of some was not so of all. A vast deal of mischief to the cause of freedom in Britain and America has arisen from not attending to this fact. Each estate has its own history. And, probably, there was a great variety in the mode of treating the people, in different parts of the island, or at least on different properties. In some places in the leeward parishes, at least, the work-people on the estates continue to occupy the same negro villages which they occupied in the time of slavery. There were no ejectments. There were equity and forbearance towards the people, and there was therefore no interruption to the working of the estates. Yet Goshen is a sample of a class of cases, which was too numerous, and which must be considered as sufficient to account for much that is to be deplored in the history of emancipation, but which many have most unrighteously, either from ignorance or malice, laid to the charge of the freedmen. Surely every impartial judge will agree with us, that such treatment as that which was experienced on this, one of the finest and most productive' properties in Jamaica, was simply suicidal, and did not deserve to succeed. But while the people on other properties may have been treated as foolishly and unrighteously as those on Goshen, there was no Mr. Barkly to correct the mischief by a timely remedy ; and thus the people were permanently alienated and scattered, and the properties became what in Jamaica is called a ruinate, where fields once fertile are covered with useless bush, and expensive buildings are in the last stage of dilapidation and decay. And some of these properties, in the palmy days of Jamaica, afforded revenues on which proprietors lived amid the refinements and luxuries of British society.

We venture one other remark here before we copy the conversation between Minister and Nelson,—it is due to the slandered peasantry of the West Indies, and it is, that for the unjust and ruinous treatment of the people the proprietors were not altogether, and, in many cases, not at all to blame. We would not that our remarks were supposed to criminate, in the very smallest degree, the proprietors of the Trinity estates, who were upright and honourable men. Living at home, they did not know what was being done by their managers, who would have acted very differently had the properties been their own. The interests of both proprietors and people were thus wantonly sacrificed in many cases by coarse, immoral, wrathful men, who were utterly unfit to manage such gangs of people. While slavery lasted, and the horse-whip could be used at pleasure, the sugar was duly made, and the rum duly distilled ; but when arbitrary power was taken away, these men lacked the moral and intellectual fitness for their altered circumstances; and, worst of all, they lacked that self-control without which no man can rule his fellow-creatures. The history of Jamaica and of "Freedom" has yet to be written. Pity will it be if that noble passage in British colonial history shall fail to find a worthy writer—a man with the qualities of head and heart which it demands and deserves—with powers of research, and sympathy, and eloquence worthy of the theme—one with leisure to perambulate the mountains and valleys of the sunny isle, and hear with his own ears what is said by the now lessening generation on whom slavery vented his last expiring rage, and to search out the records and correspondence of the time.

To this day, the people of St. Mary's speak of Kelly, the overseer referred to above, as a man who was fit for any deed of violence or cruelty. They say that when he had charge of another property, before he came to Goshen, he used to grind people on the grindstone. From his wanting a finger, they, to the day of his death, used to call him "tumpy-finger Kelly." He became a proprietor, and died a few years ago. The people say that his death-bed was horror; and that in his delirium he called for the Goshen people to come and get the money of which he had defrauded them. We do not vouch for the truth of these stories; but there were worse things done in Jamaica than Kelly was charged with—done, too, by men who had been born in Christian Britain.

Let us now hear the conversation between Minister and Nelson :—

"*M.* 'Well, Nelson, how d'ye?'

N. 'So, so, Massa.'

M. 'What are you doing now?'

N. 'I am carpenter on Goshen again.'

M. 'You were ejected, were you not?'

N. 'Oh, yes, my good minister, everything taken from me; put out of a house which I built myself; cut the timbers with my own hands, on my Sabbaths, when a slave; brought them

from the wood on my own head ; and paid *fippence* (3d sterling) for every bundle of thatch that I put on it.'

M. 'Did your grounds suffer ?'

N. 'Grounds suffer, Massa ! !   Ay, Massa, my grounds were
destroyed.   There were plenty of provisions in them—good
provisions, Massa—and Busha not only took them from me,
but gave them to the hogs, ate them himself, and sold them.
But my Master in heaven is good, Massa.   Jesus better to we
than we deserve.   He turn things for the better.   Massa
Barkly come out and put things to right.'

M. 'Where did you go when you were set off from Goshen ?'

N. 'A man on Guy's Hill had compassion upon me, and
gave me a piece of land to build a house upon, and plant some
provisions.   I built a little hut, and planted a ground and
fenced it, but the gentleman's cattle came and eat all my provisions—every yam and cocoa in my field.'

M. 'What did the gentleman do for this ?'

N. 'When I told him, he was very sorry for it, and came
and saw it, and gave me five shillings.'

M. 'Five shillings ? did he not give you any more ?'

N. 'He said he had no more at present, but would remember
me again.'

M. 'Did you ever get any more ?'

N. 'No. He was kind to me in my distress, and I do not
wish to trouble him.'

M. 'Have you got any provision grounds since your return
to Goshen ?'

N. 'To tell you the truth, my good minister, my labour
has been so often abused, that I have not strength (courage)
to raise any more provisions.'

M. 'How do you get provisions for yourself and family ?'

N. 'I buy them in the market.'

M. 'But you have every confidence now in Goshen.   Mr.
Barkly has done all he can to restore confidence, and to secure
you quiet possession of your houses and grounds.'

N. 'True, Massa.   But Mr. Barkly goes home, and we do
not know what will take place after that.'

M. 'You knew Mr. Grigor of old, when he was book-keeper on Goshen. You all loved him then; and it was the fond recollection which you had of him that induced Mr. Barkly to raise him to the office of attorney.'

N. 'True, my good minister; but men sometimes very good when book-keeper, but very bad, wicked, when big attorney.'

M. 'True; but I know Mr. Grigor a little, and so far as I have been able to discover his principles, there is no fear. I would have none, and I do not think you need have any.'

N. 'But Mr. Grigor may die, and another may come who will pull and mash us?'

M. 'No; Mr. Barkly has taken good care of that; and after what he has done to those who were here before Mr. Grigor, none will ever venture upon such a course again.'

N. 'I do not think it right, Massa, to build a good house for myself, or repair my old one, so as to make it quite comfortable, when I must, at the same time, pay rent for it.'

M. 'Well, but Nelson, Mr. Barkly gives you cattle to bring your timber from the wood; he gives you doors and windows, and he gives you £4 currency (£2, 8s. sterling), to purchase nails, etc.'

N. 'Massa, I am a carpenter; I know my trade, and I can tell you that is nothing at all to the expense of putting up a good house. No, Massa, I do not think it good that when I pay such a big rent for my house, I should spend my time, and labour, and money in building it. Now, my lord—'

M. 'Nelson, don't give me these fine names; I don't want them, and I can't suffer them. Call me minister; but 'lord,' or 'papa,' or such stuff as you give to your leaders, don't give to me. Besides, these names you ought to give to Christ, and him only. He is your Lord, he is your Father, and the man who receives such titles or names from you is proud and presumptuous, and takes what he has no right to.'

N. 'Beg pardon, Massa; beg pardon, minister.'

M. 'I only tell you, that so you may know what is right. Well, what were you going to say?'

N. 'Well, my minister, suppose I desired to leave Goshen, and I went to Massa and said, Massa, Nelson is going away, he is not to work any longer on Goshen. Or, suppose Massa called me and said, Nelson, I have no more work for you; therefore, you can seek work where you can find it. Would it not be a good thing if I had nothing of my own to leave on Goshen, if I could carry with me all that belongs to me?'

M. 'True.'

N. 'Well, minister, you see, if I build the half of this house, giving my time, and labour, and money for it, and Massa never give me anything but poor £4, the loan of his cattle, and a door and a window or two; and, at the same time, make me pay a rent of £6 a year, Massa is never paying me for my work and everything, but I am paying Massa; and when I leave Massa, I leave what I have made with my own hands, and with my own money, and for which I have never got thanks.'

M. 'Well, Nelson, what would you like?'

N. 'I would like if Massa would build us houses, and give us proper grounds about the houses.'

M. 'Would you take one of these houses?'

N. 'Take one, Massa! I glad to take one. I very happy to pay rent for it. Then if Massa and I parted, I would not be the worse of Massa, and Massa would not be the worse of me.'"

Mr. Jameson adds:—"I have given this conversation at length, as it contains the pith of the rent question, which, at present, is the subject of discussion among us. It discovers a shrewdness in the negro which, in a little time, will utterly discomfit all attempts to settle such great questions on any other basis than that of equity. Proprietors may meet the people half-way; and such advances, combined with kindness, the people feel and generally appreciate. But so long as entire equity is wanting, so long as the people are required to spend a considerable portion of their time, and labour, and wages, to erect houses for which they are charged rent fully equal to their value; so long as this rent is levied, not according to the value of the houses and grounds, but according to the will, and as it best suits the convenience of the proprietor and manager, in the way which will raise most money to enable the estate to pay the wages at the least possible cost to itself, the payment of rent will be unsatisfactory to the people. Any peace which now happily prevails, arises out of the contrast with a worse state of things, which has now passed away ; but it is only the healing of the surface of the wound, whilst the root of the disease remains to fester and to break out anew. Another consequence arises out of this state of feeling. The people, whenever they are able, are purchasing patches of ground, of three, or five, or six acres ; so that the population, advancing in the purchase of land at the same ratio, may soon be proprietors of the soil. A father purchases a few acres to settle, as he says, his children when he dies. This practice, rendered desirable and necessary by the base practices of many managers, since the commencement of freedom, is yet of very questionable expediency in advancing the future prosperity of the country. It is for the interest of the proprietor, for the ultimate benefit of the emancipated population, for the prosperity of the country, and for the success of freedom, that a system be adopted without delay, by which the labouring population will be lodged and settled in security and comfort, and with entire equity.

" In the transition from slavery to freedom, the negro had the same right to compensation for the house which he built, as the master for the slave which he bought. The same arguments which hold good in the one case, hold good in the other. This would not only have been a matter of equity, but of expediency. It would have prevented much of that misunderstanding and asperity of feeling which told upon the fields, and now tell upon the pockets of so many. It would have set at rest the question to whom the houses and grounds belonged ; and it would have prevented the belief that the Queen was to make over to the people their houses and grounds—an impression which was everywhere prevalent, and which required to be rectified by a proclamation from the Home Government. It is true that the existence of such a belief among the people was openly denied by a few, and the Government proclamation was pronounced wholly unnecessary. The reason that induced the few individuals referred to to adopt such a course, is best known to themselves. But true it is that what was declared to have no existence, existed in my district, and, so far as I can learn, existed everywhere ; that the Government proclamation, instead of being unnecessary, was the very thing needed ; and that since that proclamation was made, the impression has wholly disappeared. And what I say is, that had the people received compensation for their houses for which they were now to pay rent, the erroneous impression now referred to would not have existed, a Government proclamation would not have been required, the value of the houses would have been distinctly ascertained, and a just rent would have been of easy introduction."

But amid all the excitement of the crisis through which they were passing, Mr. Jameson's ardent piety, as genial and tender as it was manly, seems to have suffered no abatement.

The following, dated January 2d, 1840, to Mr. Bryden, is both touching and beautiful :—

" In your last, of July 3d, you mentioned the loss of two of your children. Oh ! gladly I say and think with you, ' they are not lost.' The thought that our beloved dead were lost, would be altogether insupportable. The knowledge that our sweetest flowers are decayed in the dark and lonely grave, is hard enough to bear ; but, if there were no spring time, no morn on which to meet again, if there were no celestial paradise, where our lovely flowers are now richly blooming, no house from heaven with which their spirits are clothed upon, how, oh, how could we bear up ? Blessed Jesus ! for taking our nature and destroying him who has the power of death ! Blessed Jesus ! for throwing such light upon a world unknown ! May we follow our loved ones in due time ! Happy the meeting ! no parting again !"

Mr. Jameson attended a meeting of Presbytery, in the beginning of 1840. Mr. Cowan and he returned home in company. He talked of Mrs. Jameson's death a great part of the way home.   Mr. Cowan had never seen him so much over-whelmed.   He reached home on Saturday night, and after the Sabbath services, was seized with fever.   Mr. Cowan went to see him, and found him suffering much.   His mind reverted to Mrs. Jameson's death, and he feared that his own end was nigh. His people were all anxiety.   "Mr. Cowan was met, on all hands, on his way home to-night, by people running to ask for him. One, in his own peculiar style, said, 'If anything happen to minister, it will knock us all to pieces !'"   The above notice is from a letter written by Mrs. Cowan, on the 8th of February, 1840, before Mr. Jameson had recovered.   She adds : "I trust his valuable life will be spared, for the work's sake, and for our sakes.   To us his loss would be incalculable, and much more to the cause here."

The following extract is dated February 25th, 1840 :—

"The masons are now preparing stones for the building. The people busy themselves, on Saturdays, at the lime-kiln. Yesterday (Sabbath) afternoon, the congregation spent an hour in supplicating the Lord's direction in this important under-taking, and His especial blessing on the friends who are so deeply interested in their welfare ; also upon the contributions which they themselves and others had made, and were making, to forward the work."

From a letter to his aunts we take the following (February 27th, 1840) :—"Catherine is getting very like her mother.   I hope she will prove like her in her many estimable and endear-ing traits.   For of all whom I ever knew, although she had never been mine, Nicolis possessed all that was amiable and lovely.   She used to say I was too good for her ; but the reverse was the case.   She was riper for glory than I, and has sooner entered on its full enjoyment. . . . . . Oh, if we understood what it is to be with Christ, and were our hearts truly raised above this transient scene, how little would we hanker after the earthly society of departed friends.   We would envy their present con-dition ; we would be animated with their success ; we would rejoice in their glory and happiness ; we would prepare to follow them, and long to embrace them in that world where all is holiness and beauty and love. In my musings, I sometimes find myself talking to Nicolis. I know not whether she is near me or far away ; still I like to cherish the thought that though unseen, she may yet be near. Oh, how much do we owe to the Redeemer for bringing heaven so near, yea, for making its very angels ministering spirits to the heirs of salvation, and for preparing for us a house from heaven after our earthly tabernacle is dissolved. If the apostle had illustrated this subject from nature, as he illustrates that of the resurrection elsewhere, he might have pointed to the caterpillar drawing along its sluggish and limber body, its only enjoyment being to feed on leaves, and to this same creature, when it appears in another form, full of life, sportive and gay, speeding through the air, dancing in the sunbeam, and visiting spots which, as the sluggish caterpillar, it never could have reached. Who knows what ' the house from heaven is,' with which the soul, unwilling to be found naked, is clothed when this earthly house is dissolved ? . . . . Tell my mother to dry up her tears, and to be cheerful and happy. Dear Nicolis has overcome, and has sat down with Christ on his throne. If I saw my mother above this trial, its bitterness to me would be past."

From the first, Mr. Jameson tried to induce the people to help themselves, and they felt and responded to his appeals.

" On Friday, we met, and read your letters, and agreed to raise the school fees. The congregation will make another collection on the 1st of August, and thus they will be trained to that duty, which they will be called upon, sooner or later, to discharge. I am glad to say that they appear to be willing to do everything in their power to assist in the great work.

" We are now overhead in church building ; twenty masons have been at work during the last three weeks. Our greatest difficulty is in getting carriage. Wains we have been promised, over and over again, but when the time comes, there is something in the way. If getting up the shed was trying, the church is to be still more so. We have fine timbers and stone, and plenty of water. Sand is the article most difficult to be got, having to be brought a distance of three miles. God is with us, and your hearts and prayers are with us. The expense of getting the whole set agoing is very great. Mr. Barkly's £300 we have not yet touched, but we will soon, I fear, have to set upon it also. Can you put at our command £600 ? We will begin to pay it up as soon as the church is built. Mr. Moir is better ; my little one is well ; and I am quite recovered. Mr. Cowan and I visited the school a few days ago. The progress is astonishing, and the children are in a high state of training. Mr. Barkly has gone into the proposal of building a house for Mr. Moir at the church, the interest and part of the principal to be paid annually."

But the prospects of Goshen were again disappointed in the wisdom of the Lord, who sees it needful to lead his people through hard experiences. Mr. Moir's health gave way under his arduous labours. He tried a visit to Manchester, but with no permanent advantage, and, at last, was forced to return to Scotland. The following letter was written on the 3d of July, 1840, the day on which Mr. Moir left Goshen.

" Mr. Moir has this night left us for the ship, and once more our little family is weeping. All is silent and sad. It looks as if death had been again at work. The evening is closing about us, and the silence and gloom which reign in our little dwelling, recall this time last year with its sadness and woe. The last week has been a busy time at the Pen— every one bringing something to teacher before he went away. They brought baskets of cocoas, yams and plantains, abundance of eggs, pines, and cocoa nuts, and fowls in dozens. He leaves this with the tears and deep regret of all who know him. Should he recover, I hope he will pursue his studies, and take license, for he possesses many fine qualifications for the ministry."

At a meeting of the Jamaica Missionary Presbytery, held July 3d, 1840, Mr. Jameson was requested to take charge, for a short session, every year, of those students who had made considerable progress in their studies. These had gone to Jamaica as catechists, in connexion with the Synod's Mission, and with that of the Scottish Society, and were desirous of preparing themselves for the ministry. Mr. Goldie, who expresses himself gratified in "adding a stone to the cairn" of his old teacher and friend, says that Mr. Jameson was well qualified for superintending their studies, "as he had himself enjoyed the opportunity of receiving a thorough education, and had evidently well improved it. At the time of the vacation of our schools, we went up for a month to Goshen, and were domiciled with him, while he and we did our best to improve our short session. The studies to which we chiefly gave our attention were New Testament Greek, Hebrew, and Divinity. In this last he did not prepare any lectures, so as to give a system of his own, but adopted Dr. Dick's work as a text book, and taught by examination. I do not recollect that there were ever more than six in the class, so that he was able to give all necessary attention to each of his students ; and he and we had full opportunity of becoming acquainted with each other, and with the subjects to which our attention was directed. Some of the parts of Horne's Introduction were also regularly brought under review ; and short essays and discourses were prepared on topics and texts named by Mr. Jameson. He was in the custom also of giving to each of us a somewhat extensive subject, on which an essay was to be prepared, and brought up next year.

"Being brought into such intimate association with Mr. Jameson, we could not but know him thoroughly. He was one of the most unselfish of men I have ever met with. His own comfort, his own honour, his own everything, he thought not of, if, by any sacrifice of them, he could promote the comfort and wellbeing of others. Moreover, he was most eminently a man of God. Latterly, he was a man of one book, and that book was the Bible. All leisure time was devoted to its constant perusal. Thus, 'though in the world, he was not of the world, but had his conversation in heaven.' And, as I have heard the late King Eyo say, 'He spoke of heaven as if he had been there.'"

The following notice of the work at Goshen Hall is from the Rev. William Anderson, of Old Calabar :—"We are quite busy and quite happy. I feel that it is good to be here. We meet at 6 A.M., to read Greek, and dismiss at half-past 8. Then we have worship and breakfast. We meet again at 10, read Hebrew, are examined on a portion of Dick's Lectures, and one of us reads an essay. This occupies till 3 P.M. We then dismiss for dinner, and have the afternoon for study. At both meetings we receive a great deal of instruction from Mr. Jameson."

As fruits of Mr. Jameson's labours in this department, we can point to Mr. Elmslie of the Grand Cayman, Mr. Aird of Jamaica, Mr. Anderson of Old Calabar, and Mr. Goldie himself. All these brethren have been honoured to do much in the Lord's work; and the last has translated the whole of the New Testament into the language of Old Calabar.

The following letter shows the busy missionary taking time to notice the kindness of young friends, and to remind them of the claims of Jesus on their hearts and services. It is addressed

"To the Rose Street Church Sabbath-School Association, and to the Young Men's Sabbath Morning Class Missionary Society, and to the Juvenile Missionary Society.

"September 15th, 1840.

"MY VERY DEAR FRIENDS,—I thank you for the very beautiful engraving of the church which you have sent me, and for the number of these engravings. I thank you for your consideration of our funds. I know not, very dear friends, whether my feelings are proper, but I will state them, and leave you to decide. I would prefer giving to each family in the congregation one of the engravings, as an additional token of your kindness, a memorial of the wife of their first missionary, and a view of their first church. My feelings with regard to selling are perhaps foolish and childish, but having few to consult with here, I will not move until I get your advice and approval. I feel deeply your generous consideration, in the desire which you express to return to me the original painting. It is needless to say how highly I value this production of my dearest friend, but it is on that account that I wish it to be yours and not mine. It was executed for you, and I have much satisfaction in carrying out the desire of her who is now removed from my side. Please, beloved friends, to accept the small gift, as a memorial of the wife of your first missionary, and as the first fruits of your labours in the gospel in a foreign land. I am more than pleased with the numerous copies of the engraving, and with the very beautiful manner in which they have been executed.

" I have still one object of thanks, and that is, the very valuable letters which you have sent to the congregation. The letter from you all as a class is peculiarly precious ; and your advices as to the making of contracts, time of working, and hours of resting, are of the highest importance. The people do not like to be called idle, or to get the name of being inattentive to their work. They say that ' Backra newspaper tell false on them ; cane never rot here, except when want of rain keep back the mill ; we must make sugar for massa, else we no get wages.'

" Now, my dear friends, let me express my hope that you still continue diligent in your daily labours, and especially in your Sabbath class. The knowledge of Christ is the pearl of great price. His name is as ointment ; it is a strong tower ; and, oh, what is it not to the child of God ! Will some of you commit yourselves to the work in Jamaica ? You say we will never see or meet our dear friends again in this world, but we will meet in heaven. Why not meet with Goshen Christians as well here as in heaven ? Why not cross the Atlantic as well as the Jordan ? You *must* cross the one, and why not say you *will* cross the other ? We much need help. Six weeks ago, I began this letter, and only now am I finishing it. School and congregation, church building, and the students of theology, all claim my time. I do a little at everything, and fear I make as little progress as a body between equal and opposite forces."

In a letter to Andrew Fyfe, Esq., S.S.C., Nov. 24th, 1840, he wrote :—" I long much to hear from you. Last letter I received contained the welcome intelligence that the Synod had agreed to send out Mr. Millar. Since that time, I have received from the proprietor a note, in his own handwriting, giving the house at Bonham Spring for five years, and pasturage for two horses. For some time, I have considered it my duty to give up Bonham Spring, as my general health has been unsound, owing to frequent fevers, and as I have had more to do at home than I could accomplish. The people, however, are wearying much for one to teach their children and themselves. I hope the Lord will provide. My sister has been telling me of your untiring efforts to secure a teacher from the Synod. Accept, my dear friend, of my warmest thanks for your interest and care, and give my best acknowledgments to the committee. May the Lord make our way prosperous.

" The Synod's cutting off her Colonial and Missionary Churches from a share in her aid is leaving them to struggle against a strong current. It is a severe measure. Other bodies of Christians are liberally supported by the House of Assembly and parish vestries. The Scottish Kirk is pushing hard to be taken under the wing of the Government. The different English Societies are carried onward by their churches at home. Our people are not made of money. The most of those attending our churches are labourers, receiving 7s. 6d. per week, and there has been no such outpouring of the Holy Spirit as that recorded in Acts iv. 34, 35. There is, however, a system of money-raising, which, for the welfare of Christ's kingdom, would better be broken up. We, who belong to the Secession, desire to cling to our Bible, and to the customs of our fathers, as far as practicable. We desire to be Voluntaries ; we desire to walk according to the law of Christ, that every man give as the Lord hath prospered him. We desire to defend the purity of Christ's Church in this ordinance as in other ordinances. Hence, although needful of money, I have considered it my duty to return certain sums which were sent me, considering that principle is of more importance in the Church than money. These transactions I will give at large in my journal. All things considered, I think that the Synod has crippled us sadly, by withholding what would enable us to keep pace with a rising country, and putting us in a position for showing the efficiency of the Voluntary method.

Mr. Jameson's principles were high and honourable. Once he remarked, that the vile behaviour of some of our country-men, made it almost pollution to put their gifts into the treasury of the Lord ; at the same time, admitting that there is a limit to the rejecting the voluntary gifts of such men. But one such gift—a liberal one too, and proffered at this time of need, when he did not know where he should find the funds necessary to carry on the heavy work on hand—was promptly and decidedly refused. A neighbouring proprietor had promised £50 to the building fund. In the meantime, he had used unholy freedoms with one of his servants, a young woman attending, says Mr. Jameson, " my classes, who has, in consequence, been expelled. He sent part of his subscription, which I considered it my duty to return, stating that the money of one who shamed and grieved us, and tended to destroy us, I could not receive." The money was sent back with the following note :—" The disclosures which ——, formerly a member of my classes, made to me, some time ago, regarding your conduct towards her, forbid my acceptance of the sum you offer to the church."

The arrival of his eldest sister, in November, was a happy event for all concerned. She had cheerfully devoted herself to promote her brother's comfort and usefulness ; and the mission was, in every respect, the gainer,—the people, by the presence among them of one peculiarly fitted for usefulness among the children of Africa,—and the missionary, by the companionship of a beloved sister who could enter thoroughly into all his anxieties, and hopes, and plans. She was recognised, and is still warmly remembered by the people as being, in all respects, the counterpart, and the worthy coadjutor of their beloved minister. The friends of Mr. Jameson and of the mission rejoiced in this arrangement, having reason to believe that, amidst his many duties, and in the desolate state of his own home, his personal comfort was neglected, and his health endangered.

The following extracts refer to this matter, and they give us a near view of the marvellous affectionateness of the man's heart, who, at the same time, was able to make so thorough a consecration of himself to the public cause of the Redeemer :—

"*December* 3*d*, 1839.—However much comfort my coming home at present might afford me, yet it is altogether beyond my power. Baby is yet so tender, that I fear it would injure her. She is thriving so well under the kind care of Mrs. Cowan, that I should not like to remove her. Besides, I cannot bring my mind to leave the grave of my beloved Nicolis. I feel as if that would be tearing myself from her arms. She left her earthly all for my sake ; she loved me ; she nursed me ; she watched over me with unwearied and most anxious care. Now she has left me, and all that remains for me to look upon is her grave. I delight to visit it, and cannot yet depart so far from it. This may be considered an infirmity. Call it so. Call it what you please. Still its existence is a reality ; and the consolation which it gives is ever grateful. Such, moreover, is the nature of my engagements here, that I could not possibly move from the spot, without seeming to desert my post at a most interesting emergency, and without retarding the work to a very serious extent.

"As to your coming out, I know not what to say. After what has befallen me, I am afraid to say, 'Come.' I feel more and more, every day, the comfort you would be to me. Since my beloved Nicolis has left me, there are none but yourselves whom I should desire to take her place in the management of my domestic concerns. And it would be a great happiness to have my dear child at home with myself, which cannot be in present circumstances." The above, as well as the following, was to his sisters :—"*July* 6*th*, 1840.—I am afraid to ask, far more, to press you to come. My poor heart got one terrible wrench ; another such would, humanly speaking, be far more than I could bear. I am willing, according to the grace given to me, to endure my present loneliness with patience, and to bear all the sadness and sorrow to which, for some months, I have been no stranger, rather than bring other friends whom I love to this land of sultriness, fever, and rapid death.   But, oh, my dear sisters ! if you want to see Goshen, I want to see you.   If you desire to put hand to the glorious work, haste and come.   We need you in the house, and we need you in the field of labour.   .   .   .   .   .

"I never felt the loss of my beloved Nicolis so overwhelmingly as now.   All in the Presbytery returned home with light hearts and joyful.   But my heart was heavy, heavy—as my father used to say, big with woe.   I laid my feverish head upon the pillow, and looked in vain for the solace of her who is gone from me for ever.   I can venture no farther.   Do not show this letter, and expose my weakness.   I must bear up before the world ; and it is only to you, or to my mother, that I venture to lift the sluice to the pent-up flood."

Again, July 10th, 1840, to the same :—"I want you to look after my house, and to herd my income.   Since Nicolis left me, I cannot do this myself.   I know not how my dear wife managed to make the ends meet.   I wish you to come for this, although it were for nothing else : for, if the management of the house is left on my shoulders, along with everything else, I shall very soon founder.   I have not time to attend to it. And I feel that debt would endanger the cause of Christ as much as anything else."

In the following letter to Mr. Bryden, February 9th, 1841, Mr. Jameson acknowledges the receipt of gifts from his friends in Edinburgh, which came timeously, and were welcomed during that season of anxiety.

"I have to acknowledge the receipt of the boxes.   On Saturday, they arrived in safety from Ocho Rios.   I know not what to say to you and all friends for this kindness.   The medicine chest is most valuable ; please, tender the warmest thanks of the church at Goshen to Miss Logan, Lauriston, for this valuable gift.   I am sometimes overwhelmed when I think of all that is done for us by you at home, and of the poor return I make, even on the score of acknowledgment.   All that I can say is, that you have the deepest thanks of myself and congregation, and that your kindness is ever before me and ever encouraging me.   My apparent remissness is always lying like a weighty burden upon my heart; but incessant employment makes me altogether unable to attend to other duties in which I take much delight.   No sooner was the Hall closed, than the Presbytery came.   No sooner was the Presbytery over, than Mr. Taylor fell sick, and I had to turn into the school.   Thus I happen to be, for the present, minister, teacher, and catechist at Goshen and Bonham Spring.   Of late, I have become builder also.   I formerly referred to the carelessness of the contractor for the walls of the church.   His men refused to work any longer for him, and he had to retire.   By the advice of all my friends, I have employed the headman mason, and all are now working cheerfully.   With one thing and another, I have not a moment from the dawn till I lie down to sleep away the cares and toils of the day.   Keeping books and paying money are departments with which I am not well acquainted; but when we rise to duty, and face difficulties, the way becomes smoother, knowledge is gained, and habits are acquired which more than repay the loss of ease and comfort.   The traveller's way may be toilsome, along rugged tracks, and in uncongenial regions, but his increased information more than repays the toil.   I know that He whose name is a strong tower, is with me; and that your prayers go up daily on my behalf; and truly I have reason to rejoice in my infirmities that the power of Christ may rest upon me.   As a blessing has been upon the coffee and sugar we sent you, we cannot but repeat, and, if possible, double the quantity of Goshen and Salisbury produce, this year, for yourselves and kind friends.   I am glad to learn by Mr. Fyfe's letter, that your soirée succeeded so well, and that your noble subscription was so speedily raised.

"It is said of Britain, that she has only to will a thing, and it is done; how much more truly may this be said of the Church of Christ!   Her treasures lie in her will.   And Calvary, and all the blessed ordinances of divine grace, and the mighty working of the Spirit of God, conspire to this one end—the making of a willing people.   The widow of Zarephath found that the more she gave to the Lord's cause, the more she got to give.   Ever giving she ever increased.   She learned what God's people, at the present day, more, perhaps, than at any other period, have learned, that there is a giving which enriches, and a withholding which tends to poverty.

"I have appointed this afternoon for the examination of candidates for the Lord's Supper. We intend to observe this ordinance on Sabbath eight days. There will be upwards of thirty new members. Among these there are three young females of Mrs. Jameson's training, who are hopeful characters. The sower goes, but the seed remains; the sower dies, but the seed lives; the sower must decrease, but the seed must increase."

In a letter to the Rev. John Parker of Sunderland, who, along with his congregation, took a deep interest in Goshen, and aided the work there in various ways, Mr. Jameson (February 11th, 1841) gives the following account of the fall of our first parents, from the lips of an aged negro, at the examination of candidates referred to above :—" Massa (God) say Adam must nyamee (eat) all de fruit in de garden, but de tree of knowledge. But he say to Adam, 'Adam, you no must nyamee dis fruit, else you dead.' De serpent come, say to mammy Eve, ' Dis fruit bery good, it make you be wise.' Mammy Eve take lillee (little) bit, and bring de oder half gib daddy Adam. Daddy no will taste it fust time, but mammy tell him it be bery good. Den him nyamee de oder half. Den daddy and mammy been know dat dem be naked. Dey go hide in a bush. Massa come from heaven, but Him no fin' Adam all about. Den Massa strike him foot on de ground, and say, ' I wager Adam been nyamee de fruit.' Massa go seek Adam and fin' him hidin' in de bush, and put him out of de garden. Daddy and mammy take leaves and sew dem for clothes."

Another said, " Oh, yes, me know me be bery great sinner; me sleep in sin; me sit in sin; me drink sin; me nyamee sin; me do notin' but sin; dis wicked heart make me sin."

The members of Goshen church were well instructed in their duties. They were encouraged to cherish and express their gratitude to the friends who had sent them the gospel, and to pray and give that the gospel might be spread in Africa. There are extant many short letters which were addressed to their friends in Rose Street and in Sunderland, one or two specimens of which we shall insert here. The first is from an aged African female, still alive. It is not easy to follow her when she is speaking; but what she lacks in utterance she makes up by expressive gesture.

"So long time me come from Guinea, my tongue heavy. Jesus so good as spare me to this hour, and send minister out here to tell me good word. Bless we teacher and we minister, and all the society family at home. With all my heart, and with all my mind, I 'member Jesus till last day come.

"CECILIA HARVEY."

"Jane Byefield thank Mr. Simpson to give we minister from the Rose Street family, and our minister write home for a teacher for we; and we thank him give we a kind teacher, and we love him; he learn we the word of God. I can neither read, write, nor see, but we thankful for the word, and we very glad to have we minister and we teacher to give we knowledge of Jesus Christ, and we satisfied for minister and teacher to stop with we if God spare them. We cannot deliver up our teacher to Middlesex people. We loved minister's wife as we love himself. She teached we the same as minister himself, when he was not there; we lose her; we cannot help it. We love the little one left behind. If the Lord spare her, we shall be very thankful for it. Mrs. Jameson was kind to Jane Byefield; and I like her family, though I don't see them. I send my love to Mrs. Jameson's mother, her brother, and her family, to Mr. Jameson's family, Mr. Moir's family, and to the family in Rose Street; my duty to them all.   JANE BYEFIELD."

The following is from one who can write himself. He writes with his left hand, with the paper turned upside down, a very legible hand. He has been a consistent member and faithful elder of the church, and can express himself with great feeling and fluency.

"MY DEAR FRIENDS IN SUNDERLAND,—I love to send you

a letter. Hope the Lord may be with you. The Lord able to send my minister to me. He also able to send minister over to Africa. When minister come here, we were in children practice. He gave me first lesson-book ; the second day of freedom, he gave me New Testament. And now I have the whole Bible. I learn my Sabbath morning hymn through the week. The hymn I am now saying is the fifty-first ; 'Soon shall this earthly frame dissolved.' Our verse is 2 Cor. iv. : ' If our gospel be hid, it is hid to them that are lost.' We are reading in Judges, and in Acts, the story of Peter healing the lame man. My kind regards to Mr. Parker and all the congregation. ROBERT HAMILTON."

The writer of the following is also an elder—one who is still bent on self-improvement :—

" MY DEAR MINISTER PARKER,—We have received your interesting letters, and our minister has read them to us. We hope the Lord may bless their interesting words to our souls. As God has given us the Bible, may he grant us the Holy Spirit, that we may carry it with us wherever we go. We have heard with much pleasure what you say about supporting the gospel. Our church building takes away from us, at present, all the money we can spare. When it is finished, we hope to join you in doing more to support the gospel, and to send it to Ethiopia that she may stretch out her hands to God. We send you, through the family in Rose Street, a little coffee and sugar for your tea party, and hope that soon we will be able to do much more. HARRIS ANDERSON."

Many may despise these simple effusions. But not so the thoughtful, who consider nothing interesting to a human creature, foreign to their business and bosoms. See an African in Africa—such an old woman as Cecilia Harvey ; heathenism and superstition have shrivelled and withered up almost everything human about her. Her thoughts rise no higher than the instincts of a mere animal. It is almost impossible to say anything that can pierce that dead intellect and petrified heart. But yonder, in Jamaica, see her, in the very evening of her days, with opened heart and awakened intellect, stretching forth her withered hands to a compassionate Saviour, declaring that with all her heart, and with all her soul, she will remember Jesus till the last day. Jesus shall win such trophies even in the wilds of Ethiopia herself. The voice that shall wake the dead ! can it not rouse even the dead soul of an African in Africa ? It can, and it will. O Jesus ! the hour is coming. Let it now be.

How fine is the following scene, which took place in Goshen church, and is told by an eye-witness ! Mr. Jameson was faithful in requiring obedience to the law of Christ, on the part of all who were admitted into the church. He was not one of those who think that either doctrine or duty should be modified to make it easier for the heathen to receive the doctrine, and perform the duty. Some appear disposed to relax Christian morality, even to the extent of opening the Lord's table to the polygamist.

One of those who had been chosen as elders, although he was a sincere Christian himself, had a very unruly family. His children scorned control, and laughed at decency. On one occasion, Mr. Jameson saw it proper, for the sake of religion, to request the old man to consider himself no longer an office-bearer of the church, simply on account of the ill behaviour of his children. The old man rose and said : " Yes, my minister, me will do what minister say, because it be good. My family make me be 'shame. But although my house be not so with God ; yet hath he made with me (pressing his hand on his heart) an everlasting covenant, ordered in all things and sure : for this is all my salvation, and all my desire." The earnest look of the old man, and the burst of genuine feeling, in words which he did not expect to hear, melted Mr. Jameson into tears. The old people's class had been learning the verse, some time before.

CHAPTER VII.

Jamaica Presbytery meets at Goshen—The missionary dedication—Seasonable aid—The fatherless child sings himself into Canaan—Vindication of the African Mission—Church discipline—Mr. Donaldson arrives—Miss Mary Jameson—Battle against the caste of colour—The Divinity Students—Death of Rev. James Paterson —Review of 1842—Church completed and dedicated—Mr. Donaldson's departure and death—All ours is God's— Review of 1843—Heartless corrupters.

THE following, from the pen of Miss Jameson, gives an interesting account of the meeting of the Jamaica Presbytery in July, 1841, at which it was resolved to embark in the mission to Africa. The Presbytery met at Goshen, and Messrs. Blyth, Waddell, Anderson of Bellevue, Niven, Scott, Simpson, Cowan, and Jameson made up the band.

"They had two days of anxious deliberation in regard to Africa, and of earnest prayer to God for direction in the deeply important matter which they were considering. Mr. Waddell introduced it, and read extracts from Buxton's work.[1] After he sat down, all was silent for a few moments. Then each minister rose in his turn, and solemnly devoted himself to Africa, if God should call him. I wish, my dear friends, you had witnessed the scene. Looking at every difficulty and danger, and many such await Christ's servant in wild, untamed Africa, these eight devoted men solemnly pledged themselves to the enterprise of a new mission there. Do you ask how I felt? I was lifted above myself at the noble bearing of the men."

Let us pause for a moment and contemplate the scene that took place on that occasion, when of these brethren, after two days' deliberation, each in turn arose and solemnly devoted himself as the leader of the forlorn hope in a new assault on the kingdom of darkness. This had been brought about, partly

[1] *The Slave Trade and its Remedy*, by Sir T. F. Buxton.

through the desire of many of the people to see something done to extend in Africa the same glorious gospel which had given them joy.   At the time when this self-dedication was made, they had in view no particular part of the Guinea Coast.   They only desired to put themselves at the disposal of the Lord, who seemed, at that particular time, to be asking, " Whom shall we send, and who will go for us ?"   The Spirit of God moved them all to say, " Here are we, choose thy messenger. By thy grace we are all ready to be offered for thy cause in wretched Ethiopia."   The vow was heard in heaven.   Two of that band were sent.   One of them laid his bones in the dust of Africa ; and of the remaining six, one died in Jamaica, while the other five live to see the result of that day's dedication. The seed which they thus planted, has begun to spring.   We look to thee, O God, for the power from on high, that it may grow up a tree of life and liberty for countless living and unborn thousands.

The following letter to the Rev. John Parker of Sunderland (August 5th, 1841), mentions a striking instance of the seasonable aid with which our Father in heaven favours his children :—

" Your very welcome note came by last packet ; and it was read to the church last Sabbath morning.   It strengthened my hands and encouraged my heart, for your arguments against dreams were like those which, from time to time, I had brought before them.   I asked the people why Mr. Parker said the same thing that I said.   Because he gets it where I get it. The blessed Bible is the book of my friend in Sunderland, as well as our book, and it teaches us all the same thing.   ' Achan ' I read to them yesterday, in their 1st of August meeting.   May the Lord bless your esteemed labours among us, as well as at home.

" I have, my dear brother, things innumerable to thank you for.   The *Bethel Flag* is a beautiful periodical.   I circulate numbers among the young people's classes ; all read them with interest and delight.   ' Canaan ' is a simple and beautiful piece.   We had the two first verses of old ; the other verses are a happy addition. There was a run upon it, and some of the children have carried it off.

" The boxes, my dear brother, stand identified with the most striking interpositions of Providence on our behalf. Our outside walls were finished, and paid for, when it was found necessary to build three strong walls inside, to support the flooring. This work I had to begin with an empty purse. Your box, and the box from Montrose, instead of being landed at Ocho Rios, were carried to Montego Bay, where they lay for two or three months. A few weeks ago, I heard that they were at Ocho Rios, and sent for them in my straits. They arrived, two Saturdays ago. The following week, £30 had to be paid. I told the people that the boxes were come, and that they must buy their 1st of August clothes out of them. On Thursday night, at eight o'clock, I had just reckoned the masons' accounts, —which amounted in whole to £17, 9s. 7½d.,—when my sister came up stairs, and, putting the sale-bag upon the table, said that it contained £17, 9s. 7d. I thought, surely she has been looking over my shoulder, and I could not believe. On counting the money, we found not only the sum mentioned by my sister, but one quatty (1½d.) more, which was the remaining halfpenny, and a penny to the bag. I was then compelled to own that a higher One was looking over my shoulder, and, in His own way, providing for our need. ' Well,' said my sister, ' the Lord will provide the remaining sum before it is required.' Next morning, the masons came in for their money. On being paid, they went to the box and bought, so that the money returned again to the fund. I paid ; the people bought ; the money came back ; and now our debt is paid, and £9 remain to meet other expenses. Truly, we are the children of many mercies. With what gentleness does God rebuke our fears ! How richly does He supply our wants, and enforce his own blessed injunction, ' Be careful for nothing, but in everything, by prayer and supplication, make your requests known unto God.' How blessed to live in the hearts of a praying people ! Prayer begets these boxes. Prayer brings them to us in time of need. Prayer draws down upon them God's enriching blessing, and makes them answer the purpose designed. My dear brother, pray for us. Tell our kind friends, when they send us boxes, to continue in prayer for us : for prayer is our wealth, and strength, and aid."

"My dear Brother,—Your two letters on the influence of children, are to us most valuable. They have introduced me to a wide field of instruction, which, I hope, will be blessed both to church and school. Your words to us have been spirit and life.

"I have to acknowledge your kindness in regularly sending the *Herald*. I have read the paper of Φιλοπαις with much interest. The 'Missionary' particularly interested and over-whelmed me. You will, I fear, consider it heavy work to cor-respond with me : for I am slow at the pen, whilst yours is the pen of the ready writer. For two years, my thoughts have been so much among stones and mortar, and my hours so occupied in school, that I feel it no easy work to call up my scattered thoughts ; and, as to the pouring them out at railway speed, that is out of the question. I hope you will have forbearance with the infirmity of a brother, and not ascribe my slowness to indifference. I often sigh over those days when it was my happiness to sit down quietly in my room, and enjoy those hours of retirement, which help to raise the mind above the harassments of this world of toil and care, and to fit us for communion with God, and for his blessed work. But those days are gone by. Still, ' there remaineth a rest for the people of God !' Sweet rest ! Blessed the day when the soul enters upon the enjoyment of it !

"I hope Jamaica will be forward in the great work which is to be commenced in Africa. The building of our churches is, at present, a barrier to missionary enterprise. Five of us are struggling with this millstone ; but we hope, in due time, through God's goodness, to overcome ; and then we will arise and give ourselves with more energy to the work.

"We have just laid in the grave an interesting little boy, a son of the late Mr. Kay.[1] I took him under my care, on the death

---

[1] Mr. William Kay was sent as a catechist to Jamaica in February, 1838. He died

of his father. He had been two weeks at his new home, when he took scarlet fever and died. He was about the age of my little daughter, three years. The last day he was in company with his little playmate, he sat and sang 'Canaan.' The last word he was heard to utter was 'Canaan,' and now he is in the happy land."

Early in 1841, Mr. George Millar from Edinburgh arrived at, and took charge of, Bonham Spring. The school which he taught there was a blessing to the district. Boarders were also received, and several missionary students were among the number.

Friends at home thought that the Jamaica missionaries were going rather fast in the matter of a mission to Africa. Existing engagements were heavy ; and how could they enter on a new enterprise of magnitude and importance, until the Jamaica Mission had taken shape, and been somewhat consolidated ? The following letter, dated January 4th, 1842, dwells upon this point, and indicates the claims of the brethren to credit for sound sense and moderation, as well as zeal and faith :—

" I have, to-night, received letters from two of my brothers who appear to be under the impression that I am on wing for Africa. By last packet but one, I received your kind favour also, which alluded to the same subject. I purposed to write you by return of post, but being engaged with the students, I had not a moment's time. I find it necessary, however, to let other duties stand for the night, and betake myself to this one. Instead, therefore, of writing my brothers, I address you on this important subject. I am not aware what peculiar aspect the Presbytery's measure may have assumed at home, or upon what grounds I, more than any other of my brethren, should be considered as about to go to Africa. I have not the least idea that I shall be honoured with a trust of so vast impor-

in 1841, after three years of faithful service at Mount Horeb, ten miles south of Montego Bay. The Jamaica Presbytery recorded in their minutes (January 19, 1842) " their sense of the great loss which they sustained in the death of Mr. Kay, whose unwearied diligence in the cause of his divine Master, whose unassuming manners and sincere piety had endeared him to the members of the mission, and gained for him the affection of those among whom he laboured."

tance and difficulty.   But if the appointment falls upon me, I shall accept of it only upon condition of its receiving the entire concurrence of the Society, whose agent I have the privilege to be ; and provided another be found to take the oversight of the work and flock here.

" These two points were expressly referred to when considering the question, and they enter as elements into the measure.   So much for the position of the question in relation to myself.   I would now direct your attention to the reasons which led the Presbytery to adopt these resolutions.   It seemed to us that a wide door was about to be opened for missionary labour in Central Africa, and, in consequence of this, that there was a loud call to the Church of Christ to make preparation, and to hold herself in readiness to enter, and to occupy the field. It was also impressed upon our minds that, in this great enterprise, the Church in Jamaica should show herself not only interested, but forward in undertaking the work.   If coldness appeared among Ethiopia's children, where was zeal to be looked for ?   We felt also that it belonged to us, the ministers, to guide our people.   In considering the question, we also felt that as yet we were but minors, and could not act with the full freedom and vigour of manhood ; but we considered it our duty to act according to the circumstances in which we were placed. We therefore proposed that each member of Presbytery should devote himself, individually, to the cause of Africa, and that he should feel himself bound to carry the gospel to that benighted land, should Providence call him to the work.   In the spirit of this resolution, it was also agreed to offer ourselves to the churches at home, as willing to be their agents there, should they desire to occupy that field.   To this we were induced, from the consideration, that agents will be more easily found to come to Jamaica, than to go to Africa,—that we were, in some measure, already acclimatized, and, therefore, better prepared for a more trying region than persons from home,—that we were also, in some degree, acquainted with the manners of the negro, and inured to the toils and trials of a missionary life, —and that, enjoying the confidence of our people, a number of the best people in our churches might be induced to accompany us as colonists. We also proposed to support the agent who went from among us, feeling assured that, by so doing, the funds which are necessary for the carrying on of the work here, would not thereby be damaged. Such are the reasons which led to the resolution recorded in the minutes of last Presbytery. As we are yet under tutors, it remains with the church at home to say whether any portion of Central Africa shall be occupied by us as a field of missionary labour. We feel that we cannot go and leave our flocks in Jamaica uncared for. Our places must be filled with efficient agents. It would be false philanthropy to leave our people destitute, for the purpose of carrying the gospel to those who are not a people. But any one of us is willing to submit, once more, to the pang of separation, to break the dearest ties, and to face the deep, the perils of an African climate, and the trials of an infant mission, for the benefit of our churches,—that Ethiopia may stretch out her hand to God,—and that we may bear a part in working out the most rational method yet proposed for the amelioration of Africa, and the destruction of the slave trade. . . . I am happy in Goshen, and I hope I am useful. I love my people ; and were I to consult my own feelings, I would much rather live and die among them. And I confess it is my most earnest wish never to be long out of sight of the grave of that dear one who left all, and accompanied me to this distant land ; and much do I desire that my grave should be in hers. But Jesus calls upon me once more to take up the cross. I trust that I shall be found preferring him to my chief joy, and that you will be ready to bid me God-speed. But of this, my dear friend, there is no prospect, at present ; yea, during the past year, responsibilities and difficulties of various kinds have been increasing, which will serve to tie me down here for years to come. Of these I will tell you more afterwards. If God has work for me elsewhere, He may soon remove them all. But one thing is dutiful,—never to leave the Church of Christ in a state of disorder in one place, for the purpose of establishing it in another. To dishonour it where it is established, is not to contribute to its stability in any quarter ; and, to speak without mystery, I must stay here till the debt on the church be paid."

In reviewing the work for 1841, Mr. Jameson wrote to the President and Directors of the Missionary Association in Rose Street Church, February 4th, 1842 :—

" I sit down to give you a brief sketch of our proceedings at Goshen during the past year, in which it will be seen that there is much cause for humiliation, as well as for gratitude and praise. There are 177 families on our list, most of which are whole families ; while, in the case of others, some of the members come to us, and some go to other churches, or to no church at all. Ten families have joined us since last report. Five or more of our young people have married, and set up separate families. Seven persons have been admitted to the communion of the church. The smallness of this number arises not from want of applicants, but from the necessity of being cautious. There have been eight baptisms, and eleven marriages. On the same day, and at the same time, an old father and mother, with their young son and his bride, were united in the bonds of matrimony.

" A few of the members and catechumens have been suspended, — three for quarrelling, and one for allowing his daughter to leave his house on the Sabbath-day, with her hoe and her basket, for the purpose of being ready to go to work next morning. An elder, I am sorry to say, was deposed for carrying his tools on the Lord's day, and bringing them with him to church. One of the catechumens was excommunicated for killing his neighbour's ass ; he hacked it with his cutlass till it died. Others have been admonished by myself and the session ; but, on the whole, I have much reason to be satisfied with the peaceful, sober, and consistent behaviour of the congregation. Their attention to the means of grace has been regular, and the progress of many in knowledge satisfactory.

" The week-day classes for religious instruction have not been so regular as I could have desired ; neither have I been able regularly to visit the congregation. This arises from the necessity of being daily in the school, and from the numerous and varied matters that are continually pressing upon me. I feel, however, more and more, the want of this minute inspection. Our Sabbath audience remains much the same; the house is as full as is convenient. I have reason to believe that, when we get into our new house, our audience will be considerably increased. Subscriptions and collections have been regular. Subscriptions, £105 sterling; collections, £50 sterling. Along with this, we have raised a fund of £8 for medicines and medical attendance. Altogether, our contributions amount to £163. The law of the medical fund is that every one who pays 1s. sterling, is entitled to medicine and medical attendance. In this way we aid one another, and, by a united effort, we help the weak and poor among us in sickness.

"The building has been standing still, for the last six weeks. The roof is finished and the estimate ended; and I have not had leisure to arrange for the laying down of the floor. This I intend to begin with as soon as possible. Providence has brought help to my hand in this time of need. Mrs. M'Dowall, a very excellent lady, a member of Port Maria congregation, is to give us the loan of £500. I am to pay six *per cent.*, to give a bond on the property, and refund the money in six years. I am much concerned to see the sad distress at home, and the more so, as I am not in circumstances to ease you of the heavy burden which this mission imposes. I will make every effort to relieve you as far as possible. I intend to establish a regular system which will be permanent. I feel much for my native land, and pray the Lord to remove his hand of judgment. I am sorry to see a falling off in the Synod's Mission Fund."

On February 25th, 1842, he wrote to Mr. M'Gilchrist :—

"I am truly happy that the report of the Station for 1840 gave so much satisfaction to the Directors, the Society, and friends. I hope the Lord is blessing us, but often fear lest he withdraw his gracious presence. Oh, there is much barrenness among us, much that is wrong, little that is right. I often think that all we possess is in answer to the prayers of dear friends at home.   For myself, I have to cry out, My leanness! my leanness!   When I became a missionary, I expected to have nothing to do with the world's troubles and bustle.   Whereas, I have everything to do with it; for nothing can move but through my poor instrumentality; and I do assure you, touch it in whatever way, from whatever quarter, and by whatever motive, your soul must partake of its plagues.   But the fact that we enjoy your kindness, your sympathy, and your prayers, cheers, supports, and comforts us. Our sacrament, on the last Sabbath in October, was delightful to us; and the thought was most sweet that you were with us at the same work.   I often think, on the Sabbath morning, that it is good for us that the sun rises upon you first: for your morning prayers are at the throne for us before we begin. Thus, I sometimes think and say that we are the better of you in this matter; and it is a strong consolation to ask God in my closet, family, Sabbath-school, and morning prayer, to hear the prayers which we know are presented for us, on the morning of this day, by dear friends in Rose Street, and to bless those who have been praying for us."

On hearing that Mr. Peter Donaldson had been appointed to the office of teacher and catechist of Goshen, Mr. Jameson thus expresses his feelings:—"I am delighted to see that Mr. Donaldson is appointed to be my fellow-labourer among the young.   I cannot feel grateful enough to you, and to our dearly beloved friends in Rose Street, for this new expression of deep interest and love.   It will be a great relief to me, and enable me to attend more fully to the congregation.   We have got a very comfortable house fitted up for him, near ourselves; it is far from the school, but he will have a horse."

The amount of school fees collected during the year 1841, was £32, school having been held during only nine months. There were 125 boys and 112 girls on the list, in all, 237.

Referring to her brother's activity at this time, Miss Jameson, April 22d, 1842, wrote :—

" Our beloved William has much need of relief.   Ever since the Hall ended, he has had the whole work of a school of more than 100 children, besides his ministerial duties. Our doctor says, ' Parson Jameson is an iron man ; the climate has no effect on him at all.' I never saw a minister at home go through the half of what he does. Every night I think he will come home to me sick."

Thus does he again weep with those that wept, in a letter to Mr. M'Gilchrist, May 20th, 1842 :—

" I was sorry to learn that the Lord has, once more, visited you with affliction, and removed one of your tender lambs to his own fold above. The loss to you is great, but the gain to the dear child far exceeds our utmost thoughts. Your cup is bitter, but hers is unmingled sweetness. Oh yes ! my boy and his mother, your darling and her grandmothers, have all met, long ago, and met many more dear departed friends, and have talked over scenes in Goshen and Rose Street which are full of interest to their now glorified spirits. I cannot but look to heaven as my home, as the dwelling-place of the partner of my soul, as the home of my kindred, as the meeting-place where I shall once more shake hands with those from whom I have been long and far separated, and where I shall be introduced to dear ones in Christ, whom I never saw in the flesh.

" The blessed God has not stripped your garden of all its pleasant flowers. I rejoice to hear that another bud has appeared upon the stem that, so lately, was bereft of its lovely blossom. May this tender bud long bloom, and be an ornament to her father's house, and bear fruit to the glory of God."

The following letter refers to an arrangement by which the mission family at Goshen obtained an addition to their happiness, and the congregation another zealous and efficient labourer for their good. Miss Mary Jameson arrived in Jamaica in January of 1843. When Mr. Donaldson was removed in August of the same year, she aided in conducting the school till, in 1846, the family was broken up by Mr. Jameson's departure to Africa. She then became the wife of William Milne, Esq. She came to Scotland with her husband, in the year 1848, and died in 1855. Like her brother and sister she is still held in affectionate remembrance at Goshen. Possessed of good natural talents, and a cultivated mind, she was distinguished for her amiability.   Her piety was deep and fervent, and her end was peace.

It is a family letter, and one which, on that account, might be withheld.   But it is so like the man, and breathes such a spirit of devotedness to the Lord's cause, and such elevated sentiments throughout, that we cannot deny the reader the benefit of seeing it.   Would to God that the same spirit of simple confidence in God, and entire consecration to his service, lived in every genuine Christian bosom !   The best affections of the heart would not then stand in the way of the Lord's cause, but parents would give their children, when the Lord had need of them ; and far more Christian men and women would offer themselves to the work of the Lord in heathen lands, while the treasury of the house of God would overflow with the givings of a willing people, at length girding themselves, in right earnest, to the enterprise of gospelling the whole human family. Oh, the grim silence of death covers, like a pall, the face of many nations ; and how few are at the work of removing it ! We are only at the outskirts of vast Ethiopia.   When shall the messenger of peace from the west, shake hands with his brother from the east, in the centre of her desert wild ?   When shall the voice of mercy awaken the echoes of numberless valleys, and hills, and forests which are yet unknown to Europe ?   Oh, thou King on God's holy hill of Zion, may we not soon see a willing people, beauteous with holiness, and many as the morning dew-drops, hurrying to and fro, with thee on their lips and in their hearts, preaching thy unsearchable riches to these most miserable outcasts in the land of Ham !   Let the Church of God know assuredly that Africa is not to be gospelled at small cost of time, and toil, and men, and money.   That vast stronghold of the devil is not to be conquered by the " awkward squad," or by a handful of raw recruits.   To save " God's black but comely child" will be no child's-play.   It will, as indeed the whole mission work, looked at in its grandeur, as for the honour of our blessed redeeming God, require the true manhood and womanhood of the Church of Jesus.   Let this be understood.

" I am afraid, my dear Aunts, that you will think hard of my asking Mary to come to Jamaica. But you brought us up for the Lord, and you gave us to the Lord ; and surely for your dear children to be engaged in the regeneration of a lost world, is the best portion, and the greatest honour. The separation is painful, but the meeting will be the sweeter, whether it be on this side the grave, or on the other side. I cannot say when we may be home. This is entirely in the hand of God. At present it enters not into my calculations. I feel much happier to attend to the work in hand. God controls our every movement, and his promise is,—' With mine eye set upon thee, I will show thee direction.'

" I feel with reference to Mary's life as I do respecting my own, that they are in his hand. We can only fill up the measure of our days ; and neither the cool climate of Scotland, nor the warmer latitude of Jamaica, can add one moment to this measure, nor take one moment from it. All who believe the word of God must be satisfied of this,—that as hirelings we must fulfil our days, and that the number of them can neither be increased nor diminished by any movements of ours. But the being over solicitous about this frail spark may cause a halting in our Christian race, and may fill the end of our days with regret. Nicolis was honoured with but a short period of warfare in the mission field, but who can doubt that she fell at the post assigned to her, or who can say that she would have lived a moment longer in the house of her mother, or in any house in Scotland ? She had work here to perform. She lived to do it ; and when next we see her, Jamaica will beautify her crown with its brightest lustre. The Lord prepared the way for Jane to follow. She is happy, and blesses the day that she put hand to the work. Mary desires to join the company. I dare not forbid, lest I should quench a fire which the Spirit of the Lord has kindled. I do not forget that I may die, and that without being able to lay up a fraction ; but the earth is the Lord's, and the fulness thereof ; all that I have is the Lord's, and it all goes in his service. I cannot accuse myself of extravagance in my stewardship. I know that He will provide for my sisters and daughter, and not the less so, because they have followed the Saviour in the regeneration.   I am truly glad to see how well and happy Jane is in this distant land.   Catherine thrives amazingly under her care ; and what more can I desire ?   The Lord has emptied my cup, but he has filled it again.   His billows have passed over me, but his tender mercy has calmed their raging, and placed me again by the waters of quietness.   How long the calm may continue he only knows. I desire to hold every blessing with a loose hand, excepting Christ, the rock of my salvation.   The likeness of my dear Nicolis, which our aunt in Edinburgh has so kindly sent me, is very precious to me.   She all but speaks.   She looks, but sees me not.   But hush ! farewell !"

The arrival of the portrait above alluded to, was the occasion of a renewal of all Mr. Jameson's tender recollections.   After all had retired to rest, Miss Jameson heard him come down stairs softly.   She arose, and, on opening the door of her bedroom, she saw her brother with a candle in his hand, bathed in tears, standing before the portrait.   The females, when they visited the Pen, were wont to drop a curtsey before it, in testimony of their fond remembrance of their departed friend.

The arrival of Mr. and Mrs. Donaldson is thus intimated to the Directors, June 14th, 1842 :—

" MY DEAR FRIENDS,—Mr. and Mrs. Donaldson have at last arrived, after a long passage of eleven weeks.   For preserving them through so many perils, I trust we feel thankful to the God of our mercies ; and for this fresh token of your interest and love, next to the great God, would I return the thanks of my poor heart to the Board of Education and to you.   Yes, my dear friends, my heart is too full to utter all its thoughts. May the God of heaven bless you !   May your abundant sowing produce for our blessed Master prosperous fruit !

" Mr. Donaldson has commenced his labours, and promises to be all we desire,—anxious, vigorous, and affectionate.   The children seem to be much interested in him, and he happy with them.   The school-house is rustic, and, to a stranger fresh from the metropolis, sufficiently uncomfortable ; but our friend is not put about.   He walks over the rough floor, and gives his word of command, as if he had long been accustomed to such things. His quadruped is a mule, named Kitty, a young bud of the mission tree, reared and trained by my boy William.   She is saddled every morning at eight, when she moves off with her charge, as if she felt happy in being the bearer, and careful lest she should inflict any injury, this being her first outset in the work.   Mrs. D. also enjoys good health.   I have advised her not to teach any, for some time.   She must first get a house beside the school, and, even then, it is necessary that she should do but little.   We are much delighted with Mrs. D.   She is well fitted to be a blessing to her husband, an auxiliary in the work, and a comfort to us.   They went into their house, last night.   Their abode is of a rougher texture than the one they left on the other side of the Atlantic, but we have made it as comfortable as we could.   God's blessing and presence will make them happy ; and His grace, I hope, is making them content."

Writing to Mr. Bryden, June 21st, 1842, Mr. Jameson says : —"There is one circumstance to which we have not ventured to give prominence. Robert Jarrit, whose name you will observe in the list of successful candidates for prizes, is a negro.   At his entrance into the school, the brown parents and their children stormed, and threatened to withdraw. We determined to adhere to a righteous principle.   He has made honourable progress, and his superiority has silenced the clamour of prejudice.   His appearance at the examination was injured by his modesty.   He trembled like a leaf, and the big tears rolled over his dark cheeks, while his voice was quite smothered. Several specimens of elegant penmanship were laid on the table, in competition for the prize.   After considerable difficulty, two were fixed upon, as best and second best, by the gentlemen present.   It turned out that both belonged to Jarrit."

The following extract is from a letter of Mr. Donaldson, October 21st, 1842 :—

" On Monday morning, I commenced my labours in the school, and I had no great difficulty in conducting it, even from the first.   Mr. Jameson assisted me the first week, and showed me the system he had been pursuing.   It nearly resembled the most approved systems of the schools in Edinburgh, especially that of Circus Place Academy, and was, in fact, as nearly as possible, the system I intended to adopt.   Mr. Jameson is an excellent teacher,—as good as any I have ever seen.   He is a complete missionary, and I assure you that between the church building, the school, and his other duties, he has enough of work ; indeed, I am surprised how he gets on at all.   Highly as he is esteemed by friends at home, he is by no means overvalued by them.   I had heard much about him, before coming to Jamaica, and now being his associate and assistant, I can say all things I heard of this man are true."

The following pleasing picture is from Miss Jameson's pen, in a letter to the Misses Pringle, December 20th, 1842 :—

"You will like to know about our Divinity Hall.   It met last week, and is a real good concern.   There are five as substantial Scotchmen as you could wish to see.   The Professor seems quite in his element, and has the best of health.   The students seem to be happy and comfortable, and come in from their studies always in high spirits.   They sat very close last week, and were the worse of it.   William, therefore, determined that they should take a ride every day after dinner.   About four in the afternoon, they mount their horses and scamper off like boys when the school is out, every one whipping up his neighbour's horse, and trying to pass him.

"To-night, I joined the party.   We rode round by the bottom of our Goshen hills.   The scenery was most beautiful ; everything was rich green, and the trees were hanging with yellow oranges, and shaddocks, a fruit like the orange, but twice as large.   William said, in his own droll way,—' Really, lads, we are a formidable party.   I think we may take the name of the Theological troop !'   You cannot imagine how happy we are.   I cannot believe that this is the Jamaica we dreaded so much when I was with you."

One of the marks of true magnanimity is a generous appreciation of what is excellent in the character, and praiseworthy in the exertions, and honourable in the success of fellow-labourers. Out upon the littleness that makes us niggardly in our sincere commendations of brethren and their works ! Flattery is nauseous ; mere lip compliment is unworthy of a Christian, and incompatible with godly sincerity ; but it is a luxury—the heart that is so humble and unconscious of self that it takes true delight in preferring and honouring other brethren. This was characteristic of Mr. Jameson. Sincerely and gracefully did he, on suitable occasions, render honour to whom honour was due. And what did he, or what do any, in such cases, but praise and magnify the Giver of every good and perfect gift, to whom all the virtues, and all the exertions of his servants are, in reality, due ?

The Rev. James Paterson was the first missionary sent by the Secession Church to Jamaica, where he arrived in the spring of 1835. He laboured with remarkable zeal and success, under the immediate auspices of the church in Broughton Place, Edinburgh, commencing the prosperous station of New Broughton, of which the Rev. Andrew Hogg is now the pastor. After labouring for eight years, Mr. Paterson was, in a very sudden and distressing manner, removed to his rest and reward.

Thus does Mr. Jameson refer to that event, in a letter dated February 2d, 1843 :—" It is my painful duty to announce to you the death of another beloved labourer. My friend and brother, Mr. Paterson, was on his way, last week, to the Presbytery, in company with Mr. Robson ;[1] when going down a declivity at a rapid pace, the gig gave a jolt, by the wheels passing into a hollow excavation in the road, and Mr. Paterson was thrown out. His companion was mercifully preserved, and on his reaching the spot where Mr. Paterson lay, he found that life was extinct. This sad event has covered us with the deepest gloom. But we desire to be still, and know that this is God. O that we may improve these repeated admonitions which, of late years, the Lord has been giving us. I had a few lines from Mr. Robson, who says that Mrs. Paterson and the family are bearing up, but the stroke is overwhelming.

[1] The Rev. Dr. Robson

May the arms of the everlasting God be underneath them, to sustain and comfort them. I trust some one will be willing speedily to come out, and occupy the place of our beloved brother whom the Lord has removed. The climate is most salubrious ; the drudgery and toil of an infant mission are over. There are a large and flourishing congregation, and a new and substantial church and school-house. Little remains to be done but to attend to the more delightful departments of the Christian ministry. Our faithful brother and his worthy wife and family have toiled in season and out of season, yea, beyond measure ; and when about to enjoy the fruit of their toil, the Lord has removed his servant to his higher reward, and left to another this enjoyment in the vineyard here below. How mysterious is this dispensation ! But we know that all is well."

Reporting progress during the year 1842, Mr. Jameson writes, February 2d, 1843 :—

"Another year has passed, leaving behind it many tokens of the Lord's mercy, as well as much on our part that is calculated to humble and abase us. For while the Lord has been giving, and we receiving, how little gratitude have we manifested, and how little zealous and sincere activity has marked our steps ! Truly, while the multitude meet the first moments of the new year with shouts of acclamation, it best becomes the Christian to be lying at the footstool of his God, confessing the multitude of his transgressions, and imploring grace to enable him to redeem the time, during the remainder of his years."

"I know but little difference between our congregations of 1841 and 1842 ; a few have joined, and a few have left us, in consequence of marriage, and removing to other quarters ; but so few, that it affects us but little in either way. I may say of the congregation generally, that it remains steadfast, and is making progress in the knowledge of Christianity. During the past year, fifteen persons have been admitted, for the first time, to the Lord's table, making the total of full members admitted, since the commencement of the station, 137. Ten children have been baptized, eight couples married, and four persons belonging to the church have died. Several have been suspended for quarrelling,—a sin to which the people in this country are much addicted ; one has been excommunicated for adultery, and another for stealing corn from the field. These latter cases were of peculiar aggravation, and filled the whole church with shame and horror. While such sins are now and then committed by individuals among us, it is pleasing to observe the general feeling of abhorrence with which the report of them is received. This is a token for good, and indicates an advance in moral sentiment : for the time is not yet long gone by, yea, among a certain class, it is even now present, when such practices were of frequent occurrence, and, of course, excited little or no remark.

"I have endeavoured to set agoing meetings for prayer more generally throughout the congregation, this last year. Hitherto, I have not given much encouragement to them : for I have not considered my people qualified to undertake the duties which they impose. Many of the congregation can now read the Scriptures ; and I have requested that all in a certain quarter should meet and read the word of God with one another, and pray, and read a tract which I give in my visits, or upon the Sabbath-day. The elder in this case is not, as he has been represented to be, the teacher or leader. He has never been with us an instructor, as I do not consider him capable of being so employed. The elder, with us, is an office-bearer, not for *teaching*, but for *ruling*, and for *oversight*.

"The week-day and Sabbath-day classes for religious instruction are still kept up. Mr. and Mrs. Donaldson have begun to gather together the younger portion of the congregation, which I was unable to undertake. My sister, whom the Lord has brought to us in safety, will take my class, and I will devote a little more of my time to the instruction of the old, and of those who cannot read. The Lord has strengthened our hands greatly. May it be for His glory, and for the progress of His cause."

The year 1843 saw the church completed. The anxieties and efforts of the missionary were honoured and crowned with success.   A substantial house was erected, which will serve for generations as a house of prayer.

Having summed up the entire cost, and entered the accounts in the church books, he, in one sentence, penned at the foot of the last page, gives utterance to his emotions of gratitude, in these words—words which will form the inscription on the cope-stone of the completed temple of the Lord :—"To the Most High God be all glory and praise.   Not one word He has spoken has failed.   W. Jameson."

The entire cost of the building was £2204.   Of this sum £780 was raised at the station, from 1838 to 1844 inclusive, a period of seven years.   The magnificent donation of Messrs. Davidson, Barkly, and Company, the proprietors, amounted to £300 sterling, besides materials.   Friends in many parts of Scotland and England contributed, by boxes of clothing and donations in money, £316.   About £73 were given by the other stations and friends in Jamaica.   The late Mr. Gibb of Edinburgh devoted pictures, which were sold for £100, to the work, and there was left on the building a debt of £605. £500 of this bore interest at six per cent. ; and, aided by a grant from a legacy left by Mr. Gibb, the whole was extinguished in 1857, the church at Goshen having paid the interest, and the congregational expenses, and spent the surplus in reducing the debt, while the Missionary Association of Rose Street Church, during a period of twenty years, paid the salary of the missionary, besides liberally helping to maintain the teacher.

The following extracts describe the opening services, and the feelings with which the undertaking was regarded by the missionary.   It was a day replete with interest to him, "being the answer to many a prayer, the realization of long-cherished hopes, and the blessing of a gracious God on his feeble attempts to glorify Him :"—

"GOSHEN, *April* 12*th*, 1843.

"MY DEAR FRIENDS,—The long-looked-for day has at last arrived, and our church is opened ; or rather, I should say, it has been dedicated to our God, for whom it was built, and who enabled us to build it.   We met, and presented our offering with cheerful hearts, and may we not hope that our gift Jehovah, through Christ, has accepted, that our prayers he has heard, and that he will not withhold the blessings which we, his people require. There was necessarily but a short time between the fixing of the day and the event, as I wished to have the presence and assistance of my early friend and much respected brother, the Rev. John Robson. . . . . .

"On the morning of the 31st ult., at half-past ten o'clock, the Rev. Mr. Beardslie, an American Independent brother, opened the services by singing the last four verses of the 24th Psalm, and by reading 1 Kings viii. from verse 10 to the end of the chapter, and by offering up the prayer of dedication. The chapter was read from a new pulpit Bible, which the male friends in the congregation had presented for the use of the church. The preliminary services being concluded, Mr. Robson preached from 1 Kings ix. 3. The words of the text were, 'Mine eyes and mine heart shall be there perpetually.' In the discourse he showed the care of God over his Church, and His kindness to her, as implied in His heart as well as His eye being upon her, and this he did in a way so simple, that all appeared to understand him, and with so much beauty and power, that all seemed delighted and impressed. On my asking some of the people if they understood Mr. Robson, they all replied that they understood every word, and one said, 'Yes, minister, and I eat every word, for it was very beautiful.'

"After the sermon, the Rev. Mr. Simpson addressed the congregation, giving a brief but clear account of our doctrines and government. After this, the Rev. Mr. Cowan addressed the church ; then the Rev. G. F. Waters, curate of the Church of England ; and, last of all, the Rev. Mr. Beardslie. The addresses were all most suitable ; and, I trust, impressions were made which, through the mercy of God, will result in glory to the divine Saviour, and in everlasting good to immortal souls.

"I ought to have mentioned in its proper place, that, at the close of Mr. Robson's discourse, a collection amounting to £37 sterling was obtained. Since that time, the sum of £10 has been presented by Mr. Simpson as a donation from his people, who could not come to Goshen. This makes the whole £47. The services of the day were finished at three o'clock, until which time the audience remained with exemplary quietness and attention ; and, in a short time after this, all was still about the church, which, during the day, had been the scene of so much animation.

" On Sabbath, the Lord's supper was dispensed. Mr. Simpson preached a powerful discourse from John iii. 14 ; and Mr. Robson explained the nature of the ordinance, and served the table. Altogether, this has been a season which will be long remembered by all in Goshen, which, I believe, will be talked of by some of us in heaven, and which will bring glory to Him who loved us, and gave Himself for us.

" Mr. Robson is looking as well as ever I saw him, healthy and vigorous. He is truly a messenger of comfort and joy to the churches in Jamaica. Whether he ever return again is known only to God. For this short and flying visit we are most thankful. He has been enabled to say much, and to do much that will contribute to the establishing of the cause among us."

To the Rev. J. Parker, April 12th, 1843 :—" Thus, my dear brother, through your kindness, and the kindness of your people, combined with the Christian efforts of many other beloved friends in England and in Scotland, have we in Goshen been able to carry through, or nearly so, our arduous undertaking. I need not tell you that it has been a work full of difficulty, and that it has required the exercise of patience and faith. I was an utter stranger to the varied crafts required in a work so extensive, and totally without means to meet the expense of it. Nothing would have moved me even to think of such a work, but an irresistible conviction of its necessity for the good of the cause. In surveying the history of Goshen church from the beginning until now, I am astonished at the wondrous interpositions of Divine Providence, and inclined to break forth into loud shouting of ' Grace ! Grace !' I feel that, without your prayers, I would have been as helpless as without your boxes. The former brought down the blessing of the God of the widow of Zarephath upon the latter, so that the gifts of your Christian kindness never failed to supply our wants, and to cheer our hearts. Allow me, my dear brother, in my own name, and in the name of my people, to return thanks to you, and to beloved Christian friends in Sunderland, Greenlaw, Newcastle, and wherever there is a friend who has given us his aid."

Mr. Donaldson's health gave way, in the beginning of 1843. He endeavoured to go on with his work, with various intermissions, till the end of July, when he was ordered home, as the only means of preserving his life. He went on board ship, on the 8th of August ; and, on the evening of the 10th, he breathed his last, "and was admitted, we doubt not, to join that happy choir, whose song is unbroken by sickness or pain, and from whom sorrow and sighing have for ever fled away. His tomb is under the waves of the ocean, but his spirit rejoices before the throne of God and of the Lamb."

On the 21st of August, 1843, Mr. Jameson wrote to Mr. Bryden :—" Your welcome letter came by last packet. The letter to which you refer did not reach me. It must have been in the ill-fated 'Solway.' You will see, then, why I have not acknowledged, long before this, the extraordinary kindness of our worthy friend, Mr. Gibb, and why his generous gift has been permitted to remain so long in your hands. The fact that God guided his servant to make a surrender of his paintings to our necessities, was not forgotten by me, but I wished to wait patiently God's own time and way of sending the result of the sales. I feel that this new display of our heavenly Father's mercy has come in the very best time, on many accounts. It is a testimony from himself that his eye is ever upon us, that the work is his own, and that he will not leave us. My poor heart, by late scenes, has been well-nigh overwhelmed, and the sovereign dispensations of an all-wise God have filled me with trembling. The failure of Mr. Donaldson's health and his removal from us have pressed heavily upon me. My hopes seemed to be blasted, my plans thrown into confusion, and my strength made weak. But behind that frowning cloud I cannot but see the beams of mercy, and from such an abundant supply in time of need, I cannot but hear the voice saying, ' Be not afraid, it is I.' Oh, I desire to be humbled, and to ask why it is that the Lord contendeth. I desire to be truly thankful, and, with my whole soul, to magnify and bless his holy name."

The following letter to his brother Alexander, September 10th, 1843, is both interesting and instructive, and full of important principle :—

" You are greatly entitled to call me a careless brother. I desire now to write you a few lines in reply to your late cheering letters. My heart rejoices in the work of mercy which the Lord is carrying on in your soul. Yes, *Sandy!* we are all the Lord's from top to toe, from the hat to the shoe-tie. If there be anything about us, of which the Lord cannot and will not say, ' It is mine,' to that thing we have no right, and of what avail will it be to us ? It will be our weakness and sorrow, and not our joy and strength. Somehow, we think that our Bible is the Lord's, that the Sabbath is the Lord's, the church is the Lord's, the *bawbee* in the plate is the Lord's, our prayers and our family worship, and our prayer-meetings, the session, and the visiting are the Lord's. But as to my boots, shoes, stockings, trousers, waistcoat, coat, shirt, neck-cloth, hat, and staff, my penknife, my scissors, and my etc., what has God to do with these ? Yes ! the more we understand that passage, ' Ye are not your own, ye are bought with a price,' the more will we perceive that, if the person be the Lord's, his purse is the Lord's, that all connected with his house is the Lord's, and that whatever is not the Lord's, the person is better without.

" These remarks were suggested to me, dear Alexander, by seeing in your last letter, your wish to get Christians to save all that necessity does not require, to put into the treasury of the Lord. I rejoice in this as an evidence of the work of the Spirit in your soul. If the Church of the living God would act thus, if her members would eat nothing, and drink nothing, and wear nothing, but what health and real comfort, not to say necessity require ; and if they would devote their savings to the great cause of the Redeemer, oh, how vast would be the treasury which the Church would put at the disposal of its Lord! Its extent would shame the treasuries of earthly monarchs, and it would humble those who say that the kingdom of the King of Righteousness must have aliens as its paymasters. Let the Church do her duty. Surely she is as able to give the money as the men."

The events of 1843 were thus reviewed in a report, dated January 18th, 1844 :—

" In reviewing the events of the past year, mercy and judgment are found mingled in the cup which our heavenly Father has given us to drink. Our hearts have been kept constantly alternating between hope and fear, joy and grief. Sickness has been wasting some among us ; death has been thinning our ranks, and breaking up our limited circle ; difficulties have, now and then, been threatening to obstruct our path, but as they approached, a way of escape has been opened up ; they passed like the mountainous iceberg, in frowning silence, and the trembling heart was left to sing its song of deliverance.

"During the course of last summer, I visited the congregation, at least, twice, and some parts of it three or four times. I went into every house, and talked with every family apart. I then gathered several families together, and spent some time in public catechetical examination, and in reading the Scriptures. I felt much pleasure in this department of work, and I hope it proved profitable to the people themselves. I have been unable to continue it since I resumed the work of teaching, but I hope soon to be able again to begin it, Mr. Jarrit having come to take my place in the school.

"Two classes have been kept up regularly for religious instruction ; the one meets on Tuesday evening, at the church, and the other, on Wednesday, at my own house. Since we received the lustres from Dr. Young's congregation in Whitby, we have commenced a monthly prayer-meeting. It is upon Thursday, when the moon is nearest full, and has hitherto been pretty well attended. I have also been in the practice of going, as often as I was able, to Bonham Spring, on the Thurs-

day, for the purpose of preaching.   We generally have a good
attendance, not only of Mr. Millar's scholars, but of the neighbours around.   Since August, we have endeavoured to enjoy
the Lord's Supper, on the last Sabbath of every month.   This
we have not been able to accomplish, but, upon an average, we
have had it every second month.   I was delighted to find that
you had been directed to make similar arrangements.   We will
take your days, and we will be in the midst of the work, when
you will be around the family altar at your evening worship.

" Our church has not increased in numbers, during the past
year.   None have joined it who were not with us before.   It
was reported that many were waiting until the church was
opened, to give in their adherence, but none of these have as
yet come forward.   This, I believe, is chiefly owing to the fact,
that the duty of serving our God with our money is an element
in our creed.   There are Established Churches (Episcopalian) on
both sides of us, where this divine ordinance is not only not
enforced, but where the want of it is considered a glory ; consequently few will leave a church where they are never called
upon to give, and join one where giving is enforced as a Christian duty.   A man and his wife have gone out from us, because
of their aversion to pay their monthly subscription.   During
last year, they resisted the calls of the collectors, and two
months ago, they started off to the Established Church, where,
as the negroes say, they will be permitted to eat and drink their
money.

" A painful case of backsliding occurred in the congregation,
two weeks ago.   A young woman, one of my first scholars,
taught by Mrs. Jameson, and, until her apostasy, a full member of the church, has been seduced by a white man, and led
by him into a state of concubinage.   The man set himself to
gain her eye, her ear, and her heart, and to harden her conscience ; and this he has accomplished so effectually, that, in
the face of day, she left her father's home and proceeded to the
house of her disgraceful servitude.   This is one instance, out of
many, which the history of the mission churches in Jamaica
can supply ; and now I feel constrained to ask how long is

this to be tolerated ?   Shall our churches and schools be thus
invaded without end ? Shall the minds of our youth be poisoned
continually, their consciences seared, and they themselves rendered fit for anything, however base it be ?   Can you do nothing
to arouse the moral sense of Britain to this stain upon her
colonies ?   To proclaim to every believer in a righteous Providence, that Jamaica can never prosper so long as such abominations are tolerated, yea, defended as necessary and right ?
As truly as God turneth a fruitful land into barrenness, for the
sins of them that dwell therein, so truly are these men the
enemies of their country, and of the prosperity of the island,
as well as the enemies of their species.   Why should not this
abominable system be made to quail before the public gaze ?
Why should it not be swept out of existence by the force of
public opinion and Christian principle ?   If slavery were bad,
this is no better.   If the one brought down upon itself public
execration, why should the other be allowed to pass with im-
punity, yea, and be tolerated upon the ground of necessity and
right ?   Might not the Government be requested to institute
an inquiry as to the extent of the evil ?   Surely, if it be so extensive, and every one knows it to be so, who is acquainted with
the state of things in the colonies,—and if it be accompanied
with untold evils, no country can thrive, physically or morally,
with such a curse in its bosom."

The case referred to above is a specimen case.   Many such
are chronicled in the book of remembrance, as having taken
place in Jamaica, and indeed wherever missionary labour has
had to be carried on among Ethiopians in the neighbourhood of
godless Europeans.   Ministers naturally feel a deep concern for
those young people whom they have taught from childhood, and
admitted to the fellowship of the church, or whom they expected and longed to see cast in their lot with the people of
God,—whom they hoped to see grow up strong in virtue, and
a blessing to their families. Alas, how often are these buds of
promise nipped !   How often do these blossoms go up as dust!
How often are these hopes blasted by the selfish and degraded
vices of those whose position in society gives them facilities for

the seduction of the young !   How true is it that "one sinner destroyeth much good !"

The evil of which Mr. Jameson wrote with so much holy warmth and indignation, still exists to a fearful extent, entrapping once hopeful youth, disgracing families, degrading the people, shaming the churches, withering the hopes of ministers, and causing them to writhe with indignant scorn of those conscience-seared men who thus recklessly sport with the happiness and souls of their fellow-creatures.   When we look at these and other abominations, we cannot wonder that Jamaica has sunk, scathed and blasted with the lightnings of God's wrath ; we wonder not that families who once rolled in wealth, are now plunged into beggary ; that their properties are hopelessly embarrassed, and that useless bush rankly vegetates over thousands of acres which once were the scenes of a busy, but blood-stained industry.

CHAPTER VIII.

Painful controversy—Can a European Missionary depend solely on a negro church?—Reluctance of Preachers to engage in foreign service—Rebelling against discipline—Report of 1844—The African Mission—Clifton—Illness of Mr. M'Gilchrist—The Missionary sick—Last Goshen Report.

BETWEEN the years 1831 and 1843, a controversy arose in Jamaica respecting certain corrupt practices which were said to exist in the Baptist churches. I should be glad, could I see my way clear to pass over this matter in silence. I take as my own the words of the Rev. Mr. Hinton, in his " Life of the Rev. Mr. Knibb," on this very question :—" I should gladly have avoided all reference to it, had such a course been consistent with my duty as Knibb's biographer." And I can also say of Mr. Jameson, what he says of Mr. Knibb :—" The portion of his correspondence which refers to this dispute is too large, and the development of his character to which it gave rise is too important to allow me to overlook it."

The American Baptists (see page 34) " had the most obscure and limited notions of divine truth ; and their system was a compound of superstition and error. Being the first which they knew, and being so suited to their own superstitious notions, this system made a deep and lasting impression on the people," and numbers of them became these men's followers. Mr. Gibb's disciples numbered hundreds in St. Ann's, St. Mary's, and St. Thomas in the Vale. When these men died, the bulk of their followers joined the " White Baptists," through the influence of their leaders, and " because they liked the wash, that their sins might be washed away." The " White Baptists" adopted the leader system, thus made to their hands, and " plenty" of those whom Gibb had " set off to pray" (p. 34) became leaders as well as members in their churches.   These *nuclei* carried with them their old leaven of superstition, which could not be purged out easily or soon ; and it was alleged that the important work of preparing and certifying candidates for baptism was too much left to the leaders ; that many of them being wicked, and most of them ignorant, the leaders were worse than unfit for such a trust ; that they gave to their classes no instruction worthy to be called sound and religious, but required them to bring dreams, which were called their " work," " travel," or " experience ;" and that fitness for baptism was judged of by these dreams.   It was alleged that the ministers baptized numbers of people without any intimate personal knowledge of them, merely on the certification of the leaders that they were fit for the ordinance ; and that while they preached to the people in the mass, the discipline of their churches was mainly left in the leaders' hands.   This state of things, it was alleged, prevailed so much in the Baptist churches, that it became the duty of other Christian societies to remonstrate against it.

The first remonstrants were several Baptist ministers—the Rev. Messrs. Coultart, Whitehorne, Reid, and Kingdon.   The last three also broke up the leader system in their own churches, and were disowned by the Baptist Missionary Society.

This state of things also forced itself on the attention of missionaries of other denominations.   Mr. Jameson wrote :—" We came to know these things, not by prying into other churches, but by our people appealing to us for protection from a corrupt system, when its superstitions were spread out to allure them.   As we proceeded in denouncing this system among our own people, facts were laid before us, showing that it was daily practised in the leaders' meetings.   Our people live among the Baptists, and these things cannot be hid from them."   Mr. Jameson was too honourable and too upright to join in a senseless hue and cry against brethren who had incurred odium ; and whether right or wrong in his convictions, his motives were unquestionably pure.   He was concerned for the honour of his Divine Master and the true interests of religion among the negroes. His convictions were the result of a most patient and laborious investigation, and of six years of faithful missionary labour, during which he had followed the people to their homes, taught and catechised them in the most careful manner, and knew them as intimately as any missionary ever knew his people.

We quote a few of his remarks on this painful subject :—

"I am solemnly persuaded that in the Baptist churches there is a most pernicious system at work, which is perpetuating, instead of removing superstition, and which, while it swells their numbers, ruins their purity." "Evils, many and great, have arisen from employing an ill-instructed native agency. I refer you to the mass of evidence from almost every Christian body in the island, and from Baptist ministers of the highest respectability—evidence brought forward without collusion, and from the purest motives." "If the Baptist ministers will only look narrowly into the state of their churches, if they rigidly examine their people, separately, if possible, from the influence of the leaders, they will find the charges brought against the system fully substantiated." "Such being my deliberate conviction, it would be poor brotherhood indeed to the Baptist churches, to sit still any longer, and allow this system to pursue its secret and destructive course. It would be unpardonable cowardice, and conscience and the word of God forbid me, to be silent about these enormous evils. God forbid that I should be guilty of purchasing peace at a price so costly."

In Mr. Jameson's papers there is abundant proof of his charity towards the Baptist brethren. Neither he nor those with whom he acted, ever accused these brethren of abetting or approving the evils of which they complained. Mr. Whitehorne wrote :—"The minister can know nothing of the people, beyond what the leader thinks fit, nor can he discover from the people anything of the leader's character." While the practices of the leaders were concealed from the Baptist ministers, they were revealed to other ministers by their own people. The leaders knew that their ministers would have frowned upon them as sternly as any.   Other brethren complained that the Baptists knew so little about their people as to be unaware of these evils, and that instead of receiving thanks for offering help in sifting them to the bottom, they were treated as enemies.   Among other odious names, they were called " slanderers " and " filthy scavengers "—a title which, if their services were really needed, reflected less dishonour on them than on those churches which they sought to cleanse. The purity of these mission churches was dear to all genuine missionaries.

Mr. Knibb, a great and good man, ever to be mentioned with honour as one of the most courageous and generous champions of the down-trodden slave, came to England, and eloquently defended the Baptist churches, amid the plaudits of a crowded meeting in Exeter Hall.   But that was the last place to sift and settle such a question.   Writes Mr. Jameson :—" Mr. Knibb has been in London, denying in the most solemn manner that there is anything wrong in their leadership system, and denouncing as slanderers those who are of an opposite conviction."   " To whatever extent our motives may be impugned, or our characters misrepresented, yet truth, gospel purity, and the best interests of Jamaica demand faithfulness and sacrifice."   " Holding these views, I deeply regret that the majority of the Baptist missionaries have uniformly ascribed the testimony which has been borne to the existence of these evils, to the working of jealousy or envy." " The London Baptist Society has repudiated all evidence respecting the corruptions of the leader system, and has ascribed the testimony—bearing to the worst passions of the soul." " From the aspect which the present controversy has assumed at home and here, I object to the Baptist missionaries and their churches being made judges.   A Board which sat in Edinburgh upon this question, recommend an investigation in this country.   At such an investigation, I and my brethren will at once and gladly adduce the evidence which has led us to believe that serious abuses exist in the Baptist churches in this island."   " With reference to Mr. Cowan, I am sure, from my intimate knowledge of his character, that he has made no charge without having what he considers satisfactory evidence of its truth. I know that once and again he has brought the fact of particular abuses before individual Baptist ministers. And I may say for him, for myself, and for my brethren of the Presbytery, that the strenuous denial with which the charge of these abuses has been uniformly met, both here and at home, the excision of Mr. Whitehorne and his brethren for protesting against the evils of the leader system, and the extraordinary statements of Mr. Knibb during his late visit to England, made us feel that to be silent any longer on this question, would be to sacrifice truth, and to shield errors the most pernicious to the purity of the gospel, and to the best interests of the mission cause in Jamaica and Africa."

We must believe that these good men were persuaded, by what they thought sufficient evidence, that these evils existed. They were not *diaboloi*—malicious accusers—seeking to destroy the Lord's work, by blasting the reputation of his servants. We cannot believe that they had any *animus* against their brethren. It was not Christianly kind to accuse them of envying the popularity of these brethren, or of being irritated by disappointment, because the latter were followed by hundreds and thousands, while their own congregations were small. This explanation will, we are persuaded, satisfy no one who looks at the question in all its bearings, and has had sufficient data for a calm and deliberate judgment. With the convictions held by Mr. Jameson and his brethren, silence would have been treason to the best of causes. Their representations ought not to have been scorned, their motives ought not to have been maligned, and their characters ought to have been respected. They were honest and pious men, and their allegations should have been honestly examined. Had it been proved that they were misinformed, they would have been ready to allow it. But they could not be tranquillized by "the triumph of Mr. Knibb at Exeter Hall," because that triumph did not meet the merits of the case.

Some may blame me for awakening a dispute which had

better be allowed to sleep.　But I dared not pass it over, without being unfaithful to my duty as Mr. Jameson's biographer. If I sin, it is in the good company of Mr. Hinton, who, in his Life of Mr. Knibb, has shown no particular tenderness to those with whom the subject of this Memoir acted.　From the part which Mr. Jameson took in this matter his memory can receive nothing but lustre.　It cost him vast labour, and led him often to his knees.　That the controversy was necessary was not his fault. That he and others braced themselves to such a duty is all to their honour.　But Mr. Jameson cherished not a shade of sinful bitterness towards the brethren with whom he differed. He fought sternly with the evil, but could take the brethren tenderly to his heart.　And sure I am, that more good than harm has come of the controversy.　Some of those who contended sharply here on earth, have embraced one another yonder in heaven ; and the rest will, in due time, join the loving circle, where all will wonder at the Lord's patience with their respective errors and infirmities, and at His condescending use of their unworthy services in the Church below.　And I am equally sure that all evils will be, at length, rooted out of our mission churches, as the children of Ethiopia, guided onwards by light from heaven, cast off more and more the slough of old-time ignorance and superstition.　Most heartily do we say amen to the following words in which Mr. Jameson reviews this controversy :—

" I hope that this painful discussion will be of ultimate benefit to the Church and the mission field.　One thing we learn from it is, that a native agency ought to be employed with caution, narrowly watched in its operation, and trained for its work ; that, at first, it may be used to superintend, but, ere it be employed to teach, the agents themselves should be well instructed, and their minds freed from the trammels of their former superstitions."

With the views above expressed regarding the employment of a native agency, the following remarks are not at variance. He and his brethren were only anxious that the agents should be faithful men, and really able to instruct others.　With respect to Africa he asks :—" Will not the Synod undertake a mission there, and use the tools they have prepared in Jamaica? Why prepare tools, and not use them, especially when they are so much required? Why begin a mission in the South Seas, where all is new, and take no advantage of an instrumentality which they have prepared or are preparing—an instrumentality so well suited to Africa—a field of missionary labour no less necessitous? Will no presbytery or congregation make a commencement in Calabar? Surely some will be found to wipe off the reproach which is ever thrown upon us : 'You Scotch Presbyterians are slow in your movements, and always last in reaching the field.' I wish Goshen were at its manhood, and had broken its fetters,—then would you see me in the midst of you to plead the cause of Africa, to entreat you to turn your efforts to that melancholy land, and to make offer of my services as your missionary there. Some of my people wish to go, but I tell them that they must think well about it ; that it must be a matter, not of feeling, but of principle, not of excitement, but of calm deliberation and of earnest prayer. The hardships of the missionary life will soon cool down effervescent feeling ; and if there be no root in the agent, he will desert the cause, and yield himself to the vices of the surrounding heathen."

How true these views are every mission field can witness.

In 1844, J. H. Young, Esq., of Glasgow, visited Goshen. Anxious to promote the interests of the mission, he suggested that the people should offer to maintain their minister, provided the debt of £605 on their church were paid for them. The people agreed to this ; and, at first, Mr. Jameson himself acquiesced in the proposal. But, on due consideration, he changed his mind. He found that the greatest sum which the congregation could contribute, would be utterly inadequate to meet their expenses, and supply the mission family with the necessaries of life. He concluded, therefore, that it was not his duty to peril his own comfort and usefulness, run before Providence, and, like Peter, *ask* to be bidden walk on the water. At the same time, were his Master to call him, he should be dismayed at no difficulty, and shrink from no privation.

The Directors thought with their Missionary. At the same time, several friends who had lent £105 to Goshen, generously offered to make it a gift, if the people should raise the sum of £300 during the year. An effort to do so was made, but it came short of complete success.

There can be no doubt that Mr. Jameson's views were sound. When men go out as the messengers of the churches, these churches are in honour bound to maintain them at their post. And they must feel under their feet, firm and sure, the rock of home support, while the breath of home sympathy must come across their bosoms, to cheer and nerve them in doing the Lord's work among an alien people. If an African church were to invite a minister, and he were willing to cast himself upon their support, the case would be different. But the home church says : 'Who will go for us, as *our* missionaries, to preach among the heathen the unsearchable riches of Jesus Christ ?" If one of its ministers or preachers says, " Here am I, send me," and he is sent, wafted on the breath of prayer, and cheered by the warm sympathy of Christian hearts, a bond is thus formed between that missionary and the whole body whose missionary he is, as sacred and as binding as exists between any individual minister and his congregation. Missionaries, when honoured to raise up infant churches, have to teach and train them to perform all Christian duties. Among other things, they must teach them to cast their gifts into the treasury. And the parent church must not be impatient to get quit of the obligation to furnish the missionary with the means of living. Neither must the missionary be cast entirely upon the support of any properly mission church. We cannot conceive the possibility of a case where it would be proper to say to him that he must look for no more support from home, however short his people may come of giving him food and raiment. An apostle has before now suffered hardship from the neglect of duty on the part of Christians, and few modern missionaries have it in their power to weave or dig for their daily bread.

"To J. H. Young, Esq., Glasgow.

"*August 19th*, 1844.

"I must tender you my heartfelt thanks, and the deepest gratitude of my family also, for the great interest you take in our welfare and prosperity. And I am also requested to give you the best thanks of my Session and Congregation for your expressions of kindness to them, and especially for the munificent donation of £50 towards the funds of the church, for the present year, and the same amount for the year ensuing. I have seen much of God in the building of our church ; and in your coming here, and in our brief term of intercourse, I would remark not the least of God's mercies."

Writing to his brother Alexander, September 5th, 1844, he says :—

"I am glad to hear that A——— has been so safely brought through the dangers that lately encompassed her ; and that you both have to sing a new song of deliverance. Once in my case it was mingled with judgment, when I laid my first-born —the very image of myself—in the grave, on the day of his birth. On another occasion, it was clear sunshine without a cloud. But last of all, my hope and joy was herself removed, and I was left to pour out the strains of the sorrow-stricken heart, alone. Yet surely I have reason to say, that when brought low, the Lord helped me.

"We are moving on as usual. Mary and Robert Jarrit are busy with the school. I am there also when time and other engagements permit. Notwithstanding all our efforts among the young, both in church and school, while some are a comfort, there are others whose pride and perverseness threaten to distress us much. The hallowing impressions which arose out of emancipation are becoming more and more blunted, the farther we recede from the day of freedom, and the generation which knew not slavery, being now from twelve to sixteen years of age, is, as a whole, wild in the extreme. The old people, having been schooled in slavery, are docile. The young, who were not long enough under its yoke to be broken in, are in general proud and self-willed. Drunkenness and revelling, which were common in slavery, and which 'for a season' had disappeared, have revived with more violence than ever. At the midnight revel and dance, all sorts of evil are carried on. Some of our young people had gone to these scenes on the 1st of August last, and when called to the Session to be admonished, one of them very gravely told the elders that he would not be ruled by black men. I stood firm, and made the fellow sign a recantation ; then the Session considered his case along with that of others, and found that they all had been at the dance ; and they were separated from the church. Dancing is held at home to be a harmless amusement, and so, perhaps, to a certain extent, it is ; but it is not so here. It gathers the most filthy and disreputable characters ; and a professor of religion cannot be there without compromising his character, and associating in his amusements with the enemies of his Saviour."

On October 2d, 1844, he thanks the Directors for their kind assurance of entire confidence in him. "Indeed, your long-continued kindness to us, and the many substantial proofs of your Christian beneficence which have come, year after year, to cheer us in our work, have prevented us from ever for a moment calling in question the confidence you repose in us. Allow me, my dear friends, to reciprocate the assurance, and to say, that to enjoy your entire confidence I have daily striven, and do daily strive ; and, although I seek not honour from men, yet it is my aim, and it will be my joy, to be by you accounted faithful."

The following facts, extracted from the same letter, bearing upon the pecuniary means of the emancipated peasantry, are important :—

" It has been common to represent the negroes as being well paid and well off. This is true to a certain extent, but those who mingle most with them, who visit their dwellings, and are eye-witnesses of their sicknesses, their sores, and their hardships, know that they are not so well off as is said. For instance, when, in a case of distress, I advise a doctor to be called, the very common reply is, ' Minister, it is impossible ; we cannot pay his charges,'—which are from 16s. to 20s.

"The rate of wages is being considerably reduced. For instance, a piece of job-work which was done last year for £6, was done this year for £3. As freeholders have to pay taxes as well as school fees and medicines, it is manifest that they have enough to do. Their grounds supply them with yams and other vegetables. Without these they could not live. The value of a provision ground as a means of support, however, depends upon its extent, and upon the having facilities for carrying the produce, as well as the proximity of a good market."

Mr. Jameson neither advocated nor practised the "let alone" system. None of our Jamaica missionaries flinch from what, at home, is thought to be best left in the hands of intelligent Christian laymen. But he had the good sense to see that to press the people to give more, while they were getting less, might cause an unhealthy reaction, and do more ill than good.

On November 19th, 1844, he addressed Dr. M'Kerrow upon a subject on which he felt deeply, and wrote often, viz., the unwillingness of the preaching staff of the Church to engage in foreign service :—

" REV. AND DEAR SIR,—I have read with much pleasure your address to the probationers on the subject of missions. I hope the Lord will make it effectual in moving many, not only to consider their duty, but also to do it. It is affecting to see so many men of talent, learning, and piety, lying at home with scarcely half work, and in an over-stocked field, while millions, daily sinking into hell, are crying, ' Come over and help us ;' and while the Saviour, to whom the heathen are given as his inheritance, is asking his servants, ' Whom shall I send, and who will go for me ?' To such a question shall the servant reply, ' I have married a wife and cannot go,' or, ' I am entangled with matrimonial promises and preparations, and cannot go,' or, ' I am afraid my constitution will not stand the climate, and therefore I cannot go ?' Suppose such excuses were tendered to her Majesty's Government by any of her soldiers, under orders for a foreign station, how would they be treated ? What would the answer be ? ' Before you enlisted, was it not in

your power to take up any other calling ?   But since it has
pleased you to offer your services to your Monarch, it now becomes your sacred duty to comply with all the engagements of
her high service.   Two of these are the following :—1*st*, That
personal and domestic engagements, except in extreme cases,
must give way to the public good ; and 2*d*, In her Majesty's service there must be no cowards.'   These two principles were
also woven into the very constitution of the Christian Church
by its own King and Head, at the time of its first formation,
and cannot be violated without sin, and without damage to the
public cause.   This appears evident from Matthew x. 37-39.
The Master, in sending forth his disciples to preach the gospel, says,   ' He that loveth father or mother more than me, is
not worthy of me ; and he that loveth son or daughter more
than me, is not worthy of me : and he that taketh not his
cross, and followeth after me, is not worthy of me.   He that
findeth his life shall lose it ; and he that loseth his life for my
sake shall find it.'   Those who refuse compliance with the
orders of our King on the ground of health, or of constitution,
and in whose ears these things are constantly rung by friends
who grudge them to the Lord's foreign work, would do well seriously to consider also the preceding verses, from the 28th to
the 34th.   And then let them ask themselves whether, on a
mere idea or supposition, they are at liberty to set aside an
express command of their divine Master.   It was thundered in
my ears incessantly, that in going to Jamaica I was going to
my grave.   ' My constitution was not fitted for the climate.
I would not live many months, etc.'   Now, what is the fact ?
My advisers have all been mistaken ; and my blessed Master,
whose public cause I was enabled to prefer to every private
consideration, has blessed me in this distant land with the very
best of health, for the period of eight years.   Again, in Luke
xiv. 26, 27, the same principle—that of subordinating private
and domestic interests to the public good—is distinctly stated,
as an essential element in the kingdom of Christ.   Now, those
who have devoted themselves to the service of Him whose commission is, ' Go ye into all the world, and preach the gospel to

every creature ;' and who have encompassed themselves with entanglements of various kinds, so that, on the ground of these, they seek to be excused from going to any other field of service than that which suits their entangled circumstances, should consider this passage with its context, beginning at the 18th verse. In these remarks, I refer to those whose place in the vineyard Providence has not yet pointed out. Hence, I direct the attention of those who purpose devoting themselves to the service of Zion's King, to this same chapter, and especially from the 26th to the 34th verse. Let them consider whether it be right for the man who offers himself to the work of Him whose field of operation is the world, so to encumber himself, while a student, that, when called to the service of his Lord, he will feel himself shut up to say : ' My Master must take my services at home, or want them altogether : because, for such and such reasons, I cannot go beyond the boundaries of my native country.'

" I hope that I shall not be considered presumptuous while I thus speak. I feel that I am exposing myself to this charge ; but God is my witness, and to his bar I appeal. I speak of brethren in all respects far better than myself. Still they are brethren, and with myself, the servants of the Church's great and glorious Head. My lot is cast in the mission field, where I desire to spend and be spent. Around us death has been doing its work, and one labourer after another has been removed ; and one infant missionary church after another has been suddenly reduced to destitution. Year after year has rolled past, and numerous appeals have been made on behalf of those desolate portions of God's heritage, but all has hitherto proved unavailing. Hopes have been excited, but they have as often been disappointed ; and now those infant churches, gathered out from a darkness even worse than that of heathenism, languish under the heart-sickness of hope long deferred. All this is taking place, while in the mother church the supply is considerably ahead of the demand ; and while not a few could be spared to the mission field, if the parties themselves were only disposed to follow the Saviour in the regeneration of a lost world. 'Ye,' said the Saviour to his disciples, 'are the salt of the earth,' and this expressly with reference to that gospel which they were commissioned to carry to all nations. Now, if we, intrusted with interests so vast and important, shall make our public commission bend to our personal convenience,—shall hear the cry from the heathen as if we heard it not,—and shall prefer the easy, and comparatively indolent work of supplying vacancies, to the toils and perils of the mission field, then, let us examine ourselves, lest we be as the salt which has lost its savour, and is henceforth good for nothing but to be cast out and trodden under feet of men."

These are weighty considerations, and they are well put in these earnest and impressive sentences. It should be difficult for the unemployed preaching staff of our British churches to sit easy under reasoning and expostulation like the above. Would to God that we could lay them, written in characters of fire, before every probationer and every student, and fix his attention on them, till he were forced to take the matter into the court of conscience, and the presence of the Master, and have it well settled that it is his individual duty to stay at home here, waiting his chance of a vacancy in some little corner, surrounded by steeples and echoing with the sound of the church-going bell, while yonder, waste on waste lies in the grim silence of death, and the name of Jesus is unheard ! Let it be known that a missionary must count upon having to endure hardness. He goes alone and unarmed, among selfish and covetous barbarians, who may regard him as a lawful prey. If he is a father, he will have to leave his children in their tender years behind him, and the pang of this separation may be second only to their death or dishonour. He may be exposed to malaria, and frequent and consuming sickness. But none of these things must move him. It has been the duty of some of the Lord's people to face death for his sake, and it is the duty of some of them, at the present day, to make the sacrifices that are necessary in establishing his kingdom in every land. The true spirit of Christian missionary enterprise, however, is an inspiration from above ; and it is better to send a handful who have it, than a host who have it not, or who, from their want of love, and prudence, and faith, may hinder, rather than help on the cause.

Of date January 13th, 1845, is the report of the station for 1844, written with his usual fluency, and showing the same entire consecration to the Master's work, and the same warm zeal for its progress, in the growing holiness and numbers of the church. All Mr. Jameson's reports breathe of piety and devotion ; and ever, amidst the details common in such documents, he breaks forth into expressions of joy or gratitude, or earnest longings for success.

" In reviewing the past year, I hope I can say that the blessed work has been making progress. . . . By means of domiciliary visits, some have been brought out, who were living without God and without hope in the world ; while others who were walking in the abominations of the country, have been induced to marry, and to rank themselves among the fol- lowers of the Lamb.

" During the year, divine service has been regularly enjoyed by the congregation. When supplying for Mr. Cowan at Carron Hall, on the first Sabbath of every month, my place was taken by Mr. William Millar, who expounded a chapter of God's word, and read a sermon out of some approved book ; and I feel true pleasure in stating that these services were very acceptable to the people. In my visits among them, they have referred, once and again, to the words which he addressed to them.

" The district prayer-meetings, ten in number, and held two or three times a week, have been in constant operation. In certain quarters, I found that there was a meeting held on the Sabbath morning, before day, for special prayer, the reading of the Bible, and the revising of the hymns, and questions, and passages of Scripture, which form the exercises of the public class. These meetings break up at sunrise, when all go home, and prepare for the house of God, to which they come at nine o'clock. I was much delighted, encouraged, and comforted, by the discovery of such meetings, yea, a thousand times more than if they had been begun at my suggestion. The fearers of the Lord spake, and they still speak, often one to another, and the Lord hearkens and hears, and of them he says : 'They shall be mine in the day when I make up my jewels.' Blessed day ! when long-parted friends shall meet again, and when the redeemed family shall meet with Him who bought them with His blood. The monthly prayer-meetings in the church have also been regularly kept up. At these, two persons, an elder and a member, usually officiate ; on which occasions, more than at any other time, I think I see the spiritual profiting of the people. It is delightful to hear with what appropriateness some of them use, at the throne of grace, the hymns and verses of the Bible which they learn, and to notice the unction, the earnestness, and point of their prayers. The Lord's Supper has been enjoyed among us, on the last Sabbath of every second month, the day on which dear friends in Rose Street were also sitting around the same festive board. The mutual mingling of our prayers and of all our religious exercises, and their ascending together to the throne of the everlasting Father, supply to the heart thoughts which tend to quicken, strengthen, and comfort.

"During the past season, I have visited the congregation twice, and many parts more frequently. In the course of these visits I have enjoyed much delightful intercourse with the people, by which my soul has been refreshed, and theirs, I trust, edified and also refreshed. At the same time, I have met with persons of a very different description, and have had to look on scenes of a mingled character, some painful in the extreme, some revolting and disgusting, and others ludicrous. But through these visits, I hope, good has been, and is being done. Such is a brief summary of the year's operations. But it is time to bring before you the report of the school.

"The number upon the school-list during the year has been 124 ; the average attendance from 70 to 100. I feel much pleasure in stating that the children have made satisfactory progress in the different branches of education. They appear happy at school ; and, some weeks ago, when I desired them to say when the Christmas holidays should begin, I was quite taken aback by their choosing just the week before Christmas. I asked them if they would not have it two weeks before Christmas. Forty or fifty little things cried out : 'No, we want to come to school.' The older children, however, came forward and stated that they wished to work to get a little money before Christmas. Feeling that the vacation was as necessary for the teachers as for the scholars, I held to the point previously fixed upon, and dismissed the school for a term of four weeks, amidst, I believe, the regret of teachers as well as scholars, all parties being more disposed to remain than go.

"Saturday last brought the long-looked-for box to Goshen, containing the school-books,—Mr. Whyte's[1] precious gift. The sight of his fine paper and pens induced me to sit down and re-write this report."

On March 7th, 1845, Mr. Jameson expressed his pleasure at seeing an old friend, a Methven man, George Cunningham, Esq., who went to Jamaica in quest of health. "He was so much improved during the voyage, that, although he had to be carried on board ship, he has just completed an overland journey, under a tropical sun, without pain, and with no other discomfort than a little fatigue."

In this letter he rejoices over the arrival of the Rev. Messrs. Hogg and Main, who have been spared to this day, and still labour in the most interesting circumstances. "It is cheering," he says, "to receive such a reinforcement. Manchester will once more be well supplied. I hope that God will carry on His work there, and increase the results yet more and more. May those who have come, be long spared in life, and health, and strength !"

On March 17th, 1845, writing to Dr. M'Kerrow, he details his efforts to meet the wants of the Mile-End district, and deprecates the forming of a too high estimate of the piety and general advancement of the people. His views on this latter point were most correct and judicious. "Action and reaction are equal, and in opposite directions." And the African mind

---

[1] Mr Andrew Whyte of Edinburgh, a generous friend of Goshen.

having been repressed, controlled, and bent by slavery, has a tendency to recoil from the extreme of cringing subserviency, to that of unreasonable self-esteem and contempt of all right and due obedience to superior authority.

"Clifton is situated about two miles from Bonham Spring, and six or seven from Goshen. It is in the neighbourhood of a number of families belonging to Goshen church, who are prevented, by the distance, from attending divine ordinances regularly, and whose children, for the same reason, can derive no benefit whatever from the school. These families are the oldest Presbyterians in the quarter; they were, at first, connected with Port Maria, and through them the station at Goshen was begun. They have once and again been disappointed, in not receiving that pastoral superintendence which they expected. Still they have continued stedfast to the cause, and take a deep interest in its prosperity. One or two of the young people were taught at Mr. Millar's academy; and all availed themselves of the Sabbath instructions which were enjoyed during Mr. Millar's residence at Bonham Spring. On his removal to Montego Bay, I was unable fully to supply the district. In the meantime, Mr. Thomson came, and, not succeeding in obtaining Bonham Spring house for our purposes, I procured Clifton, which is equally central and healthy. Although we were first in the field, we have been the last in getting a settlement. In consequence of this, hundreds whom I have taught, now tell me when I meet them, that they have joined the Baptists, or Wesleyans, or Church of England. The design of our present operations is not to bring back those that have left us : for this I have no desire to do ; but to benefit those who have adhered to us through good report and bad report ; and to endeavour to bring in those who are still standing afar off, by seeking to do good to them and their children."

Mr. Thomson's health failed ; but Mr. Jameson kept the Clifton school agoing during the season, until the lease of the premises expired. The Wesleyan Methodists, who have laboured in Jamaica with their characteristic energy, afterwards built a chapel in the district which Mr. Jameson thus earnestly sought to cultivate. There are very few in that neighbourhood now connected with Goshen. But the labours of Mr. Jameson, and the man himself, are fresh in the memories and hearts of all there. And whenever the Goshen minister pays a visit to Mile-End, he is sure of a lively and interested audience.

The following is an address to his people, on being absent on Sabbath, April 20th, at Clifton, where he went to intimate the cessation of Mr. Thomson's labours :—

"In consequence of the illness of Mr. Thomson, and the necessity, on this account, of giving up, for a time, the station where he was employed, I deem it my duty to leave you, for the purpose of visiting the friends there, to lay before them the painful tidings. Our mutual friend, Mr. Millar, has kindly promised to be with you, to read and explain God's most blessed word. I hope you will listen with attention and interest ; and I pray God, in his infinite mercy, to bless the truth to the souls of you all. 'Hear, saith the Lord, and your souls shall live.' 'Say not of the Sabbath, It is a weariness ; but esteem it the holy of the Lord, and honourable ; and honour Him and His Sabbath, by not thinking your own thoughts, or speaking your own words, or doing your own actions.' In God's house, and out of it, let quietness and solemnity mark your whole conduct.

"In your prayers, remember that portion of our church family at Clifton, whose hearts will be filled with sorrow at the tidings which I have to bear to them. Pray the Lord to restore to health his young servant who was labouring there, and to fit him for many days of usefulness.

"What need you have to improve your Christian privileges, lest the forbearance of God come to an end, and He remove your candlestick out of its place ! Then you will lament and say, 'The harvest is past, and the summer is ended, and we are not saved.'

"Pray, also, the Lord to prepare you by his Holy Spirit, for drawing to his holy table next Sabbath. See that you are in love one with another. 'He that dwelleth in love, dwelleth in

God, and God in him.'   Examine your own selves, and know your own selves, how that Jesus Christ is in you except ye be reprobates.   Purge out the old leaven—the leaven of malice and wickedness.   Crucify the flesh with its affections and lusts; and be ready to meet with the Lord at his table, and to give yourselves wholly to him.

"Let those who are not members of the Church of Christ—who have been sitting at ease, and allowing precious opportunities to pass away unimproved, consider what they will say to Christ, when he examines into their misimprovement of the means of salvation.   Oh, thoughtless hearers of the gospel! what will you say? what *can* you say?   You must stand condemned: speechless must you stand.   Be wise, therefore, before the day of mercy pass away for ever.   Seek, at once, the salvation of your precious souls.   Break off your sins which are so fatally entangling you.   Turn to the Lord, and join yourselves to the company of his people."

The following remarks are a specimen of the manner in which Jamaica missionaries deal with their people, in endeavouring to train them in the duty of giving to the Lord :—

"On Thursday evening, there will be a meeting for prayer. I hope that many will attend to cry to the Lord for his presence at his table on Sabbath, and in behalf of the heathen world. Same evening, I will read over the names of those who have paid their subscriptions, and the amount paid by each.   I hope none of you are putting off the payment to the end of the year. Come, at once.   Why delay in the Lord's work?   You may be dead long before August; and will you appear before your Judge for your crown, while you have slipped away, having neither fed the hungry, nor clothed the naked in his Church, nor done anything at all to aid the Church in her necessities?   Why should the Lord's professing people keep the Lord and his Church standing, month after month, outside their door, while they are serving themselves and the world first, and then come up, at the very last hour, when the long year is just expiring, with only the third, or the half, of their offering, and, with a sorrowful countenance, saying, 'I have no more, and can get ho more ?' Good reason why ! You have taken the Lord's portion—the portion which He gave you for his church—and you have mixed it up with your own worldly portion, and spent it all during the course of the year. He towards whom you act thus deceitfully, is God and not man, and to you he saith : ' Be not deceived ; God is not mocked ; whatsoever a man soweth, that shall he also reap. He that soweth to the flesh, shall of the flesh reap corruption ; he that soweth to the Spirit, shall of the Spirit reap life everlasting.' "

Writing to Mr. M'Gilchrist, September 17th, 1845, he announces his determination to send home his sister and daughter, as this step seemed necessary for the health and education of the latter. Alluding to a scheme for the following year (1846), he says :—"This measure would require my presence in the congregation ; and such indeed is the pressure of evil upon the church from the world without,—a pressure which, alas ! is causing many to fall,—that every missionary should be at his post, unless he has strong reasons for leaving it. While I thus write, I do not think that there is any cause for being alarmed at the present state of things. The church is just casting off her bad humours, and this will, in the end, promote her health and peace. . . . I rejoice in the hearty response of the church to the call from Africa. I hope that the painful discussions in the Synod have been brought to an end, and that past differences will now be lost in the union of love and zeal, in executing the great commission of our Lord, ' Go and teach all nations.' "

In the latter part of this year, Mr. Jameson was prostrated by a severe illness, which kept him from his loved employ about three months. Who can doubt that it was to him a season of great spiritual improvement, and had a bearing on his call to Africa, and his removal to heaven about two years afterwards ? Severe discipline not unfrequently precedes a new demand on the zeal and faith of the Christian. Thus, the bonds that tie him to earth are weakened, and he is the readier to gird up his loins, and grasp the pilgrim's staff or the warrior's sword, as the work and the service may require.

The intelligence of an event which affected the people of God with sorrow and sympathy, reached Mr. Jameson in the latter part of this year. To Mr. M'Gilchrist he had conceived a most devoted attachment, which was not less warmly reciprocated on the part of that honoured and devoted servant of the Lord. The men were formed to be brothers, from their geniality and congeniality of temper and character. The esteemed pastor was in the van of the philanthropic and Christian movements of his most exemplary people. The stroke which deprived them of his ministrations, and plunged his family into mourning, was also felt in Jamaica, and the following letter which Mr. Jameson wrote, November 4th, to Mrs. M'Gilchrist, testifies of his warm affection for his " brother beloved :"—

" MY VERY DEAR SISTER,—The present packet has brought us a letter from our sister in Perth, detailing the circumstances connected with the deeply distressing and mysterious affliction of your beloved husband, and of my beloved friend and father. A report of this sad calamity reached us, by the last packet, but it was of such a nature that, while it raised . our fears to the highest pitch, it yet left us in ignorance of all the circumstances ; and we were waiting for the present packet with an anxiety, the intensity of which I am unable to describe. I often tried to pray for that dear friend, towards whom I cherish all the affection of a son, but I felt all uncertainty, and wished that I had wings like a dove, that I might fly far hence, and see, and know, and be at rest. Jeanie's letter, which we have just received, has brought before us those sad scenes which have been passing in your happy family ; and, while it has delivered us, in some measure, from the pain of uncertainty, it has overwhelmed us with the account it gives us of the state of our dear friend. I feel thankful to the God of all mercy, however, that his life is continued, and that there are symptoms of improvement. Would to God that his useful life may be spared for your sake, my dear sister, for the sake of the dear children, for the sake of the devoted people who are attached to his ministry, for our sakes in this distant corner of the vineyard, and for the sake of the Lord's cause generally !   Humanly speaking, his is a life which we can ill spare.   For myself, I feel as if I cannot want him at all, and hundreds feel as I do.

" My dear sister, I hasten to say how deeply we all sympathize with your dear husband, with you and your family, and with the congregation.   I may say for every praying individual and family in Goshen church, that we cease not, day or night, to make mention of you all, and of your great affliction, in our prayers.   We entreat the Lord of life to lengthen the days of his servant, and to restore to its vigour a life so useful.   We entreat the God of all grace to bear you up under this heavy stroke, and to make all consolation to abound toward you.

" God will do what is right with our dear friend ; and we may rest assured that this is just what is best for him, best for you and the dear children, best for the congregation, and best for us all.   True, we may not at present see this.   These harrowing scenes fill the eye, and rend the heart.   By them the eye of faith may be dimmed ; and the child of God, cowering under the pelting tempest, may feel as if all these things were against him.   When the heavens are pouring out their floods, the lightning flashing through the sky, the thunder disturbing its peaceful bosom, and the tempest rending the lofty oaks, and stripping the forests of their leafy shade ; the poor traveller, with a sinking heart, says to himself, ' What good is there in all this ?'   In a few days, the parched ground is covered with its green mantle, and all nature seems to put forth new strength.   So, my dear friend, wait and see the salvation of God.   A little time will show that all is well, that this dark cloud is full of mercy, and that it comes at the bidding of that God, who has encompassed your path hitherto with so many blessings.   In the hands of God, our merciful High Priest, would I leave our dear afflicted friend, feeling assured that he will do all things well with him.   And upon the same kind and gracious care I also cast you.   I trust that every consolation may abound toward you, and that our God may supply all your need.   I also hope that the Blessed

Shepherd will himself look after the flock, for the purpose of sanctifying to them this very trying dispensation, and of maintaining among them all the ordinances of the blessed gospel. And I do fondly hope that our dear friend will soon be raised up to break again the bread of life."

The Secession students attending the University of Edinburgh, had formed themselves into a Missionary Society. They were wont, at that time, to meet in the Session-house of Rose Street Church. In April, 1845, they wrote to Mr. Jameson a friendly letter; and the following are a few passages from his reply:—

"*Dec.* 18*th*, 1845.—Your interesting and to me delightful letter of 5th April last, reached me about June, and refreshed and cheered me very much indeed. The spirit which it breathes, and the means which it shows to be in operation for awakening and increasing missionary zeal among you, who, if spared, will be the heralds of mercy in future years, cannot fail to excite devout gratitude and joy in every pious heart.

"My dear friends, I rejoice to aid in furthering your important design. Being the Lord's servant, I am the servant of his Church, and I am only doing my duty in complying with your request.

"I know how real an interest is felt in our work here by dear friends in the distant land. And for that interest I desire to be ever grateful, and to do nothing unworthy of it. But all we can say about our labours is that we desire to be faithful. But, alas, how imperfect and feeble are our efforts, and how infinitely far short do we come in all our attempts to promote the Divine glory ! We are most unprofitable servants ; and if God makes us instruments of mercy to any, to Him—to Him alone—be all the praise and glory !

"In casting our eye over Jamaica, we see parish churches and missionary churches, and school-houses ; we see large congregations and well-filled schools. But let us not suppose that the land is Christian, because it bears the name. The apparatus which God has promised to bless has been set up, but it does not act like a steam-engine. Look at the corn field over which the sower plods his weary way. Watch his silent, but laborious work. Look at the slow and peaceful growth of the seed. Now, it lies in the bosom of the soil. Now, its verdant leaf covers the naked clod. Now, its growth is accelerated by the genial mildness of spring, and again, it is hindered, and even threatened with destruction, by the cold winds, the scorching sun, or the heavy rains. At length, harvest comes, and barns are full. So will it be with the word of God in Jamaica, and every other where. Here, dear brethren, the seed is being sown; it is growing in many fields; but harvest-day is still far off. And many, many, unfriendly blasts are sweeping over us. But those who have root in themselves, from being the subjects of the Holy Spirit's saving operation, are still standing, and will be the joy of the Redeemer's soul, and our crown of rejoicing.

" Jamaica claims the continued care of the parent church, not only for her own sake, but for the sake of Africa. For a while, our people may be encouraged to give themselves to the work of God there, under the care of the ministers with whom they are acquainted. Thus, you will have to fill our places, while we, from time to time, lead forth bands of Ethiopia's children to their fatherland.

" One thing more would I say to you. Having enlisted in Christ's work, be soldiers indeed. The territory of our King is the wide, wide world. Say not, you will go here, or you will go there; you will not go to this place or that, but to the other. Dear brethren, say not so. But as the eye of the servant is towards his master, yea, as the whole British army is at its Monarch's beck, ready without a murmur to go to the utmost bounds of her vast dominions, upon the shortest notice; yea, to penetrate into the heart of the enemy's country, to vindicate her honour, and establish her throne, so, as soldiers of the cross, say ye to your Master, ' Here are we ! Send us where thou hast most need of us.' Now, avoid those entanglements which, in after-life, and when the day of active service comes, will leave you no liberty, and which will make it necessary for the Church either to take your service at home, or not at all."

The following are extracts from the last report which Mr. Jameson sent to Rose Street :—

"The attendance upon divine ordinances is much the same as was stated in my last report. In good weather, it has been regular, and although numbers be not flocking into the house of the Lord, but the reverse, still those who are in it, are making progress in solid attainment. And I have reason to bless the God of all grace for the steadiness and faith of many. I am sorry, however, to report that the past season has witnessed a greater amount of backsliding than I ever remember to have taken place in the congregation, in the course of a year.

"What shall we say to these things? While the love of many is waxing cold, while those who had a fair profession, are turning back to the sins of the world, while the young are giving their hearts to know madness and folly, and while men of rank, education, and influence, are lowering themselves by becoming seducers, shall we suppose that these are all symptoms of a dying cause? No, verily! The opposite is the fact. The devil finds that his kingdom is menaced : and he cannot rest. The wickedness of the wicked cannot be any longer concealed amidst those dark clouds of ignorance which, in former years, enveloped this country, and, therefore, it lays itself out to secure, as far as possible, the countenance of the Church to its works of darkness, by enticing her children to follow polluted pleasures.

"But He who is for us, is greater than all who are against us ; and He will assuredly cause Zion's righteousness to go forth as brightness, and her salvation as a lamp that burneth. When we look at our churches, and see the many who are walking consistently with the truth, what reason have we to rejoice and bless God! It is ours to sow the seed, and it is God's to bless the seed sown. The greater part of our old scholars are now away, busy at work, and have been so, during the last season ; thus furnishing a complete refutation of the charge brought against the missionaries, that their schools were making the young people lazy. It has turned out here as at home. The children come to the school, until they are able to read and write a little. Then, when farther advanced, they work part of their time, and attend school another part. And, at last, they retire altogether. Three young men are about to go to Montego Bay to the Academy. They have got on a considerable way with their learning, and they wish to be teachers. Through the kindness and liberality of our friend Mr. Gibb, I am enabled to further their desire. I fondly hope that these young lads will be blessed by God, and made a blessing.

"I am very desirous of having my dwelling-house removed to the church. We should there be in the midst of our people, and could secure a meeting, at any time. Besides, I should avoid those night exposures, which I feel are telling upon me. You may ask why I did not see all these advantages before now. I saw them, but, somehow, the way of obtaining them did not occur to my mind until lately. I built the church larger considerably than the congregation requires, in expectation that, by my visits and invitations, the large population who were sitting at ease, might be induced to come in. But in this, to a certain extent, I have miscalculated. For, at the present time, the general population is drawing off from, rather than drawing near to, religion. And to those who are desirous of having a connexion with religion, and of enjoying its ordinances and its sacraments, with little trouble and pecuniary outlay, and with little or no sacrifice of worldly indulgence, our Erastian Establishment affords every facility. This feature of the present time will live out its day. It has come, and it will go. But it will take its time. And a season will follow, in which the fruits of present toil and of present prayers will appear. Let us wait patiently for it, and by persevering labour do all, under God, to bring it about. Then we shall gather strength, and when the church requires that portion of the building which is now intended for the minister's residence, she will be able to erect a dwelling for the one which she takes away.

"I must now lay before you a view of our pecuniary contributions. But here, I am afraid, you will think that we come far below the mark which you set for us. I have done what I could do with propriety, in order to raise the sum to the highest possible mark. But I find, this year, that a pressure on one point is in danger of causing a relaxing in another. I have been well sustained by a number of the congregation, who are always willing. I have endeavoured, by private exhortation, as well as from the pulpit, to stimulate those who are backward, and whilst, in some cases, I have been successful, yet in others, feelings have been awakened which have led some to absent themselves from the Lord's table, and others to keep away from the church. I am more and more satisfied that this pecuniary contribution is not a thing which we can drive. Unless the Lord open the heart, we cannot expect an open hand. There have been some encouraging instances of activity and faithfulness, especially among the old and the children. Some have a ground, the produce of which they devote to the church. Others have taken pieces of work, the profits of which they allot to the church. One little girl at school, nine years of age, sewed a shirt, for which she received two shillings, which she gave as her subscription. Another little girl, about the same age, raised from her ground the same amount, and she also brought it, and put it into my hand. A few among our adult youth have been exemplary. But the greater number appear, at present, to be laying out the most of their earnings in dress and folly. I have frequently urged upon them and their parents the consequence of this, in a coming age, when the present generation of church members shall have passed away. One affecting instance of the debasing love of money I cannot refrain from narrating. It is of a woman, whose master generously returned to her, as he did to all his other slaves, the compensation-money which fell to himself. The individual referred to received as her share two hundred dollars, or £40, and her children as much. During 1845, she has been paid £30 of the amount. Her subscription not appearing, I told her that she for one could not plead poverty. At last, out of the hundred and fifty dollars which she had just received, she gave one dollar. I thought of returning it, but wait to see what effect the word of God which I spoke, may have upon her. In a word, as we have not the intelligence nor the church machinery of home, we cannot expect that uni-form consistency among our members, nor those vigorous and well-sustained efforts, which mark the high attainments of the parent church. You cannot judge us by the figure of the four living creatures which are before the throne. You must take a lowlier figure, that of the parent bird teaching her newly-fledged young to fly. She sits upon the topmost branch, invit-ing and entreating, promising and reproving. Some are moved by her persuasion, and make a willing effort to reach the point where the mother sits, but when half-way, they plunge, they flutter, and come far short. Some are too timid to try ; while others, in a sulky mood, look as if they saw not, and listen as if they heard not. So is it here. Our best people are willing, although unable, to do what they desire. Others have the means, but want the heart. And, in such cases, we find that we can do no more than hold to their eyes the torch of truth, and looking upwards, cry aloud,—' Come from the four winds, O breath ! breathe on these slain, and they shall live.' "

In giving the statistics, Mr. Jameson mentions that, up to the end of 1845, he had admitted 192 persons into the church ; and that of these, thirty-six had died, or been excommunicated, while eleven were under suspension for carelessness and folly. "With reference to myself, I am waiting to know the mind and will of God respecting the disposal of my future service. Although I expect not a voice from heaven, yet I feel assured that God will give such intimations of his pleasure as to put beyond a doubt the path in which I have to go. And if this be to leave Goshen, and to go to the dreary moral wastes of Africa, I am ready, as soon as I see another here, to bring my family home, and to make arrangements for departing thence. I feel that some more of us must embark in this great and im-portant work, towards which the Secession Church has acted in a manner so godlike ; and what is there to hinder me, more than another, if my Master call ? "

It will interest the reader to hear from Miss Jameson of the affection which the people showed during the missionary's illness. "Never can I forget their affectionate care during William's fever. They would not allow me to buy either chickens or yams, but, every day, they supplied us with both. When thanking them, many of them would say : 'No, my Missis, it is our duty to do so. When minister well, and we sick, him visit we, him bring physic, him comfort we from the good word. Him never give we up. Now, when him sick, we love to carry thing for him comfort. We pray God to bring him round. Mind minister good, Missis, and we will bring chicken and yam till it please God to make him better.' Their grief at hearing of Mr. M'Gilchrist's sore sickness was very great. Many of them came to William, weeping, and saying : 'Oh, minister, we sorry very much to hear that we father over the water be sick. We heart bitter for him, and we pray God to spare him good life, and make him quite strong again.' "

CHAPTER IX.

The Mission to Old Calabar—Mr. Jameson called to join it—Accepts the call—
Appeals to the preachers—Finds a substitute—Farewell to Goshen—At home—
Ordination of Rev. John Campbell.

WE now come to the last and short period of Mr. Jameson's
life, which was spent in thoughts about, and in preparation for,
his work in Africa, which, alas! proved so short. Would that
it had been longer! Would that he were even now in the field
there! But the Lord is on high. He hath the residue of the
Spirit, and can make many such labourers to arise and go forth
to his own help against the mighty.

In marking out the future course of such a missionary as Mr.
Jameson, we should have pictured him grown to a good old
age among the people whose spiritual father he had been; leading on his flock from one step of Christian progress to another;
with a new generation rising up around him, whom he had
trained from infancy, looking on him with all the affection and
reverence which such a character and such a ministry were
fitted to inspire. But another lot was appointed him. A new
call was addressed to him; and, in spite of the attractions
binding him to Goshen, believing that he heard his Master's
voice saying, This is the way, walk thou in it, his ardent mind
at once embraced the call; and he started off on what he
hoped would be a long career of usefulness in deeply degraded
Africa.

The origin of the mission to Old Calabar, in the Bight of
Biafra, has been noticed in the course of this Memoir. In the
words of Dr. Somerville, "Just as the woman of Samaria,
when she found Christ, and had her heart opened by the touch

of divine mercy, felt an instantaneous desire to bring her countrymen to the Saviour, so the feelings of the negro converts in Jamaica went out strongly to their fatherland ; and the cry became almost universal, We must send the gospel to Africa."

And this was a satisfactory evidence that the work of God among the freedmen of Jamaica was, so far, genuine. In answer to this desire on the part of the people, the missionaries of the Baptist denomination sent out a mission to the island of Fernando Po, and to Bimbia and Kameroons, on the opposite mainland. And we have seen that eight brethren, assembled in Presbytery at Goshen in July, 1841, borne along by the feelings of the people, and resolved to take measures to embody them in action, solemnly devoted themselves to God, each of them engaging, if the choice fell on him, to go forth as pioneer, or leader of the " forlorn hope " in any part of Africa to which the Spirit of the Lord should call them.

We have seen that the nature of this movement was, at first, somewhat misunderstood at home, being considered as premature, while the churches in Jamaica were still, to so great an extent, dependent on the bounty of the home churches, and while some of them had heavy building engagements on hand, or buildings encumbered with debt. It was thought to be both prudent and dutiful that they should strive to do more to maintain their own ministers, rather than divide their efforts by a bootless attempt to begin a mission in Africa—an undertaking beyond their infant strength. This misunderstanding, however, was soon corrected. The Jamaica brethren explained that they and their people desired only to be agents and aiders of the home church, if the home church should undertake this new mission. They could furnish one or more brethren accustomed to missionary labour among Ethiopians, and inured to the tropics, as well as assistants of African descent ; they could be regarded as a normal school for an African mission, which they and their people yearned to see in operation.

The next step was to look out for a field of labour on the West Coast of Africa. The Rev. George Blyth went to Liver-

The Old Calabar River from Old Town; Duke Town on the left, with Mission Premises on the hill above.

pool to make inquiry at persons employed in the African trade. And Providence led to the selection of the Efik or Old Calabar people, who occupy a territory on one of the most navigable rivers on the coast of Africa. The chiefs of the Efik people sent them an invitation to come ; the Synod sanctioned the adoption of the new enterprise ; and then the Jamaica brethren proceeded to select fit agents.

The Rev. Hope Masterton Waddell was unanimously chosen by his brethren as the person, who, in their estimation, was the best qualified to conduct the first band. Mr. Edgerly was appointed to accompany him, along with Andrew Chisholm, a carpenter, and Edward Miller—the last two, natives of Jamaica. Mr. Waddell spent some time at home, visiting many places, explaining the nature, objects, and prospects of the enterprise. The Lord greatly prospered his labours and the labours of others. The utmost interest was felt by the people of God everywhere ; and the means necessary for the work were readily furnished by a willing people, devoted to the honour of their exalted King, and full of compassion for the desolate and friendless children of Ham among the rivers of Ethiopia.

Mr. Jameson, as one of the consecrated eight, had contemplated the possibility of being called upon to redeem his pledge. In a letter to Mr. William Bryden, he wrote :—" The question of Africa is exciting deep interest among us. . . . . Perhaps I may be called upon to plough the rugged soil of Africa, and another may water the vineyard here. I desire to have no will of my own in the matter. Lord, show me *what* Thou wilt, *where* Thou wilt, and *when* Thou wilt." But the call came sooner than he had anticipated ; and he was required to arise and depart sooner than, in any case, he had resolved to move.

The following sentences of a letter addressed to the President and Directors of the Rose Street Missionary Society, 26th December, 1845, will be read with interest. Rev. Dr. Somerville writes :—" There is none who peruses it, breathing as it does such deep, fervent, and believing zeal, that will hesitate to acknowledge that Mr. Jameson is just the man who is fitted to be a fellow-labourer in Africa, with our ardent and devoted Waddell."

Mr. Waddell had written to Mr. Jameson (31st October, 1845), asking him to make every effort to prepare a few more native agents, and to be ready to go at their head to Africa, in the following year. "This view of the subject," says Mr. Jameson, "had not as yet been before my mind. I felt as my brethren feel, a deep interest in the all-important work. I felt that the vows of God with reference to Africa, should I ever be needed there, were upon me ; and I thought it possible that, some time or other, I might be called upon by my Divine Master to arise and go thither. But anything like this immediate movement I was not contemplating. When Mr. Waddell's letter came, I saw that there was a speciality in it which I could not feel easy in passing over in silence. I then wrote to Mr. Blyth, and urged upon his attention the propriety of settling definitely, through the Committee, the next agent who should go to Africa, as much had to be done between his appointment and his sailing. At the same time, I said that, in common with my brethren of the Presbytery, I was at the disposal of the African Committee, and I was willing to undertake the work, if I thought that my Divine Master, through them, called me to it. The reply to my communication is as follows :—' As our eye has been upon you all along, you need not entertain any doubt of your services being accepted for Africa.' Once more, in my fleeting and ever-varying life, I am placed upon a point where every movement involves great and important consequences,—a point where overwhelming views of my own littleness—my utter nothingness—ever fill my mind,—where I discover work to be performed which fills me with trembling, and leads me in agony to cry out, Wherein lies my capacity for this ?—but a point from which also are discovered the rays of the Sun of Righteousness thinning, and scattering, and melting from the face of the horizon those battlements of clouds,—and upon which is heard the gentle voice of mercy from the most excellent glory, saying, ' My grace is sufficient for thee ; go in this thy might.' Beloved friends, I am willing to go in the strength of the Lord my God, and I am willing to remain here. I have no will but that of my Divine Master : for sure I am, that happiness, and comfort, and success in my work, depend on my being just where he wants me to be, and in doing just what he wants me to do. To serve God have I come into the world ; in this most blessed service would I spend my days ; and when I have done all that is appointed for me, I would depart and be with Christ, which is far better. It matters little where my grave—my last resting-place—may be, or by whose hands my lifeless body may be consigned to this dark and silent abode. All is in safe keeping for time and for eternity. On the resurrection morning, all will be found well—nothing the worse for falling asleep far from the graves of my fathers, and for being buried by a rude and barbarous people : for I know whom I have believed, and I am persuaded that he is able to keep that which I have committed unto him against that day.

" But it is essential that another minister be found to take my place in Goshen ; and it is exceedingly desirable to have him here before I go. We cannot weaken Jamaica for the sake of Africa ; and I cannot, with any comfort, leave my young, and inexperienced, and weeping flock, without seeing one in the midst of them to teach, to comfort, and to lead, when I resign my charge. Oh ! surely some heaven-born spirit—some heart in which lives the liberality of Christ—will be found in the Secession Church,—and that soon : for there is not much time to lose. I cannot leave without seeing one in my place to feed, comfort, and care for this flock: for there is much weeping, and this letter to-day has been frequently interrupted with sorrowing hearts and tearful eyes.

" An old African was here a little ago. It was affecting to see the old weather-beaten man wipe his streaming eyes, and to hear him say, with a look of agony,—

" ' Oh, my minister ! we cannot say to you, Do not go : for it is the Lord's work. But what are we to do ? You comfort us, and your going away will mash us (that is, it will knock us to pieces). Oh, my minister ! Oh, my minister ! '

" I brought him in, and seating him beside me, said :—

' Francis, I am sorry to see you so grieved. You know I am going on my Master's work, and he will take care of me.'

" ' Oh, my minister, I don't fear for you at all ; I am distressed about myself. No fear of you, but what become of me ?'

" ' Francis, I don't like altogether to hear you talk that way. You talk as if my mouth had given you the comfort, and as if I had done for you everything. Now, think again. Whose word has given you comfort ? '

" Francis replied, ' The word of God.'

" ' Now, am I to take all that word with me ? '

" ' No, my minister.'

" ' Well, again, who has brought this word to your heart, Francis ? '

" ' The Holy Spirit.'

" ' Now, does He leave you when I go ? '

" ' No, no ! bless God ! bless God ! He abide with me for ever.'

" ' Well, Francis, I am not going away (should I go) before another minister come ; then I will bring him round to see you, and show him all how I do with you when sick, and how I speak to you when I teach you ; and this minister will just say the same words that I speak. So you will have everything the same but the man,—the same God, the same Saviour, the same Spirit your teacher and sanctifier ; and the only difference will be'——the old man here took up the speech, and finished the sentence,—

" ' A new mouth.' "

Writing to Mr. Blyth, 25th February, 1845, Mr. Jameson said :—"I fully and entirely surrender myself to the African Committee, and hold myself in readiness to meet their views, whatever these may be. This I do in the full assurance that the Committee will use every means along with myself to have my place supplied in Goshen, so that the cause may not suffer there. The work in both places is God's, and I am sure that in obeying so urgent a demand for Africa as that sent from home, the cause of the blessed Saviour in Goshen will lose nothing, but, I trust, will, through the Divine kindness, gain much in the end. . . . . Our worthy and respected Chairman has hinted that I am running before Providence, and had better look out for Jonah's whale. I may be before the Committee, but not ahead of Providence."

In these circumstances, Mr. Jameson appealed to the preachers of the United Secession Church. He declared his willingness to obey the call now addressed to him, and told them that his chief anxiety respected the interests of the little Christian Society which had been brought into existence through his instrumentality.

"To vacate this infant church, even for a short time, would seriously damage its interests; and to serve Africa at such a cost would in the end prove highly disastrous to the cause which we all desire to serve. I am not at liberty to leave the sphere in which God has placed me, and where he has sustained me during the last nine years, without seeing another on the spot, into whose hands to resign my trust. Neither do I feel at liberty to leave my people upon the promise of occasional supply from the brethren. For I know that every brother has enough to do with his own church; and the inconveniences of travelling in this country are so many and so great, that the flock would have a very precarious subsistence indeed.

"I therefore, dear brethren, make my appeal to you. By you will my views of duty be very much regulated. If one of you be led to respond to this appeal; if he will come out to Goshen, and say to me, ' Go forth into that dark land, and the Lord go with you; and I will take your place at Goshen, and water the flock,' then shall I know that the Lord is sending me far hence, and then I shall hasten to obey his will. But if no response be made to this and other appeals, then surely I must conclude that the Lord has no work for me in Africa, but that He wills me to remain and tend the flock in Goshen. This important matter, dear brethren, I leave in your hands. Judge ye concerning it with impartial judgment. If the Lord is now saying, ' Who will go for us ?

Whom shall I send ?' With reference to Africa, I desire to say, ' Behold, here am I, send me.' And with reference to Goshen, I trust that some one will be found willing to use the same language. Oh, if our Divine Master calls us to distant work, let us not count our lives so dear, our friends so dear, or our country so dear, as that, for their sakes, the interests of his glorious kingdom among the heathen shall be disregarded. To one and all of us is the commission given :—— ' Go ye and teach all nations,' etc. From the relation in which the preacher of the gospel stands to this commission is he emphatically ' the light of the world, and the salt of the earth.' Oh, then, dear brethren, may none of us be found putting under a bushel that radiant light with which our Divine Master has intrusted us, by refusing to face the difficulties and dangers connected with the spreading of its heavenly beams among the peoples dwelling in thick darkness, and in the region and shadow of death ; may none of us be as the salt which has lost its savour, by refusing to carry to the perishing heathen, or to the far-distant missionary church, the life-giving, heart-changing, moral-reforming, and soul-saving gospel ; and this for no better reason than that we love father and mother, houses and lands, or our own lives more than our Lord. As those who hold the commission of our Lord, as those whose high and holy profession declares that we are separated for the express purpose of preaching the gospel, let each of us stand, looking up to the heavenly throne, and saying, ' Lord, what wilt thou have me to do ?' And let us be ready to go wherever we are called, and to do whatever we are bidden. Pardon me, dear brethren, for presuming to speak thus to you. My only apology is, that I am speaking out (almost unconsciously) those truths with which I require, every hour, to check the unbelieving doubts and fears of my own heart, and with which I seek, through divine grace, to fortify my mind, in the prospect of more arduous duties and of greater dangers."

To Mr. Jameson's letter of 26th December, the Society replied :——

" *20th February*, 1846.—That while they are grateful to God for giving them such an agent as Mr. Jameson, while they continue to cherish towards him the warmest affection, and have unabated confidence in his prudence and zeal, and while they look forward with great anxiety towards a separation between Mr. Jameson and his attached flock at Goshen, yet, believing that God is now calling him to go as a herald of mercy to Western Africa, they feel that they would be wanting in duty to God, to the Church generally, and to themselves, were they to throw any obstacles in Mr. Jameson's way ; and, therefore, they not only do not oppose his going to Africa, but bid him ' God-speed ' in his new enterprise. They also specially desired to make arrangements for preserving Mr. Jameson's connexion with the Society."

The Society were worthy of their missionary, and their missionary was worthy of them. With reference to the above communication, Mr. Jameson (April 3d, 1846) wrote :—
" Beloved friends, I reciprocate your affection and esteem. The period of my union with you has been indeed the sunshine of my days, and with it are connected the most blissful associations. Clouds, it is true, have once and again obscured my sky ; and my heart has been nigh to breaking, but your kindness has comforted me. Many circumstances render the present movement a trial of no ordinary kind to my poor, faithless heart ; and the thought of being separated from you whom I love as my own soul, is one which fills me with the bitterness of anguish. The thought of leaving Goshen, with its important and interesting work, and its numerous endearments, and of leaving Rose Street, with all its prayers, and zeal, and sympathy, and friendship, in one day, almost overwhelms me.

" My sister Mary's marriage will throw the school into my hands. I know the value of her assistance, now that I am deprived of it. The progress which her young charge has made, shows that in her removal the school has sustained a heavy loss. She is not going far away, but will live in the midst of the people, over whom she has acquired a salutary influence."

A minute of the Committee of Directors of the Rose Street

Society (April 18th, 1845), states that " Miss Mary Jameson had laboured devotedly in educating the young for two years, and that no remuneration had been solicited either by herself or by her friends ; and they express their approbation of labours so disinterested and abundant by presenting her with the sum of £50."

The receipt of the Rose Street communication, acquiescing in Mr. Jameson's mission to Africa, is thus described by Miss Jameson :—

" Before opening the letter, he desired me to retire with him to his room, and shutting the door, laid the letter on the table. We kneeled down, and he poured out his soul before God, praying that, whatever might be the decision, we might be enabled to meet all, and not flinch from trying duty.   He then opened the letter, and wept while perusing it.   After a long pause, he said, ' Well, well, Jane, 'tis all of the Lord, who knows the end from the beginning.   He knows well that I desired not to leave this dear people, or to break up our pleasant home.   Oh, no !   I would desire to live out my days among them, and to have my dust resting with theirs till " that day."   Being called to Africa, I referred the matter to my beloved friends in Rose Street, and besought the Lord to declare his will through them. He has now done it in a beautiful and thrilling manner, by the fine spirit which they display.   Therefore let us be up and doing, and make haste to follow as the Lord leads.' "

Mr. Jameson continued at his post, resolved to remain there till the Lord should break up his way.   On the 26th of March, he was formally appointed to proceed to Africa, by the Jamaica Missionary Board, who also proposed that Mr. Goldie, then at Negril, should take charge of Goshen in the meantime.   But this proposal was not adopted, as it was thought not to be advisable to break up Mr. Goldie's arrangements, since a missionary for Goshen would soon arrive from home.   It was now six weeks from the sailing of the last vessel of the season.

The following spirit-stirring appeal was addressed to the friends of the African Mission in Lloyd Street Congregation, Manchester, the Rev. Dr. M‘Kerrow's, 5th June, 1846 :—

" Among the many fields of missionary labour which present themselves to the eye of the Church, that of Africa is likely to occupy a very prominent position for years and ages to come. What continent has been so much neglected as Africa ? What people has been so abused as the Negro race ? Truly, they have been servants, and servants of servants unto their brethren. While the curse has been most distinctly predicted, and most completely fulfilled, so the time to favour Ham's land is no less explicitly foretold, and who can doubt that the oracle will be as fully accomplished ? God foretells the one, as well as the other; and whatever dangers and difficulties may lie between the commencement and the completion of the work, yet it must and it will be done. In Psalm lxviii., God rebukes the idolatry of Egypt. He puts down the worship of those beasts whose dwelling is among the reeds of the Nile. He shames out of existence the adoration offered to the bull and to the calf. He brings to an end that system of warfare and plunder in which the Hamitic nations especially delight. And all that silver and gold which have hitherto been expended in idolatrous worship and brutal strife, He causes to be brought into his own treasury in Zion, as a token of the people's subjugation, and of their willing submission. Then it is that Egypt's princes shall do homage to Zion's King, and Ethiopia stretch out her hands to God. Then shall all the kingdoms of the earth sing praises unto Jehovah, who rideth upon the heavens, who hath sent out his voice, and hath performed such mighty works. This, dear friends, I take to be the meaning of this Psalm, from verse 30 to the end. I feel most assured that the present movement towards Africa is of God, that the time is approaching when she who has so long 'lien among the pots, shall be as the wings of a dove covered with silver, and her feathers with yellow gold,' and that this will be brought about through the instrumentality of that powerful word which Jehovah himself hath given. I would beg leave to suggest for the study of those who have leisure and opportunity, whether there be not a plan of missionary operation laid down in prophecy. In excavating mines, all is easy when the vein is found. So in the mines of heathenism, are there not lines laid down by the Spirit of God, by finding and following which the work may be done much more effectually? Whatever may be in this, one thing appears evident, viz., that to Africa a prominence is given in Scripture, perhaps second only to that of the Jews. Besides, the claim for help which Africa has on Christendom, exceeds in strength that of any other people on the face of the earth. That claim is in proportion to her wrongs. And shall we go to the utmost ends of the earth in search of heathen, to whom we may bring the light of Christianity, and leave Africa, so deeply wronged by Christendom, to weep her woes unpitied, and her children to perish for ever? Let us act justly. Let us give the dark and degraded land of Ham, which so many nations have spoiled and peeled for ages, far more of our sympathy and care. Oh! let us send thither, and continue there, the powerful word of Jehovah. Let us strive to multiply those who preach it; and when death thins their ranks, let the blanks be filled up. If you cannot go yourselves, have you not sons who can take your place? You have already given them to the Lord: and why should they not be given to this service as well as to any other? Do you say that in this service there are too many privations and dangers? Christian friend, has it come to this with you, that for the sake of your son's ease and convenience, and your own humours, you will allow the work of your Saviour to stand? Others, you say, will go. But if it be right for you thus to reason respecting your child, it is right for every other parent, and thus none may go. How disastrous would this be! How fatal to the cause of your Redeemer! I would say to such a parent, Think again. If your child wish, and think it his duty, to carry the tidings of mercy to the heathen, hinder him not. Quench not the flame which the Divine Spirit has kindled within him, lest that Spirit forsake you, and you be left to a joyless desertion. With reference to this work, the voice of our King from his throne is : 'Thy God hath commanded thy strength.' He thus demands from his Church all that may be available for this work,—ourselves, our children, our money, our prayers. Let our earnest prayer be : ' Strengthen, O God, that which thou hast wrought for us.' "

At length, Mr. Jameson seemed to hear the voice behind him saying, " This is the way ;" and a ray from above shone out, revealing it to his earnest gaze. Thus touchingly is the last fortnight at Goshen narrated by Miss Jameson.

On Saturday, the 13th of June, 1846, Mr. Jameson was in his study preparing for Sabbath. In the afternoon, he came and said to his sister : " Jane, within the last hour, strange thoughts fill my mind. I have not had more pleasure in preparing for the Sabbath since I came to Jamaica ; and everything was going well with me, when, in a moment, all my thoughts were scattered, and nothing could I think of but our immediate return to Scotland, to make arrangements for Old Calabar." He added : " I fear I have been trifling with my duty in waiting for one to take my place, while the Lord is calling me hence, and saying that he will provide another, in his own time and way. The whole matter breaks upon my mind. I have accepted the call to Africa, and am expected there about the end of the year. Could I get any proper person to take the charge of my beloved people in the meantime, we should yet go home with the ' Copse,' which sails on the 10th of next month." His sister said : " I have been thinking, this afternoon, that Mr. Gregory, catechist at Port Maria, would do very well, if he would come." Mr. Jameson's countenance brightened, and he replied : " I see the Lord in this. He has been prompting us both, at the same moment. I came to suggest this to you, and you have named it to me. The first obstacle is already removed. The cloud which seemed to envelop me when I left my room, begins to dispel." In the beginning of the week, he learned by a letter from Mr. Fyfe, that everything was being done to secure a successor. At the same time, he received a letter from Mr. Somerville, the Mission Secretary, asking him to come to Scotland without delay. On Friday, he went after Mr. Gregory, and found him in the act of writing a letter, agreeing to go to another station. He told him to stop : for he was sent by God to bring him to

Goshen, and to Goshen he must go immediately. Mr. Gregory gave his consent. On Monday, the 22d, a letter was received from Mr. Blyth, saying that he had secured a passage for the family in the " Copse," which was at Montego Bay, but adding, " The ' Copse' does not sail on the 10th of July, as we expected, but on the 1st, which will hurry you very much. Captain Duncan has promised, therefore, to have his boat at Frankfort Wharf to convey your baggage and stores to Montego Bay, on Friday the 26th, and yourselves must be there on the 1st or 2d." Mr. Jameson was deeply moved, and, for a little, seemed lost to everything about him. At last, he said : " I fear the thing is impossible. That gives us only three days to get everything ready. My dear people know nothing of this haste." His sister told him to keep his mind easy : for that a good deal could be done in three days. The washerwomen, on being asked to bring in the clothes on Wednesday, replied, with deep emotion : " Oh, my Missis, never did we wash with such heavy hearts; yet, if Massa in heaven give we sun to dry them clothes, you shall have them." Next day, the school children were dismissed, at the close of the forenoon's work, that they might tell their parents to meet minister on the following morning, at nine o'clock, in the church, as he had something very particular to say to them. At the appointed hour, nearly all the members of the church were waiting minister's arrival. His heart was heavy, and, as he said when he returned, he thought the very mule felt the load, for it moved more slowly than usual. The people were eager to know what the matter was ; and, with the deepest emotion, he laid before them the whole case, explained why he had changed his mind concerning the time of his leaving them, and read to them the letter from home urging his immediate return. They spoke little, but their bitter weeping was eloquent. Many said they would try to give him up to God's work. Others, that their hearts would break. But, with one accord, they offered to bring provisions for the passage home. Mr. Jameson thanked them, saying that he would be very glad to receive anything they could spare ; but that they must not impoverish themselves. He reminded them that there was only one day to provide, as everything had to be at the wharf early on Friday morning. The meeting separated; and each group went home in silence and sorrow.

Mr. Jameson did not return till evening, but, long before that, many presents had come in, and ere sunset on Thursday, there was an abundant supply of the very best provisions, which the good, kind people could procure. On Friday, by three A.M., two wains came to carry the baggage and stores to the wharf; and before the sun rose over the nearest green mountain, all was again quiet around the dear home. Nothing was heard save the whoops of the cattlemen on the way to the wharf.

On Saturday morning, many people came, and bought up all the household articles, every one being anxious to possess some little thing that once belonged to minister. But, with a delicacy for which many deny them credit, they declined removing those things till minister should leave. On his saying to them, "Well, you must not quarrel about them; every person must quietly take his own;" they replied, "No, minister! we heart too sad to quarrel, at this time."

All had left; and Mr. Jameson was reclining on a couch, the tears coming unbidden to his eyes, when his daughter, going up, asked him, "What do papa?" He replied, "Sorry I am to turn Aunt and Kitty out of house and home, but it is the Lord who calls me; and I know He will supply all your need."

Mr. Jameson looked forward to the Sabbath with great anxiety: for it was the Communion-day, and the last he would spend with his beloved flock. Long before day-break, he was dressed, and pacing his study, in meditation and prayer. On his sister entering, he said to her : "Jane, I am struggling to nerve my mind for the stern duties of to-day. The Lord has promised : 'I will strengthen thee ;' I feel somewhat girded, and able to go forward." The classes were held as usual from nine A.M. till eleven, when the church became crowded with people of all classes, among whom his own were conspicuous by their sad aspect, and their eager look on minister. After praise and prayer, he read Romans xii., and addressed them from Phil. i. 27. The discourse was most affectionate and faithful. Many wept, and many trembled. An unusual number of whites was present. Them he addressed very solemnly, saying that he was glad to see them in the house of God, though some of them were doubtless pleased that he would trouble them no more. He then said: "My own countrymen, you are dear to me. Very earnestly have I sought the salvation of your souls. Some of you know well how I have admonished, and besought you, yea, wept and prayed for you. Once more, I say, Take heed how ye hear. 'I take you to record that I am pure from the blood of all men.' Think not that you are done with me for ever. No. The judgment seat awaits us ; and if you are found on the left hand, I shall be able to testify that to you the gospel of salvation was fully preached."

In the afternoon, the members partook of the Lord's Supper. At the close of the service, Mr. Jameson asked his own class, of nearly 100 old people, to stand up, and then handed them over to Mr. Gregory. In the same way, the rest of the classes were given over to the care of other friends. Before leaving the pulpit, he bade the weeping flock farewell ; and, commending them anew to the infinite compassion of the Good Shepherd, and to the care of the friends who were to remain behind, he again bade them farewell ; and requested them to retire with composure. He said he would rather not see them outside, but would visit them in the early part of the week. It was a little time ere he could separate himself from the house which the Lord had honoured him to build for his worship ; and, on going out, he was pleased to find that the people had granted his last request ; for, wishful as all were to grasp his hand, none remained about the place. The ship's boat did not come for them so soon as was expected. And thus Mr. Jameson was able to visit every family, and give a parting word to all, commending them, and especially the young, to the Lord. Mother Winter (p. 69) tells that, at parting, neither she nor Father Jameson could utter a word. They grasped each other by the hand, and parted in silence. He had just paid his last visit, and reached home, on Friday the 3d of July. The family was seated at table ; and minister was expressing his gratitude to God for having permitted him to do all that his heart had craved, and his desire that now the boat should come, for he could not again face his people, and take another farewell. Just then the servant entered saying,—— " Minister, two men come from the wharf to tell you that the boat is there." All was now hurry. Everything was got ready. But the sun was down, and they must wait till the following morning. About fifty of the people gathered to the Pen ; and they prayed together. They remained watching till three A.M., when the bell was rung. A cup of coffee was drunk ; and all assembled once more. Minister exhorted them to "pray and not to faint." Then opening his Bible, he read the 121st Psalm, and prayed. In half an hour, they had mounted their horses, sighed farewell to that dear home, and in silence were hastening to the wharf, nine miles distant. The boat was ready, and the seamen anxious to start, as wind and tide were favourable. The hurried grasp ! the embrace in which soul clasps soul ! and those embark while these remain behind. Mr. Cowan accompanied them to Montego Bay, where the " Copse " lay waiting them, and, favoured with a steady breeze, they reached it at one o'clock in the morning.

On the evening before they left, Mr. Jameson wrote Mr. Fyfe :——

" The 'Copse's' boat is at Frankfort, waiting to carry us off, to-morrow morning, to Montego Bay. We shall sail on Monday, the 6th ; and you may expect us about the beginning of September. I know you will pray for us, that the blessed God may keep us on the mighty ocean, and bring us to you in safety. Our poor people keenly feel our departure ; but, I trust, that, in answer to prayer, they will be sustained, comforted, and blessed. Mr. Gregory is likely to prove useful and acceptable.

" A Scottish emigrant from Aberdeen died, some years ago, leaving three children houseless and unprotected. One of the daughters and her brother fell into cruel hands. I entered into a prosecution, and rescued them from their worthless oppressors. The boy has turned out very ill; and one sister has fallen into the unclean ways of the country; but the other, who has been in my family, as a servant, is a very steady, well-doing young woman. I could not think of leaving her behind, to certain ruin; and have resolved to take her home to her uncle in Aberdeenshire."

The separation of Mr. Jameson from his flock was painful in the extreme, and he declared that no consideration would induce him to submit again to such a series of mental suffering. He was attached to his flock by the ties of a very strong affection—the affection of a tender spirit, and of a spiritual parent. And they regarded him as their best friend—their father— who had so faithfully spent and been spent among them. How could the loss be made up? To a people who had never before known the friendship and kindness of such a man, the removal was peculiarly bitter. But the pious among them fully understood the motive which swayed him; they felt the importance of the object in view; and although, as one of them once said to the writer, they would never have given him up to a family church,—that is, any sister congregation in Jamaica,—yet they tried to give him up to Africa.

The Rev. John Campbell, who succeeded Mr. Jameson, thus speaks of the feelings which he found among the people towards their first minister :—" My beloved predecessor has secured their confidence and affections; he still lives, and will ever live in their hearts. I have been deeply moved in listening to their lamentations, because of his departure, and in witnessing the tears of love and gratitude which the remembrance of his work and labour of love among them has caused them to shed. Truly, he has not lived and laboured in vain in this land. There is a people here whose prayers will bring down blessings on his own soul, and on the work of his hands amid the moral wastes of Africa."

The following affecting incident may be mentioned here. There was a white man, a book-keeper, or under-manager of an estate, who was, like too many of his class, entangled in the vices of the country. Mr. Jameson frequently warned him of the peril to which his sins exposed him, and entreated him to repent and live. The youth, often thus reproved, hardened his neck. One Sabbath, while the people were assembling in the house of prayer, this person was seen riding past intoxicated. Mr. Jameson again expostulated with him, and begged him to have pity on himself. The poor slave of the devil scorned his counsel. At last, minister solemnly told him that he expected soon to hear that the carrion vultures had eaten out his eyes. Just on that day fortnight, one came to tell minister that it had turned out as he had feared : for that the poor man had just been found dead, that he had fallen from his mule while drunk, and had not been discovered till the carrion crows had actually begun to devour the corpse, and had already eaten out the eyes.

Mr. Jameson was distinguished for moral courage as a minister of Christ. But he was no less characterized by love. He never shot the arrows of bitter words—words dipped in the gall of an evil temper,—when he was sternly rebuking sin. His reproofs were winged by love to straying souls. And hence, although immoral men quailed under his uncompromising faithfulness, they could not hate the man who was so manifestly godly and sincere. Men of all classes who still remember him, do honour to his memory. Not often are the same qualities found in an individual servant of Christ,—the same conscientiousness, the same forgetfulness of self, the same self-devotion, the same faithfulness in duty, the same zeal, and the same love.

The Rev. John Cowan went with Mr. Jameson to Montego Bay. The latter officiated, on the Sabbath, in the Presbyterian place of worship, and addressed a meeting on Monday. On Wednesday, 8th July, the Rev. Messrs. Denniston, Blyth, and Cowan accompanied them to the ship, and in a farewell service of prayer, the voyagers were commended to the care of our Father in heaven. The anchor was weighed, and the " Copse " sailed, having on board the party from Goshen, Mr. Robert Blyth, and Mr. Tomary, a Christian son of Abraham.

Mr. Jameson thus speaks of the voyage, in a letter to Mr. Blyth, August 29th, 1846 :—" By the kindness of our heavenly Father, we arrived in Leith Roads, on Thursday the 26th, at three A.M., after a passage of seven weeks. We have enjoyed a very comfortable time on board, being permitted to worship God every morning and evening. The captain was very attentive and kind ; and the crew were sober and quiet. On arriving at Leith, I found that friends had been looking for us daily. At noon, a number of Rose Street friends came on board, and gave us a very welcome reception. A ship will sail for Old Calabar in October, and it is not improbable that I may go out then. I long to be at the work. God orders all ; and I am ready to start whenever the way is opened."

So eager was Mr. Jameson to reach the sphere of his labour in Africa, that two months only elapsed ere his foot was again on ship-board. The interval was spent in visiting friends, settling his family affairs, and arranging for his departure. He took part in several missionary meetings ; and his addresses, which were the utterances of a feeling and devoted spirit, never failed to carry the hearers along with him. These addresses were not written, but poured forth under the genial influences of sympathizing Christian assemblies, as the memories of the past came over him, or the hopes of the future were kindled in his bosom. He was frequently in great anxiety before he rose to speak, but his heart never failed to well out in such strains as melted all his hearers.

The address, with which he made his first appearance among his Rose Street friends, remains among his papers, and from it we select the following review of a ministry of ten years :—

" In rising to address you, after so many years of separation, feelings of a varied kind agitate my bosom. I trust, however, that the chief of these is gratitude to God for all his mercies. These have been far more and far greater than I deserved. Dark clouds have sometimes encompassed my path, and once and again have they emptied their treasures of storm upon my head. But these were mixed with mercy, and now I appear in the midst of you to sing of mercy, and with you to join in the anthem of praise : ' Bless the Lord, O my soul, and forget not all his benefits.' Next to the gratitude which I feel to God, is that, dear friends, which I owe to you. Your prayers, your generosity, your sympathy and forbearance, have made myself and the church at Goshen lasting debtors to you, the dispensers of the bounties of Zion's God to that infant flock.

" But you ask, ' What good has arisen out of these ten years of prayer and of toil ?' We reply : Much ! ten thousand-fold more than we are able to tell you ; yea, incalculably more than we know. Who but God himself sees the utmost effect of the rain which waters the earth ? So it is with the word of God which has been, for nearly ten years, preached at Goshen. It has spread there the knowledge of the Saviour ; and through it has Jehovah been exalted. At Goshen, many sinners have been converted through the gospel, which you sent to them, and maintained among them. Prayerless ones have become children of prayer ; and they cease not to remember you, their best earthly benefactors, at their heavenly Father's throne. Some, also, who began their pilgrimage there, and finished their course, have arrived at the Canaan above. Ten years ago, in Goshen there was no church. Now, there is a church of 200 members. Ten years ago, there was no house of prayer. Now, there is a substantial building, which will hold 700 people. Ten years ago, none were found willing to give of their substance or labour to the service of the Saviour, and hence our temporary place of worship had to be put up, at first, at my own expense. But through the preaching of this gospel, prejudices vanished, hearts were touched, and made willing. Ten years ago, I was received at Goshen with suspicion. When I left them, they said, with tears, that they were losing a father and a friend, or, as an old man expressed himself, ' Minister, our back is broken.' By the disposal of an all-wise God, my labours at Goshen were both in the congregation and in the school. Once and again, through your kindness, I was freed from the latter, but was ever again brought back to it ; and I have found the congregation to thrive as much when I was teacher and minister, as when I was minister only.   I endeavoured to make the school a means of diffusing the gospel.   I enjoined the children to teach their parents, at home, the Bible lessons which they learned at school.   And this has been, by the blessing of God, the means of moving the minds and hearts of many.   In a word, dear brethren, there are many in Goshen who call you blessed.   Your labour of love has gathered around the throne of grace a company of Ethiopia's ransomed children; who pray for you, and glorify God on your behalf.   As for myself, I will magnify the Lord, who sent me, under your auspices, on that mission,—whose tender mercy has supported me so long in that distant field,—and whose sovereign grace has deigned to make me the instrument of bringing, were it but one soul, to Christ.   But I have taken a long and last farewell of Goshen—that spot which, by innumerable associa-. tions, is dear to my heart as the spot where I was born, and where were spent the happy years of my boyhood.   My presence among you this night, together with the scowling clouds, the thunders and lightnings, the winds and waves of the Atlantic, through all of which a gracious God has carried us, remind me that the anguish of heart we felt, and the floods of tears we shed, were not the tumultuous agitations of a dream, or the visions of a roving fancy, but a reality.   My flock in Goshen !   Must I see you no more ?   Tomb of my amiable and beloved one !   Can I never more steal a look at thee ? Like a vision, ye have passed from my eyes ; and awaking as from a deep slumber, I find myself separated from you all by five thousand miles of ocean."

The church in Rose Street chose Mr. John Campbell as Mr. Jameson's successor at Goshen ; and, at the request of the Edinburgh Presbytery, Mr. Jameson took part in his ordination, on the 29th September, 1846.   The Rev. Andrew Somerville preached a very admirable sermon on " The call of the Holy Ghost to missionary service," from Acts xiii. 2.   Mr. Jameson delivered affectionate and interesting addresses to the newly ordained missionary and to the congregation.   That to the former described the field of labour, and the duties it would entail ; and thus concluded :—" I am transferring into your hands the labour of many years—the child of my most anxious thoughts and of my most earnest prayers. With many tears, and with a heavy heart, I have bidden Goshen farewell for ever. I have left behind me much, very much, that ever will be tenderly interesting and dear to my heart. There is the flock which I have been a humble instrument in gathering to the Saviour's fold. There are many wanderers from this fold, for whom I have wept, with whom I have remonstrated, and in behalf of whom I have prayed and do pray ; but they are wanderers still—deluded, unhappy wanderers. There are the graves of beloved dead, to whom I was bound by the ties of strongest affection—to whom I preached the gospel of salvation, and whose souls, through this gospel, are now glorified, though their bodies sleep in the dust. All have I left, not out of a vain curiosity to visit new lands, or to behold new scenes ; nor, so far as I know my own heart, in obedience to any worldly influence ; but for the sake of the blessed Saviour, who bought me by his blood, called me by his grace, and who, I believe, is sending me in the way in which I am going. To that new sphere I betake myself the more joyfully, since I see you here ready to enter upon the one which I have left. Go on then, dear brother, and the Lord will be with you. Expect difficulties and trials ; but rest assured that you have your encouragements, and that you will not want your joys also. You are sent out by a beloved people, to whose sympathy, to whose kindness, and to whose generous consideration, in every respect, during the last ten years, I am indebted to a far greater extent than I am able to describe. I know not how I can more fully express the sincere wish of my heart with regard to you, than in the utterance of a hope and a strong desire, that your intercourse with the Missionary Society in Rose Street may be as sweet, as improving, as hallowed, as mine has been. You go to a people who are longing for you, and who will hail, with great joy, your arrival among them. You go in the service of a great and gracious Master, who says,

' Lo, I am with you always.'   Go then, and fear not, and the God of grace go with you."

The writer, who had the honour and privilege of being the third missionary of the Rose Street Church to Goshen, can fully subscribe to the sincere acknowledgment which Mr. Jameson made of the steady, Christian kindness of that most exemplary congregation :—" I can truly testify how considerate, how faithful, how honourable, have been all your transactions as a Foreign Missionary Society, and this for the long period of almost ten years.   Without wearying, without fainting, have you continued until now."   This congregation undertook to maintain two foreign missionaries—Mr. Jameson in Old Calabar, and Mr. Campbell in Jamaica,—at the time when they had " to incur the expense of supporting an additional pastor for the purposes of their own edification."   Were this example of zealous and beneficent exertion followed by the whole Christian Church, as it is, we are happy to say, by some congregations, the dark places of the earth would soon see the salvation of God.

Goshen Church is still under the fostering care of Rose Street Church.   The Rev. William Gillies laboured there from 1856 to 1859, with great earnestness, and was much beloved by the people, who mourned over his removal to Falmouth. The present minister is the Rev. John Welch, who was, for several years, the zealous and successful teacher at Carron Hall, and who, having studied under the Rev. Mr. Renton, was ordained at Goshen in 1861.   Including school fees, the total contributions at the station, up to the end of 1860, amounted to £2850.   From 1839, when the church was formed, up to the end of 1856, 255 persons were admitted for the first time, 50 of whom had come under church discipline ; of these there were eight alive who had not been restored, the rest had either been restored or were dead.

CHAPTER X.

Voyage to Old Calabar — Arrival — Fernando Po — Duke Town — Creek Town — Preaches through interpreters — Opens school — Calabar marketing and house-keeping — Egbo Institution — Linguistic talents needed by a foreign missionary — Death of Eyamba — King Eyo Honesty — The Warree returns from Jamaica — Closing labours — Illness — Death.

HAVING arranged that his sister and daughter should reside in Perth, under the ministry of the late Dr. Young, of whose church his brother, John Wilson Jameson, Esq., was an elder, Mr. Jameson preached in Rose Street Church, on Sabbath, October 3d ; and, on the following Sabbath, he preached his last discourse in Scotland, in Dr. Robson's church, in Glasgow. He then spent some time in Liverpool and Manchester. Having taken what proved to be a last farewell of his attached relatives, Mr. Jameson embarked on board the " Magistrate," in which a free passage was generously granted him by the owners, Messrs. W. A. and C. Maxwell & Co. His kind host, Dr. Fergusson, and other friends, accompanied him out of the Mersey. A farewell letter, addressed to the friends of the African Mission, by Mr. Jameson, is to be found in the *Missionary Record* of the United Presbyterian Church, for December, 1846. It is full of his characteristic spirit of devotion to the work, and contains a solemn exhortation to the Church, whose messenger he was, to persevere in labour and in prayer for the success of the enterprise on which he went.

Mr. Jameson sailed on Saturday, October 31st, 1846. He was thus only two months at home, and during that period had neither rest nor relaxation. His labours for ten years, and his late severe sickness, had necessarily weakened his constitution, and a period of cessation from exciting engagements was needed to restore its tone.

From a journal of his voyage from Liverpool to Old Calabar, we make the following extracts :—

" I shall not speak of partings—those tearings asunder from the embrace of friends most dear—those rendings of heart—those efforts which the whole man puts forth to suppress, or, at least, to restrain, the conflicts of nature which are incident to such scenes. May these be sanctified to me and mine. O may they lead our hearts nearer to God ; may they make us cleave to Him who will never leave, from whom no distance can divide, and who will be the everlasting portion of His people, after earth and all its joys and sorrows shall have passed away.

" The wind became contrary ; and, on Sabbath, we made no progress out of the channel. Our abode, on that day, was not in thy peaceful sanctuary, O Zion ! We were not permitted to unite in the worship of thy hallowed courts. But the roaring wind, the raging wave, the rattling ropes, and the running to and fro of men on deck, took the place of thy melodies. I thought of the happy and profitable hours which I have spent in thy services. I called to mind the circumstances in which beloved friends on shore were placed, as they sat around the pools of divine ordinances, and drunk to the full of the water of life. When I think of these things, my heart becomes as water, and I say with the Psalmist : ' My soul is poured out in me.'

" On Saturday forenoon (7th November), the Captain thought that we had passed the Tuskar lighthouse, and were now getting clear of the land ; when, all at once, the unseen hand of a gracious Providence lifted up the thick mantle of mist, and showed us, at the distance of six miles, a bold headland of barren, lofty rocks, towards which the tide was rapidly carrying us, and on which it would soon have dashed us. The captain, who is a most experienced and careful seaman, now knew that we were not so far as he had thought. A sharp look-out was kept, and, about one o'clock on Sabbath morning, the light was seen, once and again, through the fog ; and, on sitting down to breakfast, in the morning, we were full thirty miles beyond it, speeding over the Atlantic with a fair wind.

" This being the second Sabbath on board, I proposed to the Captain that we should have divine service. He declined, saying that the weather was too cold, the wind required too much watching, and, at any moment, all hands might be called. In silence, therefore, did I endeavour to worship the God of salvation. I thought on the privileges of by-gone days, when in the ' Christian,' on the way to Jamaica, I enjoyed the fellowship of a beloved partner ; and when in the ' Copse,' returning home, I was with those with whom I had sweet intercourse, even at the stormiest hours. I thought upon the Sabbath bell, and worshippers thronging to the house of God at its call, and said, ' O that I had wings like a dove, that I might fly far hence, and, once more, drink of the streams of the sanctuary, which flow so abundantly in the land of my fathers.' At length, it seemed folly to waste the precious hours in such unprofitable musings, and going to my cabin, I poured out my heart to my God—my home—my country—my friend—my all. I read the history of Elijah, and received much comfort and instruction from the remarks of Krummacher on the prophet's sojourn and exercise by the brook Cherith.

" I gave the sailors some religious tracts, and expressed the hope that we should have an opportunity of worshipping God together, when the weather improved. They read the tracts with apparent interest, and, during the day, the crew conducted themselves with the utmost decorum ; and many of them were engaged in reading their Bibles and other books. No work was done but what was necessary.

" On Thursday evening (12th November), the ocean is luminous. As the ship rushes through the waters, her track is lighted up. The rudder, which descends seventeen feet into the water, is illuminated to its lowest point, as it turns from side to side. A shoal of porpoises is sporting around the ship, and the water through which they pass is lighted up. Here, a huge one plays on the surface ; there, two are racing or chasing one another. They tumble, they dart forward with the velocity of an arrow, or like lightning, shoot down into the abyss below. Now they appear robed in light—the full shape of the monsters—and every movement of their tails and fins, is manifest. And now their huge size diminishes, and their swift movements cease, until all that is seen is a small point of light twinkling as if from the dark horizon of a distant world. Once more, this feeble and distant light begins to expand and move upwards. Your eye follows it as it ascends from the secret chambers of the deep, and, just as it begins to assume its shape, off it flies as on the wings of the wind, and you almost fancy that, having discovered you prying into the privacy of its home, it fled from your sight.

" *Wednesday, 16th December.*—Saw a water-spout, yesterday, a few miles ahead of us. To-day, we saw two at a greater distance, hanging like dark conical funnels from the sky, and seeming to terminate in mid-air. We were too far off to hear the noise which they produced, but distinctly saw their whirling motion, and the effect which they produced upon the water.

" Quantities of fish, as the dolphin and bonita, are frequently seen around the ship. Great shoals of flying-fish arise at her bow, and dart off like partridges from the huntsman's dog. The other day, one dashed itself out of the water so high, that it struck against one of the sails and fell dead upon the deck. A young shark was speared, yesterday morning, by the captain. When hoisted on board, a sailor cut off its tail, as the speediest mode of killing it. It was then skinned, and the skin was carefully preserved. In the stomach were found pieces of beef, egg-shells, and potatoes, which had been thrown overboard, a short time before. The heart, long after it was separated from the body of the animal, upon your touching it with your finger, raised itself from the spot where it lay, as if conscious of pain. After the creature had been apparently dead fully half an hour, beheaded, skinned, and gutted, one of the men cut the body into slices for the pot (for sailors eat the young shark), and every time the back-bone was cut through, the headless body writhed as if in pain, and each slice seemed full of life. So merciless, however, is the shark, when a man is within reach of its fatal jaws, that sailors look on its pain without pity.

Some localities teem with these monsters, and truly awful is the death of those persons who fall into the water, and are devoured by them."

Would that the following remarks were earnestly pondered, and heartily received by the true Israel of God.

"I have been reading Winslow's book, *Christ the Theme of the Missionary.* O that the principles stated in it were pondered and rooted deeply in the heart of every member, minister, and missionary of the Church ! It is most evident that the work of missions is the work of the Church. Who can doubt that the commission to 'preach the gospel to every creature' is given to her ? And that to her, also, belongs the promise : 'Lo, I am with you alway, even unto the end of the world ?' It is evident that the Church is the missionary society by whose agency the world is to be made subject to Christ. It is her duty to map out this vast field into its proper divisions, to keep this map on her table, and her eye on the map, and not to rest so long as one unoccupied point remains on it— one nation not blessed with the joyful sound—one being without God and without hope, because she has not put into his hand the offer of mercy through a crucified Saviour.

"The Church ought also to be a missionary seminary. Christian mothers and fathers should train their children for the work of the Lord, and give them enlightened views of the Lord's public cause, and of its claims upon them, being more anxious as to how they may best glorify God, than how they may attain rank and wealth.

"Again, we see what should be the aim of those whom the Church sends to the heathen as her substitutes. It is to make disciples, to receive them into the Church by baptism, and to train them more perfectly in the way of God, so that the converts may daily grow in faith, love, and holy obedience to the Saviour. Hence the work of the missionary among the heathen is varied and extensive. It seeks to renew the heart and reform the conduct, to purify what is vile, and put right what is wrong in heathen society.

"If the missionary keep this before his mind, and honestly

seek to accomplish it, he will have little time left to mind anything else. When the scientific traveller, or the merchant, visits a heathen shore, he is so engrossed with his peculiar pursuit, that he has neither time nor heart for anything else. He has no time to seek the eternal welfare, or the moral improvement of heathens. Each man's own peculiar work requires his whole time and strength. No less exclusively ought the missionary of the Cross to labour in his calling. And if he do so, time will not hang heavily on his hands. The day will be gone before it appears to be well begun ; and months and years will fly with astonishing rapidity. Instead of having idle hours for other pursuits, he will desire that more hours were added to the day, and more days to the year : for his work requires it all. In his work he will find variety, not sameness. In the work of preaching Christ among the heathen, he will find a continued source of interest, and delight, and refreshing."

The sharpest of all trials to parents in foreign and heathen lands is the necessity of parting with their children, to remove them at once from a climate deleterious to the body, and from a social miasma which threatens ruin to mind and spirit. It is impossible to preserve children from contamination, or to train them for honour and usefulness, in the wild wastes of heathenism. The mother may have to send her sick lamb to the kind bosom of some friend at home. And as it voyages under the care of some kind Christian friend, she, in the heathen land afar, dreams by night, and muses by day on the fragile one whom she has given out of her bosom, rather than forsake her husband and their common work. "Leave thy fatherless children, I will preserve them alive," is surely as much hers as if she stood a widow by the grave of a dead husband. Or the parents have brought home their little ones, and left them behind that they might descend again into the dark mine. When these lambs are sick, they will not be near to tend them. A thousand snares are in their path, but they will not be there to warn and to guide them past in safety. Other eyes will see their bright smiles, other ears will hear their infant prattle, other hearts engross their young love. If there be any sacrifice in the lot of a missionary to the heathen, this is pre-eminently that sacrifice. Blessed be God! that he so often eases this sacrifice to the parental heart, by opening a shelter for the lambs thus removed from the native shelter of the home roof! All honour and thanks to those loving, wise, and careful friends who act the part of parents to the children of the mission! Their loving care greatly relieves the anxious heart. And so do the gracious promises of our blessed God and Master, in whose cause such a trial has to be met.

The following, written on December 5th, 1846, is a specimen of Mr. Jameson's letters to his daughter :—

"My dear Child,—It appears strange when I think that I am now so far away from you,—that thousands of miles of ocean now separate us. As I sit in my berth, and am being carried farther and, every hour, farther away from you, my thoughts, my child, are much upon you, and my prayers to God are often ascending on your behalf. I cannot but say, that I miss your company, as well as the affectionate, tender care of your dear aunt. But it is the work of the Blessed Saviour, that has called to this separation. And as fathers leave their families, to go to foreign lands in search of riches, and of the fading glory of this passing world, it would never have done for me, a servant of the Lord Jesus, to set aside a call to Africa, so evident as the one which I possessed, because of my interest in you. My first duty is to serve the Lord, in the gospel of his Son; and while I am attending to this, you will be blessed. But should I neglect this for your sake, neither of us would do well. Now then, my child, we are separated for a season, but I trust that a few years will bring us together again, that I may spend the remainder of my days with you. This, if the Lord will: for His will, which in all things is holy and right, be done! Let us, my child, be prepared for whatever it may be. I trust, however, that should the desire, which I have ventured, in dependence upon the Divine will, to express, ever be gratified, I shall find you, my beloved daughter, the child of a beloved mother—rapidly growing in wisdom, in knowledge, and in the fear of the Lord. I would have esteemed it a privilege and a happiness, to be by your side, and to watch over the opening and the maturing of your mind, as well as to be instrumental in regulating that heart, which God himself has said is deceitful above all things and desperately wicked. But God has appointed otherwise. He has, however, blessed you with the superintendence of a beloved aunt, who came many thousands of miles to your aid when you were a helpless babe, and who, from the days of your infancy, has watched over you with a mother's care.

" When God took your mother from you, he sent you a mother in Aunt Jane. I trust, therefore, that your heart will ever cleave to her, that you will avoid every thing which may cause her grief, and that you will attend to every thing which may contribute to her comfort and happiness. You will find that the religion of Jesus is the same in Perth as in Goshen. God, and his Son Jesus, and the Holy Spirit, will be worshipped in the family, every morning and evening ; and on no account be absent on these occasions. An example of spiritual-mindedness —of what is pure, and lovely, and of good report—will be set before you by your grand-aunts. Imitate their example, and learn wisdom from their matured experience. It is a good thing, my child, to dwell among the godly, where, in company with them, you are daily led to the throne, and where you neither see nor hear that worldly-mindedness which is the death of the soul. Take care, therefore, what companions you choose. Seek not the friendship of those children, whose parents may be great and wealthy, but whose words and ways may alienate your heart from what you see at home. But seek the friendship of the good, who regard heaven as their home. Be sure that you forget not your Bible and your prayers ; and while you pray, remember your father, whom the Lord's work has called far away. Attend Dr. Young's classes for religious instruction, and wait upon the Lord in his ordinances on the Sabbath. And, my child, by the religious privileges which you so richly enjoy in Perth, strive to profit, so that if spared to see you again, I may find you both wise and good.

"We had a good day's fishing, the other day. The Captain and the sailors threw out their lines as soon as they saw some fishes swimming by the side of the ship, and, in a short time, there were six large ones, called dolphins, hauled on board. The cook fried them, and we all ate of them, and they were very good indeed. How good is God, to send us these fishes, to be a little fresh food for us in the middle of the great ocean! You want to know where I am at present, when I am writing to you. Take the map of Africa, and on the western side of the continent look for Cape de Verde Islands; then look down the edge of the map for the number 10, and between that and 9th latitude, you will see where I am. It is very hot. I am sitting with my jacket off, perspiring much. But I am well, very well indeed, for which I would be thankful.

"*Grand Sestros.*—My DEAR CATHERINE,—Again take the map of Africa, and carry your finger down the side of it, until you come to 5°; then carry your finger across the Atlantic Ocean to the continent, and you will find Grand Sestros on the coast. You see me there, then. Well, a hundred or more of naked men have just leaped on board from their canoes. But I think I hear you say, 'Aunty, what is a canoe?' A canoe, then, is a boat scooped out of the cotton-tree. But what means scoop? Turn up your dictionary, and you will find the meaning of the word there. Well, these people have no clothes on them. They swim in the water like ducks, and when they come on board the ship, they talk, and they laugh, and they roar, just like the negroes in a Jamaica market. The Captain was obliged to take a whip, and lay on all around him to keep them in order. There are eighteen of these naked men in the ship with us, going to Calabar, to help the sailors from Liverpool to fill the ship with palm oil.

"I must now bid you adieu. Give my love to your little cousins in John Street, to grandmother in Airdrie, to Uncle John, and to every body. I commit you, my child, to the Lord; and I cease not to pray to God on your behalf, that in all things you may grow up unto him, and be found in him."

On the 16th January, 1847, the " Magistrate " cast anchor near the bar of the Old Calabar river, and sent a boat up to Duke Town, from forty to fifty miles, to procure the native pilot, as is customary on the arrival of a vessel. The mate, who had gone for the pilot, brought word to Mr. Jameson that Mr. Waddell had sailed in the " Warree " for Jamaica, and that Mr. and Mrs. Edgerly, with the other agents of the mission, were at Fernando Po, where they had gone during the time of the smokes at Old Calabar. He was taken somewhat aback by the intelligence of Mr. Waddell's voyage, and must have felt his absence very much. But he knew that this was for the benefit of the mission, and was a new call upon his faith in God. Captain Garnett, who had been sent out by Mr. Jamieson of Liverpool, to take home his steamer, the " Ethiope," arrived from Fernando Po in a long-boat, while the " Magistrate " was proceeding up the river. He went on board, and having learned who Mr. Jameson was, kindly offered to carry him to Fernando Po, as he was to return thither in two days. On reaching Duke Town, Mr. Jameson was introduced to Eyamba, and thanked him for his attention to the agents of the mission. On the same day, he visited King Eyo, at Creek Town, and inspected the mission houses at both places ; and this, his first landing on African soil, and introduction to African society, took place on Thursday, the 21st January, 1847, the tenth anniversary of his landing in Jamaica, with his partner, to commence his missionary career.

Putting his things under the care of King Eyamba, Mr. Jameson left Duke Town on Saturday the 23d, and on Monday, at eight P.M., reached Fernando Po, having received many kind attentions from Captain Garnett. He there found Mr. and Mrs. Edgerly well ; and the meeting was the occasion of joy to all. One of the native assistants, Edward Miller, had died some weeks before, " full of faith and hope. During his brief sojourn at Clarence, he appears to have gained the esteem of all who knew him ; and his unexpected removal is spoken of by all in terms of regret. Thus is the memory of the righteous blessed. Humility of mind, and gentleness of deportment, never fail to secure friends, and to rear for the lowly in heart a lasting memorial." The Baptist brethren received Mr. J. with much cordiality. He writes : " There is evidently a work of grace going on here through their instrumentality. Last night, we had a prayer-meeting, and I was much delighted with the supplications offered up by some of the natives." On the Sabbath, Mr. Jameson preached at the house of Mr. Lynslager, a native of Holland, who has long been a merchant at Clarence, and, for a time, was Governor of Fernando Po. This gentleman, who has in various ways aided and favoured missionaries, " expressed his thanks for our labours, and his regret at our going away." In the afternoon of the same day, Mr. Jameson preached in the Baptist chapel, and afterwards united in observing the Lord's Supper with the church assembling there. The Rev. Mr. Clark, one of the Baptist brethren, offered the use of their vessel, the " Dove," to carry the members of the mission and their luggage to Old Calabar, on her return from Bimbia; but, in the meantime, the " Mary" of Liverpool arrived at Fernando Po, on her way to Old Calabar; and they gladly availed themselves of the kind offer of Captain Foreshaw to take them with him at once. They accordingly sailed on Wednesday the 3d, and arrived at Duke Town on Friday. Governor Becroft went with them, as he took a very deep interest in the enterprise. " He is a veteran in the service of Western Africa, and is a man of great experience, and prudence, and influence among all classes." [1]

Mr. Jameson thus describes one of the trials of the situation, incident on the removal of their things from the beach to the mission-house at the hill top. It was towards the evening of Friday, the 5th of February, when, the anchor of the " Mary " being cast, " Captain Foreshaw sent our lug-

---

[1] Captain Becroft, who was British Consul, and also Governor of Fernando Po, at the time when the mission was begun, was respected and trusted by both the whites and the natives in the Bight of Biafra. He was a man of principle, straightforward and impartial, and anxious to advance every scheme that promised to benefit Africa. He well understood the character and the customs of the negroes ; and in settling palavers between them and the traders, he dealt out justice with a clean and even hand. The consequence was, that all honoured him while he lived, and lamented him when he died.

gage ashore in the pinnace.   By this time, it was almost dark. Mr. and Mrs. Edgerly went to King Eyamba's to get the key of the house ; and on procuring it, Mrs. Edgerly hastened to the house to get a candle lighted.   Mr. Edgerly set off to get men to carry up the things, while I remained on the beach to see them landed, and to take care of them.   In about twenty minutes, a number of people arrived, and having got the various articles placed either on their heads or on their shoulders, all set off with what they could carry, Mr. Edgerly and two servants accompanying the band, some sixteen or seventeen in number, lest, on the way, any should bolt with his burden, or hide some of it for his own use.   A lantern was now also brought, and a watch was set at the different corners of the road, to prevent, if possible, any pilfering.   Notwithstanding of this vigilance, Mr. Edgerly all but lost a box containing money.   He got a glimpse, in the dark, of the fellow making off with it, pursued him, and rescued the box.   All the things being removed from the beach, I took my place as a guard, and, in a short time, everything was safely deposited on the floor of the mission-house ; and I felt, for the first time for many months, that I was once more in a home.   Mrs. Edgerly had succeeded in making the empty house wear an air of comfort.   We got tea, and after having praised the Lord for his kindness, and committed ourselves and beloved friends at home to his care, we sought repose for the night.

" Saturday the 6th dawned upon us, and we stirred betimes, to get the remainder of the things landed.   Two or three dozen carriers were procured.   But the barrels, boxes, and packages were so heavy, that the poor creatures lost heart and ran off.   And no wonder ! I was almost disposed to do so too, when I saw them writhing, and sweating, and quivering under the ponderous loads.   What with the intense heat of the sun, the gabble of the naked slaves,—some grumbling, some falling on the steep ascent from the beach, while the bundle rolled back, and others tickled to the highest pitch at the scene,—and what with anxiety about the safety of the goods, I would gladly have fled from the sight of what pained me.

But the things had to be carried up ; they must work, and I must bear. All this arose from the necessity of carrying everything away for safety, when the family removed to Fernando Po.

" In the evening, I wrote a note to each of the ship masters, inviting them to attend divine service on the following day at the mission-house. With Governor Becroft and Mr. Edgerly I called on King Eyamba, to request the liberty of meeting in his house on the Sabbath, with such as might come. But he said it would not be convenient, as he would be busy. He, however, consented to have a meeting on the following Sabbath. Governor Becroft kindly remarked to me, on the way home, that patience is required. 'Your work will not drive; it must be done by little and little. Manage prudently; and, by and bye, Eyamba may have no difficulty in allowing you to do as you please. But what he says must be attended to. Your chief efforts, however, should be directed to the young.'

" On the forenoon of Sabbath, about six or seven of our countrymen came to worship, including Governor Becroft and Captain Crompton. I preached from the text, ' How shall we escape if we neglect so great salvation ?' On this my first Sabbath in Calabar, I felt that truly I was in a heathen land, and far from the Sabbath-keeping of my native country and of Goshen.

" On Saturday, I had told Eyamba that there was a stench about the mission premises, which threatened to sicken us all, and that I supposed it proceeded from a corpse lying in the neighbourhood. The King said that it was against the law to throw dead bodies into the bush around the mission-house. On Sabbath afternoon, one of the house people said that he had seen a dead body the day before. But on going to look, we found it had been removed. About the place where it had been lying, the stench was truly horrible. The body of the poor slave is not buried, but cast into the bush to waste away in the open air, or become the food of the vulture. Thus the bush about the town is full of human bones, and the atmosphere is polluted with putrescent animal matter.

" On *Monday, 8th February*, I went with Governor Becroft to visit King Eyo at Creek Town. He received us with kindness, and promised to aid us in erecting a school-house. I said that next week I should be at Creek Town for good, and he promised, on any day I mentioned, to send his large canoe to Duke Town for my luggage. During dinner, the Governor spoke to him about the odious practice of killing human beings on the death of big men. He allowed that the practice still existed ; and, as for himself, he said that there was an old woman—his mother, I believe—at whose death some slaves must be killed, and then he would be done with it for ever. I earnestly hope that, before that event takes place, he will, by the Divine blessing, see things in another light, and fall from his horrid resolution. He is a clear-headed man, and true to his engagements, on which account, I believe, he and his father before him have been called " Honesty ;" but very determined, and, as a ruler, severe. He is one whom you must respect, and whom you must desire to see under the influence of the grace of God. After dinner, we returned to Duke Town.

" Having now got all our things housed, the boxes had to be opened, and everything put in its place. But where that place was, it was hard to say, for it did not, as yet, exist. To meet this difficulty, we got two planks the length of the store-room, and fixed them up. We emptied some of the boxes, and put shelves in them, and set them upon the planks. As I sawed and hammered, Mr. Edgerly, having the best knowledge of the kind of goods required for the market, arranged the shelves, and Mrs. Edgerly stowed away into other boxes what was not likely to be required for present use.

" It is asked, naturally, What have you to do with all these goods ? You more resemble merchants than missionaries. The simple reply is, they stand us instead of money. By these we have to buy our food, and put up our houses. This system of traffic is a very heavy part of our cross. It takes up our time ; it calls away our attention from more congenial work ; and sometimes brings us into painful collision with the people. But as it is essential to the work which we have taken in hand, we must set our faces to it, and, in dependence on promised grace, do the best we can. But it is far from agreeable to leave one's work, four or five times a day, to sell a paper of needles for a fowl, a few fish hooks for eggs, a knife, or snuff-box, or padlock, or razor, for some yams. But necessity is a stern law. It is do or die. It is Christ's work we are working ; and since he became poor to make us rich, surely nothing should be esteemed hardship which is connected with the carrying on of the great design of mercy, even the working with our own hands, that we may not be burdensome to any, like the great Apostle of the Gentiles.

"Mr. Edgerly is a hard-working, zealous man. He turns his hand pleasantly to anything which requires to be done. The same may be said, with like truth, of Mrs. Edgerly. Her services in her department are no less valuable. A mother in Israel, where such mothers are so few, is a blessing of no ordinary kind.

"14*th February.*—Sabbath has at length arrived. We had fixed eight A.M. for the meeting at Eyamba's place. It had rained all night, and was raining in the morning. But not liking to break the engagement, Mr. Edgerly and I went down. Eyamba said that there was too much rain, that his gentlemen had not come, and that we better return at two P.M. At eleven A.M. I went on board the 'Henry,' Captain Smith, while Mr. Edgerly went on board the 'Magistrate,' to hold divine service. After finishing, we called on Eyamba, and found him in the midst of his marketing. The floor was covered with yams, coppers, etc., and the place was full of people. We went home, and returned at two o'clock. Eyamba told us to go up stairs, and he would be ready in a little. After waiting fully an hour, and no call, I went down and told him that my time was too precious, and I could not remain any longer. He said he was ready, but the gentlemen were not come. I waited for nearly another hour. At last, the table was covered for dinner ; and a few minutes before the eatables were carried in, it was signified to me that the king was ready. We went down stairs, and found five or six gentlemen sitting around him, with a few slaves standing behind.   I explained the object of our work, and the religion which we had come to teach them.   Eyamba interpreted, but in a manner so careless and indifferent, that I much doubt whether he communicated the ideas which I wanted to convey. In the meantime, the smoking viands, in large calabashes, were being carried up stairs, and the eyes and hearts of all parties were turned with marked avidity to the meat which perisheth. I stopped, Mr. Edgerly prayed, and we took our leave.

"The hearts of the people are wholly bent on trade, and most firmly glued to their heathenish and superstitious practices. That they do not wish to have their minds disturbed about the opinions and practices of their forefathers they declare ; and their conduct shows how truly they speak.   God has opened a door of entrance ; and we are most thankful for being allowed to live here without molestation, and teach the young.   The want of a knowledge of the language is a great barrier to our doing much among them.   Few understand us, and these few understand us imperfectly.   The language and the truths of the word of God are entirely foreign to them.   On our interpreters little reliance can, as yet, be placed.   It is true, indeed, and this is the spring of our present activity, that the Divine Spirit, in his saving operations, is not limited by human calculations of times, and seasons, and fitting instrumentality.   For aught we know, He may, at the present moment, be preparing an Eyamba or an Eyo for receiving the word of eternal life.   Let us not cease to pray that it may be so.   But, humanly speaking, the present aspect of things strongly demonstrates that this field must be cultivated by the acquisition of the native language, the translation and circulation of the Holy Scriptures, and teaching the young to read these Scriptures, and, in some measure, comprehend the doctrines and precepts which they contain, and the terms in which these doctrines and precepts are expressed.

" On Wednesday, the 17th, I came with bag and baggage to Creek Town.   I have been carrying on a war of extermination against the white ants, which have devoured almost entirely some of the posts which support the floor.   They eat into the heart of the wood, and while a post may look well enough from without, yet when you strike it with the hammer, you find that it is nothing more than a shell; and as you lay bare the interior, thousands of the ants are seen running about in all directions."

With more than his usual zeal did Mr. Jameson throw himself into his work. He was face to face with heathenism, among a people wholly ignorant of the name and salvation of God. And his soul was stirred within him as he viewed the sad scene, and knew that he bore a sovereign remedy for all that woe and wickedness. Here was Satan's throne. Not a pillar of it hewn away! Here was his citadel. Not a breach made in it! for the attack was only just begun. The lowest depths of childish, or rather of hellish superstition have been reached by these children of Ham. Evil has become their good, and the devil their god. How can it be otherwise? Is it not thus wherever the glorious gospel of the blessed God is unknown? Is there any other Saviour from sin than Jesus? And how can men who never heard his name implore his help? Church of the living God! wake up to pity! Wake up to the high enterprise of your glorious mission! Christian men and women of Britain! let all this woe be your concern; and with the finger of mercy stoop down, in God's name, to undo this heavy burden, that is crushing millions into hell! Hasten to the rescue! Here is pre-eminently your work; and you are only beginning to begin to do it. Ethiopia is promised to Jesus, and belongs to him; and we must proclaim through her wide borders the truth about his person and his salvation. It is stern, hard work that is needed. The learning of strange tongues, the patient giving of line upon line, the telling about love Divine to callous and petrified hearts, with no encouragement, or with much opposition, from the poor blinded creatures themselves—this is the kind of work to be performed there. But there too the word of God, in the hand of the Spirit of God, is the same sharp sword, the same resistless fire-flame, the same crushing hammer, that it is elsewhere. Prophesy upon the bones, and prophesy to the winds; and shall not these bones then live? To doubt it is to doubt the omnipotence of Jesus.

The subject of this Memoir saw and believed all this ; and, therefore, he began to teach and to preach to old and young the truth as it is in Jesus.   He has left a very full journal of his work up to July 30th, within six days of his death.   Considerable portions of that journal were published in various numbers of the *Missionary Record* of the United Presbyterian Church, in 1847 and 1848.   Among these there are very full notices of the topics on which he addressed the people, who assembled on the Sabbath mornings in King Eyo's yard, when his words were interpreted to the audience by the King himself.   This Eyo was able to do, as he had a good knowledge of colloquial English, and was also much interested in the subjects which were brought to their notice.   The following extracts are mainly such as have not hitherto been published.

" *Wednesday, 24th February.*—I commenced the school with thirty-two in the morning and thirty-five in the afternoon. King Eyo sent up a bell to ring at school hours.   The children behaved well ; and some of them can read a little, while they seem most anxious to learn.   Altogether, the work of the day has gone on very satisfactorily.   I fondly hope that the gracious Lord will in mercy bless the undertaking, and make it conducive to this people's good, and his own glory.

" *Thursday, 25th.*—The school list to-day numbered forty-two.   A few who were with us yesterday, went to-day with King Eyo to Duke Town to visit the ships.   They told me that they were going, and I expressed my regret, as it would be very much against their learning.   At the close, Esien, the king's second son, a boy of about ten years old, came to say that if king say he must go, he will go, but if not, he will come to school.   He came to-day ; but the others, not being able to resist the temptation of a day's pleasure, went in the canoes. To show that I was pleased with his self-denial, I ' dashed ' Esien a knife, with which he seemed highly pleased. About twenty of the boys came up to family worship.   I made them repeat after me the Lord's prayer and the Ten Commandments.   In commencing the school, I prayed shortly myself, and then made the scholars again repeat the Lord's prayer and the Commandments. None of them appeared to understand one word of what they were saying, and for me to attempt to give them any idea of it was only confounding the confusion. I spoke : they understood not, and shook their heads. They spoke : I understood not, and shook mine. I put some to their books, and others to the letter box, making thought visible, and sound sense.

"*Friday, 26th.*—A number of Ebo people came to see the white man and his house. I asked them if they would like to see a white man in their country. They said, 'Yes.'"

Missionaries have not free access to the interior parts. Every article of commerce passes through the hands of the coast tribes. They jealously watch over this monopoly ; and lest the operations of missionaries should in any way interfere with it, they use every means to keep them from visiting places beyond. This makes extreme caution and prudence, and Christian forbearance and temper, necessary on the part of the missionary who desires to preach Jesus where His name is not known. Patience, caution, and wisdom, combined with tact and kindly firmness, will, under God, break down this barrier. Mr. Jameson soon discovered this difficulty ; and it still exists in Old Calabar with little abatement. He wrote:—"I have been told that this was the cause of the death of Lander. He was shot by a Bonny man, who went into the interior for that purpose. The murderer is alive still, and is well known at Bonny. I make these observations to show that our way will be in a great measure shut up, until those among whom we dwell, feel perfectly assured that in giving us a permit, they do not risk their trade ; and that, in the meantime, it is our duty to show them what we are, and whose we are, by diligently doing our duty.

"Some days ago, I tried my hand, for the first time, at Calabar marketing. Wanting fresh soup, I sent to the market to buy a fowl. A person who said he was my friend, sent me one, charging 16 coppers, and also some small fish for which he charged 13 ; saying that he would come for the coppers in the evening. He came, making great professions of friendship.   I went to the box and paid him 29 ship coppers instead of 29 Calabar coppers, that is 145 instead of 29. He continued to boast of his friendliness in high-sounding terms, while, at the same time, he failed not to lay his greedy hands on my best knives and forks, and padlocks, and scissors. I said to him that if this was the price I had to pay for living at Creek Town, I must go.   On thinking, I found out my mistake, and was not a little annoyed at my stupidity and simplicity, which were the more inexcusable, as I had been warned of the difference.   I sent for my friend, with a message that he must bring the coppers with him.   He came himself, but took care to leave the goods at home.   He was easily persuaded that I had made a great mistake.   But he said he would take the remainder on trust, and send me the value.

" *Saturday, 27th February.*—Wrote a note to King Eyo, saying that as to-morrow was the Sabbath of the Lord, I would be happy to hold divine service with him and his people. In reply, he stated that he would be too busy to-morrow, but that, next week, he would be ready.   As might be expected, the Sabbath as a day of sacred rest is utterly unknown in Calabar.   It comes and goes like the other days of the week. It is said to be well that we have not idolaters to deal with, but a people without any religion, to whom we seek to give one.   This sounds well far off, but when you come near to grapple with what is, you find it awfully obvious, that the carnal mind is enmity against God.   Whether idolaters or no idolaters, human power is no power.   In both cases the arm of the Lord is needed, and in both cases the arm of the Lord is all that is needed.   This great mountain, before the Lord's servants, and to speed on his cause, will sink into a plain."

In allusion to the Egbo institution, Mr. Jameson writes that, " to expose to the people, in our present circumstances, and in theirs, the delusions connected with the apparently mysterious being called Egbo, would be to peril the safety of the country, and it would prove fatal to the work which we desire to advance, by causing us to be sent out of the country.

We should act as men who want to take down an old wall. They build a new one out of better materials before demolishing the old, so that what is enclosed and worth preserving may suffer nothing by undue exposure. Our present work is to spread far and wide, among old and young, by teaching and preaching, the knowledge of the Christian religion—the best bulwark of nations, as well as the source of man's best hope for time and eternity. As we proceed, under the power of the Spirit of God, the minds of the people will be gradually enlightened ; they will become disgusted at their former ignorance and superstition ; and all classes will consent to remove the unseemly structure of former ages, and to erect the bulwarks of the country on the foundation of righteousness and truth. O Lord ! hasten this day, long desired and expected. Arise, O Sun of Righteousness ! with healing in thy wings, that this dark night may pass away from under these heavens.

" *Wednesday*, 10*th March*.—To-day the school was small. It is King Eyo's Sunday—the day on which he makes a Calabar feast to all the white men in the river. A general invitation is given by three cannon shots fired in the morning ; and all white people are welcome to come. In explaining the second commandment, I mentioned the name of the devil. The boy who was interpreting asked, ' Who is the devil ?' ' Your enemy, and the enemy of God. He tries to make you as bad as himself, that you may be punished as he will be.' ' But why did God make the devil so bad ?' I replied, that God made him good, but he became proud, and was cast down to hell ; and that now he goes about trying to turn all men against God, and in favour of himself. ' But, why does God not kill him ?' ' God could easily kill him, but He leaves him alone, as well as He leaves men who are bad. Yet a time is coming when God will punish the devil and all his followers.' Many of the children are shrewd. I humbly trust that the most blessed Spirit will prepare an intelligent and energetic agency here. Out of these stones he can raise up children to Abraham.

" *Sabbath*, 14*th March*.—Went down this morning to the

king's yard according to promise, to meet with the people. I sat there a long time, and saw no movement of any kind that appeared to favour my object. The king had sent out the Egbo drum to summon the people. On its return I was called, and on going down from the king's dining-room to the yard where they were assembled, found the attendance very good. The king commanded silence. Having prayed, I gave them some account of the creation, but directed their attention more particularly to the creation of man.

"*Saturday, 20th March.*—Hearing that the king was about to start for Duke Town to visit the ships, I went down to remind him that to-morrow is God's Sabbath, and to arrange a meeting for divine worship. Having told my errand, I expressed the hope that we should have our usual meeting. He said he would tell me when he came back. I said, 'King, I hope you will make no engagement for to-morrow that will interfere with the Lord's work : for this is your chief business to-morrow. If you lay it aside, God will be angry, but if you attend to it, his blessing may rest upon you. When you return, I will send to inquire, and will come down to-morrow, at any hour which you may appoint.' I sent accordingly, in the evening, and received a note in reply :—'MY DEAR FRIEND,—I will be happy to hear God's word to-morrow morning at eight o'clock.'

"*Sabbath, 21st.*—Went down according to arrangement, and found the king engaged in some business. I went up to the dining-room, bidding him call me when he was ready. In a little, the messenger came. The king appeared annoyed, because there were not more people, and said : 'I sent out early to call all men, and you see very few have come.' However, there were about as many as usual. When I was commencing to speak, the king turned round and said : 'I wish you would tell the people about all those things they do in abusing and killing one another. I want no more man to be killed, but all these things to be done away with.' I said that I would do so with pleasure, as I was to speak about sin, and that would just come in my way. I then said to the people, 'You see that you have a good king, one who desires your good, and he is sorry to see that there are not more of his people present. I want to see your wives and children here also, for I am sent to teach them as well as the men. All must die ; all must rise again ; all must be judged, but only the good will go to happiness ; the bad will be sent to punishment.' The king said, 'Yes, this meeting is for all alike.'"

Then follows a very full account of the discourse for that day, in which the missionary informed them of the creation of woman, the history and character of the devil, his successful endeavour to ruin man, the first disobedience, and the expulsion of our first parents from paradise.

The school occupied Mr. Jameson's time during some part of each day. Every true missionary must feel the importance, yea, the necessity, of exerting himself among the young. If his lot is cast among people who have a literature, and schools where the youth are taught to read, he need not, at the commencement of his mission, spend his time in teaching the art of reading. As in Burmah, he finds a people who can read, and are fond of reading, and he sets himself, like the apostolic Judson, to acquire a complete knowledge of their tongue, that he may at once spread the knowledge of the Saviour through tracts and books carefully prepared and widely circulated. By and bye, Christian schools will become necessary ; but the pioneer will not spend much of his time in this department. It is otherwise in Africa. Of what use are books, if the people are not taught how to use them ? Can a missionary fail to labour in the daily, exhausting work of teaching the young the arts of reading and writing ; and can he despise any means, however humble, by which the young may be encouraged to seek instruction, or allow any occupation whatever to make him either neglect this department altogether or do it remissly ? Let every labourer in the field of missions look at the noble example of William Jameson. When his hands were full of pastoral work, and his heart full of anxieties in church building, when he had no Society's funds to fall back upon, if he had not a suitably qualified helper for the school, he devoted to it his best energies. And here, in Africa, he pursued the same course. And so will every man whose heart is in his work, and who gives himself to it, with that singleness of purpose and of aim, which it requires.

Mr. Jameson spent his leisure in learning the language. He says :—" The language we are acquiring as fast as we can. I have arranged it, through the help of Mr. Waddell's vocabulary, into something like grammatical order, and translated the Lord's Prayer and some other portions of the New Testament. How far I have succeeded in this first attempt I am not yet fully able to judge, my object being chiefly self-advancement in the knowledge of the language."

Missionaries in Africa require a talent for acquiring languages, as much as missionaries in Asia. Africa has no literature, no grammar, no moonshees, no pundits. It is difficult for a European to learn an African language ; yet it is of the very first importance. No native can interpret a missionary's thoughts, and convey his feelings with fulness and accuracy. It needs much time and labour to enable him to do so himself, in vehicles so imperfect as vehicles of religious feeling and Christian truth, and so imperfectly understood. And what if, as in the case of Madagascar, the missionaries should be banished, and the converts left to themselves ! If the word of God or some portions of it are left in their hands, all will be well. The Lord, the Spirit, will make his own use of it. A seed will thus be left in the soil, and it will not be lost. To give an African tribe a good version of the word of God, and teach as many as possible to read it, is to do a great work. If this is done, then let the devil stir up his children to drive away the Lord's servants. The tree has been planted which will not die. The fire has been kindled that will not quench. That germ of life will live in the sternest soil, and the Lord of life will make a lever of it to overturn, and change, and regenerate. Church of God, in favoured Britain and favoured America ! put on new strength. Grudge not your best men to the work of rendering the sacred words of Heaven into every tongue of man that needs a version. And do not grudge the means of teaching as many as possible to read and understand it.

The following extracts, from a letter addressed to Mr. and Mrs. Milne, his brother and sister, give some sketch of Mr. Jameson's domestic experience at Creek Town :—

"My house I had got into some degree of order and comfort, when a tornado came on and destroyed it. The wind made the thatch fly in all directions. On looking out, I saw that our kitchen had been laid flat with the ground. The rain poured in on us, so that, in five minutes, the floor of the hall was running, and my bedroom, the only other room in the house, was admitting the rain in all quarters. A young man who came with me from Fernando Po, makes my food, goes to market, and looks after my house. Another young boy cleans knives, etc. Upon the whole, I am comfortable and happy : for having my work, there is no time to weary, and this, with the presence of the blessed Master, is all that is required to reconcile the mind to any place and to any circumstances. None must come here expecting much. Love to Christ and to his work can alone sustain the mind amidst the privations and discomforts to which we are exposed. He that is happy under the Cross, as well as when not under it, will find satisfaction and peace ; but every other will find a vacuum which nothing can fill. I feel thankful that I have none with me whom I love as myself, either wife or sister, subjected to see, to feel, to hear what there is in this part of the world. You must not suppose from these remarks that I regret my coming, or that I am aught but happy. If you do, you are mistaken. I am very happy, very busy, and very hot."

The whole of his correspondence at this time is most animating, full of ardent devotion to Christ, and breathing forth the intensest zeal. It is the bright and softening radiance of the setting sun. This is nothing uncommon in the experience of exemplary servants of the Lord. The nearer they come to the goal, the faster do they run. The nearer to the twelfth hour, the more vigorously do they work the work of the Lord. Some rays from the approaching glory are reflected from their countenances. Jesus feels nearer—yea, close at hand. Their joy is to speak of him, and to think of him, and to pray to him. And they are frequently favoured with a prophetic instinct, and see the light of the Sun of Righteousness beginning to gild the tops of the hills of darkness, harbingers of his sure and glorious rising—of a perfect day of gospel privilege and Christian life, in places where, from the beginning of the world until now, the word of the living God has not been preached.

The next entry in the journal refers to the sickening scenes of blood which were enacted at the death of King Eyamba. A soul-harrowing narrative of the atrocities which were perpetrated at his death, was given by Messrs Edgerly and Jameson, and full particulars are contained in the *Missionary Record* for November, 1847. There we see the earnest efforts made by Mr. Jameson and Mr. Edgerly to save life, and how fruitless were their endeavours. They remonstrated and pleaded, but the heathen heart, inured to scenes of inhumanity, felt not their appeals. Superstition neither fears God nor regards man. But these efforts and testimonies against evil and for good were perseveringly followed up by the missionaries ; and in 1856, through the Divine blessing, bore fruit. In that year, under the influence of good King Eyo Honesty, a law was made, that no more men should be killed for the dead. It should be borne in mind, that there is ever among heathens a danger of partial relapse into old customs. In so far as is known, the Calabar people have kept their own law, although it has been alleged that it has been evaded by some. The only security against a reaction is the gradual leavening of the mass with the spirit of the religion of Jesus Christ.

"*Monday, 31st.*—King Cameroons visited me some time ago, and remained to dinner. Having nothing but a tea-cup to divide the soup, and mugs to drink our water, the gentleman said nothing, but ate his chop heartily and pleasantly. As soon as he returned to his house, he sent up a boy with a divider and two tumblers, with a message, that no Calabar gentleman liked to drink out of mugs, but they all use dividers to soup, and tumblers to water.

"Another day, John Eyo, a brother of the king, was at breakfast. We wanted egg-cups, but we managed as well as circumstances would permit. He made no remark, but on going home, he sent up two wine-glasses to be used for that purpose. If I am not a gentleman at chop, it is not because I lack the kind attention of my friends.

"*June 6th.*—Speaking to the children in school respecting prayer, I asked whether any of them ever prayed. Some said, 'Yes;' others, 'No.' One boy, on being asked, replied, 'No. I cannot pray in English yet, and God no saby Calabar.' I assured him that he was in a great mistake, for God saby Calabar as well as English. He saby everything we think before we speak it, and although we do not speak it at all.

"After being so long here, I felt desirous that King Eyo should visit my house, and dine with me. I accordingly fixed a day; and he came, with a number of his chiefs. Addison, my man, rose at three A.M., and by ten o'clock had everything ready to set on the table. A little before that hour, the king arrived. He walked under the shade of a huge umbrella of various colours, chiefly red and blue. This gay canopy is five or six feet wide; the handle is perhaps seven feet long, and from two to three inches thick. Behind the king walks the bearer of the umbrella, and around him are his attendants, each carrying a sword or a musket. In this company were the gentlemen, and the greater number of the school children, who seemed as deeply interested in the proceedings as any. After dinner, or more properly breakfast, I proposed to read a portion of God's word, and pray. This I accordingly did. While reading and explaining the law of love, and the evils of quarrelling and fighting, the king said : 'Yes, I know that be true, long ago. For this same town here was broken to pieces and destroyed by quarrels. Many people were killed, and many went away to live at Duke Town. I wished to come back to my father's town, and wanted my family to come with me, but they all refused. At last, I got one or two of them to come, and we build up the place. Then one come, then another, till we all come back.' The forenoon was spent thus in a very interesting manner.   I was struck with the decorum and good manners of all who were present."

The " Warree," at length, arrived from Jamaica with a reinforcement, consisting of Messrs. Goldie and Newhall, with their wives, and several natives of Jamaica.

"*Saturday, June 19th.*—The forenoon's school having closed, I took the glass to see what signal was raised at the mission-house at Duke Town.   The letter ' W ' at last made its appearance.   This signal had been agreed upon to announce the arrival of the ' Warree.'   I immediately got six or seven of the school boys with their paddles into the boat, and set off, in all haste, to meet the friends from afar.   All were well and in good spirits ; a gracious God had encompassed them with mercy during a tedious voyage of three months.

" Mr. Waddell came with me, so that, this evening, I had the happiness of welcoming my brother to my humble abode in Old Calabar.   Last time I saw him under my roof was at Goshen Pen House.   How different the abodes !   But not different the hearts !   Not different the God whom we serve ! We pray as well in this humble dwelling, as in the great house at Goshen ; and we are as happy in the one place as in the other.   We have our work, our food, our sleep, our Christian privileges, the fulness of Him who filleth all in all, as our portion, and what more can we desire ?   We forget not all his benefits."

Of this happy meeting Mr. Waddell makes the following notice :—" The sight of Brother Jameson put all gloomy thoughts to flight.   It was delightful to meet him here in Calabar.   My beloved brother had joyfully put up with what others would have murmured at as inconveniences, and was as happy, he assured me, as ever he had been in his life.   He had bent his energies to the school, and it prospered in his hands."

"*Sabbath, 20th June.*—Mr. Waddell preached in the king's yard.   Every one was glad to see him, and welcomed him as an old friend.   He explained Rom. xiii. on the relative duties of rulers and subjects.   The people were well out, and attentive."

Referring to the same day, Mr. Waddell writes :—" In the afternoon, the children assembled in the Sabbath school, and my delight in hearing Mr. Jameson and others getting on in mingled English and Calabar, was more than I can well express."

" *Monday, 21st.*—Mr. Waddell and I, after the morning school, returned to Duke Town. We had our first meeting of committee, and agreed that Mr. Waddell retain his station at Duke Town ; and that, for the present, Mr. Goldie remain there also, until he be acclimatized, learn the language, and Providence open up another field for him to occupy ; that I remain at Creek Town, and that Mr. Newhall go there to teach the school ; and that Mr. Edgerly open a new station at Old Town.

" *Wednesday, June 30th.*—The schooner came up to Creek Town, on Thursday last, to land the house which was brought from Jamaica for this station. She anchored immediately below the town, and full in sight of the mission-house.[1] The sight of her resting on the peaceful water, aroused thoughts of interest and grandeur. Rest on, little vessel ! and enjoy the repose to which thy hard service entitles thee. May the blessing of Heaven ever rest on thee, and on him who has placed thee at our disposal.[2] And whether thou continue ours or not, may prosperous gales ever attend thee."

The house was landed from the " Warree," and carried up, board by board, to the place where it now stands. The king's people and the school children carried, and the king's brothers superintended. " About one o'clock, the children

---

[1] Over the tops of the mangrove trees, seven miles away, stand the Duke Town mission premises ; and to the left, at about the same distance, is Old Town. Signals can be interchanged between the three mission-houses at pleasure. Below, there lies the Creek ; and between the mission-house and the Creek is the native town. The most prominent objects are the king's house, and the church more to the left. The former was burned in 1859.

[2] When a ship was wanted to convey the mission to Africa, a liberal friend, Mr. Baikie of Kirkwall, gave a new sloop. But it was found to be too small ; and, just in the hour of need, one of Liverpool's princely merchants generously granted the use of the "Warree," as long as she might be needed, with an annual subscription of £100 to keep her in a sailing condition.

came beating on their bellies, signifying that they were hungry.
A potful of Calabar chop was standing ready for my dinner.
In a twinkling it was devoured, and the beating on the belly
still continued. Some of them shook their skins heartily to
show how empty they were. More chop was cooked, and, at
last, all were satisfied.

The following, from a letter to Miss Jameson (now Mrs.
Simpson of Annan), 19th July, 1847, is interesting. The
pioneer goes into the virgin forest, and by patient toil fells the
old trees, and makes a clearance. He builds a humble log-
house, and works on in the woods there. A hard life is his,
but hope keeps him up and at it. He sees, in prospect, fields
of ripe grain where now the forest waves. Posterity will owe
much to him, and to those hardy men who work and hope like
him. To such as these they will owe fruitful fields, and yellow
harvests, and wealth. These men are planting the acorn.
Children's children will rejoice under the broad arms of the
giant oak. Their rude shanties, made of the rough logs, are
the germs of stately homes, where elegance and plenty will yet
be seen. So it is with the pioneer missionary. His is the
burden and heat of the day. His it is to go forth weeping
with his precious seed, to fell the forest, to clear off the jungle,
and to sow. Others will come after and reap. He labours ;
others will enter into his labours. The sower and the reaper
shall rejoice together, when they meet in their Father's home on
high, and see the precious sheaves that have been gathered from
their united labours—a blessed increase which the Lord has
given.

"From the time I rise till I lie down, every moment is
occupied. I have upwards of sixty scholars daily. We are
also busy in putting up the house. It will be a comfortable
residence, if God dwell with us, and hallow it with his presence.
I could look upon it as a home, were you and Catherine under
its roof. But, at present, that cannot be. The natives are
kind, and I feel myself not only perfectly safe, but even happy,
in the midst of them. The children and adults go and come
with all the ease and familiarity which were shown by our

people at Goshen. Sometimes they dash (present) a fowl, sometimes a goat, and sometimes a few yams.

Sabbath Scenes in the King's Yard.—" Eyo likes very ill to
interpret the same thing over again. He has a very tenacious
memory, and if I happen to repeat a statement, he turns round
and says : ' You tell us that before ; we want to hear something we no saby yet.' Once and again I have gone with
my subject prepared ; and as soon as he discovered the drift
of it, he looked up and said : ' That no do. I tell you we want
the fashions. The people no care about these things yet. By
and bye they will like them ; but all man come to hear what
God's word want them to do.' Eyo likes the law, or the
fashions, as he calls it, but the doctrine of the Cross appears to
him but foolishness. Sometimes a long palaver arises between
him and the rest about something suggested by the discourse.
Last Sabbath, I was explaining the nature of prayer, and told
them that we must pray in the name of Jesus Christ, and not
love sin in our hearts. Eyo said : ' I wish God would take
away all sin out of my heart, that I might pray right.' And
I stated that God hears and answers the prayers of his people.
Here Eyo proposed a difficulty : ' Why so many people pray God
to give them chop, and they no get the kind they want ?'
Among other reasons, I stated that some pray but will not
work. All day, they sit and clamour to Abasi (God) for chop,
as if He would send it down to them from heaven ; but they
do not work for it. Now, God says, If a man will not work,
he shall not eat. This reason tickled the king much. He
laughed heartily, and began with *birr* to interpret. He had,
now and then, to stop to get out his laugh, in which the rest
joined him ; and, for about ten minutes, the gravity of our
meeting was completely upset. At length, Eyo said, ' That
be very good fashion ; we all saby that and like it.' What
helped to arouse the sense of the ridiculous, was the presence
of a man called, by way of nickname, *King Chop*, who is just
such a person as I had described, ever clamouring for the good
things of this life, but unwilling to do a hand's turn. Eyo feeds
him out of charity."

But—

> "The spoiler came, and all that promise fair
> Has sought the grave, to hide for ever there."

Mr Jameson's labours, prosecuted with so much wisdom, fidelity, love, and zeal, could not fail to commend him to those among whom he lived. In one department, that of settling palavers, he seems to have been singularly gifted. This work among Africans requires in Europeans great patience and good temper. Both are severely tried in hearing a full and particular account of the minutiæ of quarrels which are, in general, very childish, and arise from frivolous causes, although attended with extraordinary heat, and cherished with great tenacity. Mr. Jameson showed so much tact and temper in settling these differences, that the late King Eyo used to tell the writer that his father proposed to install him as judge for the whole town ! !

During the too short period of his life in Old Calabar, he established himself in the confidence and affection of all. Even now, after a lapse of fourteen years, his memory is cherished ; and any reference to him still awakens the slumbering feeling of regard towards the faithful servant of the Lord who spent such a short missionary life in their midst. The late King Eyo has told the writer that, at one time, during Mr. Jameson's stay at Creek Town, he was in great trouble. His mother had committed a great fault, and was put under ban by his father. Such was the shame and vexation of her son, that in his desperation he resolved to commit suicide. But God directed him to open his mind to Mr. Jameson, who sat with him the greater part of the night, and by his conversation, diverted him from his purpose. In the language of Governor Becroft, " The people idolized him, and there was nothing which it was beyond his power to accomplish." His scholars frequented his room, and he was among them as an elder brother. He was full of plans for their benefit and for the promotion of the mission.

All who are actually engaged in, or aspire to, the work of missionaries to the heathen, would do well to inquire what was the secret of the success of such a servant of the Lord. By what means, or by what attribute of character, did he acquire so much influence over men, and enter so deeply into their confidence ? There is only one answer to this question. Mr. Jameson was one who loved men for their good. His heart was large. He could love even an ugly, rude, untutored, selfish African, and that from the remarkable affectionateness of his disposition. The power of love was the power which opened to him the hearts of those among whom he laboured. No man can be a good missionary without this spirit of love. The heathen, if not attracted to the man, by seeing that he loves them, will not be drawn to the "doctrine," however ably he may preach it. If the missionary be unamiable, impatient, irascible, or petulant, if he be disposed to be angry at what is bad among the heathen, and get soured by their greed, and falsehood, and other evil qualities, they will soon discover it. And the discovery will not fail to steel them against the missionary personally, and against the gospel, which he ought to commend to them by the very opposite characteristics. They will not exercise towards him the forbearance which a pious church exercises towards the infirmities of a pastor. The evangelist must be an embodiment of gospel love. And the more ignorant, and stolid, and provoking, and even insulting the sinners are to whom he preaches Jesus Christ, the more necessary is it that he exhibit among them, and towards them, the patient love that animated our blessed Lord and Saviour, and which was reflected from such preachers of the Cross as Paul and John, and such missionaries as a Williams, a Judson, and a Jameson. If in one missionary now in the field, or in one missionary-elect, or in one young person destined of God for missionary work, this narrative of the ten years' earnest and loving labour of this large-hearted man, be the means of evoking a determination to grow in the spirit of gospel love, of which Jesus Christ was, pre-eminently, the exemplar, and of which the subject of it was so noble a specimen, it will not have been written in vain.

It is with regret that we draw near to behold the end of

this ministry. Would to God that it had been prolonged! Why, we ask, was such a labourer removed so soon? Why is he not still in the high places of the field? Our blessed Lord and Master would both try the faith of his people, and rebuke their sad tendency to make man their trust. How shall the work go on, when such a labourer dies? How shall the war prosper, when such a soldier rests? The Lord will show that he has others, and will send them forth. The fatal tendency among the churches to look away from the arm of the Lord to the earth-born arm that bears to the poor heathen the word of life, is a tendency that ever provokes rebuke and trial. Why will not the people of God cease from man—emphatically cease from man, whose breath is in his nostrils? The Lord is dishonoured and displeased, when we forget that the conversion of a soul is entirely due to His almighty grace. To this thoughtlessness and idolatry on the part of the Church we, no doubt, owe the removal of many a master of Israel. God thus teaches us that "not by might or by power" of man, "but by the Lord, the Spirit," can the world be turned to Him.

But the days of our appointed time must come to an end. "The numbered hour is on the wing that lays us with the dead." The Lord's work seems to need the devoted, and wise, and affectionate service of his gifted ambassador. To his friends he seems indispensable. His fellow-labourers cling to him in the land of dark heathenism. But is not Jesus himself alive, and present too, when the servant is removed to heaven? And is not He "all in all" to his own cause, to the bereaved heart, and to the labourers in the field, who, at the death of their brother, feel as when a standard-bearer falls?

The following, to his daughter, was among the very last which Mr. Jameson wrote :—

"*July* 23*d*, 1847.—MY BELOVED CHILD,—I am glad to hear that you are getting on at school, that you like it, that you learn your lessons, and that you are able to stand so high in the class. All this makes me very glad. But do not forget that the blessing of God alone can make your learning truly profitable, and that without this what you learn will be of little service. Strive not to get above your neighbours in the class, that you may be considered better than they ; for this is an unworthy feeling and very unprofitable. Strive, my dear child, for knowledge, which is unspeakably better than medals, or prizes, or praise. Above all, seek the knowledge which maketh wise unto salvation. Oh, Catherine, what is the world without this ? What is any accomplishment of mind or body worth, if the soul be barren towards God ? Read those books which bring before you the state of your depraved heart, and show you that you are undone, and which tell you of the love of Jesus Christ. Above all, read your Bible diligently, and pray earnestly for the Divine Spirit. . . . May the Lord keep you, my child, and may he lead your heart to himself, in your youthful years. This is the prayer of your loving father."

On Wednesday, July 28th, Mr. Jameson visited Duke Town, for the last time. During that week, he had felt indisposed, but had been able to go on with his work. The brethren had agreed to observe the Lord's Supper, for the first time, in that heathen land, on the afternoon of Sabbath, the 1st of August, and he was anticipating with joy the blessed ordinance. On the evening of Wednesday, he addressed the weekly prayer-meeting at Duke Town, on the 14th chapter of the Gospel of John. He spoke of the chapter as abounding in promises, filled with consolation, and well fitted to chase away perplexities and cares, and lead to the fountain of rest and peace those who were living in that land of sin and death. He then spoke of the pleasure which he anticipated in sitting down at the Lord's table in Old Calabar. He slept on board the " Warree," and, next morning, returned to Creek Town.

On the evening of Friday (30th), he and Mr. Waddell took a walk to a hill, about a mile distant, as it was a tempting evening for a little wholesome exercise. " I hope it will do me good," he said, " for I have not felt so well to-day, a little feverish like. The fresh air and exercise, after the heat, and dust, and confinement of the school, will help to brace me up." On their return, he took medicine and a warm bath, and, next morning, said he felt quite well.

The morning of Sabbath (August 1st) was very damp,' and Mr. Jameson did not feel well. He doubted the propriety of his going to Duke Town that day, deeply regretting that he should not be present at the first celebration of the Lord's Supper in that country. Mr. Waddell went to Duke Town, and Mr. Jameson to his usual meeting in the king's yard, hoping that after it was over, he might yet be able to join the little band around the Lord's table. But death had begun to execute his commission—to prepare the Lord's servant for his Master's presence. With that service in King Eyo's yard his ministry ended. Never again will the children of Efik hear his voice, till the day of accounts, when it may be heard testifying against those who refused to believe and obey the word of eternal life, which he and others declared unto them.

The record of the closing scenes of this devoted, godly, earnest life, is preserved in letters from those who were fellow-labourers in that land of darkness and of death. The accounts contained in these letters are exceedingly touching. About noon on Sabbath, Mr. Waddell, who was conducting a religious service on board the " Majestic," received a note from Mr. Jameson, saying that he was very unwell, and wished to see Dr. M'Losky, immediately. That gentleman went to Creek Town, without delay ; and, after the solemn and interesting service of communion at the table of the Lord, Mr. Waddell hastened to the bed-side of his sick brother, and found him attended by Mr. Chisholm, one of the carpenters of the mission. He was very composed, and much gratified to hear that they had had a comfortable service. The directions of Dr. M'Losky, who felt anxious about Mr. Jameson, were carried out during the night ; and, on the morning of Monday, there was such apparent improvement as delighted the doctor. In the evening, fever returned ; and, on the morning of Tuesday, symptoms of mental wandering appeared. When Mr. Waddell spoke or read to, or prayed with him, he was perfectly sensible.

Then he would shut his eyes a little, and murmur incoherently. Such precious words as, " Fear not, for I am with thee ; be not dismayed, for I am thy God, etc.," would cause a smile of complacency, and he would say, " Ah, that is it ! That is the good word ! That is the truth ! ' Never leave thee, never forsake thee !' " The doctor came, and took measures which resulted, by the Divine blessing, in such improvement, that the beloved patient revived, indications of delirium ceased, and he passed a tolerable night.

On Wednesday (4th), Mr. Jameson was apparently much better. King Eyo went to see him, and sat a few minutes with him. To him, and to one or two of his best scholars, he spoke a few words. Messrs. Goldie, Edgerly, and Newhall went from Duke Town to visit him. He said he was much better, and would soon go to Duke Town, for change of air. About seven P.M., he became sleepy, and about nine began to refuse his medicines. He slept till near two o'clock, but not a refreshing sleep. His skin was hot and dry, and his pulse quick. He became very restless, and moaned much, with occasionally short sighs. He was not awake nor asleep, but in a kind of stupor. Ah, that African fever was holding him in its fatal grasp, and shaking him over the grave's mouth. Towards morning, he hiccoughed several times. That fatal hiccough ! Mr. Waddell knew its deadly sound, and sent for the doctor and Mr. Goldie, with a note conveying his deep anxiety on account of the sufferer.

About six A.M. of Thursday (5th), he perspired a little, and was somewhat relieved, responding in a faint voice to the morning salutation, " Good morning, brother," and saying he felt no pain, was quite well, and only weak. The doctor, with Mr. Goldie and Captain Cumming, soon arrived. The sufferer again became insensible. All was done that medical skill could dictate ; but all in vain. Coma supervened, and the patient never revived. " I cried unto God," writes Mr. Waddell, " to whom belong the issues from death, that He would have mercy on him, and raise him up from the gates of death. But God had some better thing in view for him than a return to the labours and trials of this life. Beloved brother, must I lose you so soon, after rejoicing to meet you, and spending with you a few happy weeks? His breathing then became slow and measured, and was accompanied with some noise. I took his pulse in my hand. It beat feebly. He breathed at intervals, gasped, gave two or three slight convulsive efforts,—the ties of life were breaking, his pulse fluttered for a moment, and all was still. Mr. Goldie and I closed his eyes. I kissed the hand I held, and bade him farewell. While we bid you farewell, the Lord God, your Redeemer, welcomes you. Sin and death have done their worst on you, beloved brother ; you are past the reach of their darts now. Angels and the spirits of just men made perfect welcome you home. We sorrow, but not as those who have no hope. He sleeps in Jesus, and will come again with him. May I be a follower of him, as he was of Christ, and of all them who through faith and patience inherit the promises. At six o'clock P.M., on the 5th of August, he expired."

Writes Mr. Newhall : "Many times, during that day, our telescope was pointed towards the mission-house (at Creek Town). The sun went down, but no signal. The clock struck nine, but no messenger, and we retired. About half-past ten o'clock, some one came up the steps leading to the hall door, and knocked. Mr. Edgerly raised his window, and said, 'Who is there?' 'Captain Cumming.'[1] 'Wait a minute, and I will let you in.' He was afraid to ask the news. I did not wish to ask : for the very footsteps seemed to say, 'He whom thou lovest' has fallen asleep. The door was quickly opened. Captain Cumming came in, and faltered forth, 'Mr. Jameson is gone.' The words, which sounded like the notes of a funeral bell, passed from the hall to the side-rooms, and from the side-rooms to the basement, and there was a general burst of sorrow."

When word was sent to King Eyo, his reply was : "I am very sorry to hear that he gone to God, and leave we all. Any place you wish to bury him, you shall have for this town." Next

---

[1] Captain Cumming was the captain of the "Warree." He took out the Mission from this country, and then made the voyage from Old Calabar to Jamaica and back.

morning he came up to the mission-house to offer his help, and proposed to hoist his ensign half-mast high. The ships in the river did the same. The king seemed truly distressed. He did not come, as usual, in state. His umbrella was carried after him, furled. He said he would attend the funeral with the gentlemen.

"I am very sorry we lose him so soon," said he. "I wish he had lived here long time; he would do plenty good to them young boys."

"It is the will of God, King, who knows, and will do what is best."

"That be thing I no saby,—how God take him away so soon, after he send him here long way, for teach we good."

"Well, King, I no saby (know) that myself; some of God's ways are very dark to us. But I know that he does all things well, and must say, Good is the will of the Lord; shall not the Judge of all the earth do right?"

In warm climates, affection must hasten to bury the dead out of its view : so soon does corruption fix its tooth on the forsaken frame. A grave was dug near by, and a coffin was made of Jamaica mahogany. Friends from Duke Town, countrymen from the shipping, and King Eyo with the gentlemen of Creek Town, met to perform the last sad tribute of respect and affection. The body was coffined, and carried into the hall, at four o'clock P.M. on Friday. All gathered round; and Mr. Waddell prayed, and read appropriate passages of Scripture, but broke down when he attempted a short address. Mr. Goldie engaged in prayer. The coffined clay was then carried, in sad and solemn silence, to its peaceful bed. "Ashes to ashes, dust to dust; on the resurrection morning, my brother, we shall meet again." Mr. Edgerly then engaged in prayer; the grave was filled; and King Eyo, unwilling to omit altogether the honours usually given to the dead, in Efik, ordered three cannon shots to be fired as his farewell; and these were answered by the "Majestic," at Duke Town.

Just before he became sick, Mr. Jameson began to write to the brethren in Jamaica, and to the students in the Hall. The

letters were left unfinished ; and the one for Jamaica is supposed to contain the last sentence which he penned : " The
field here is full of interest, and full of hope."   Nearly fifteen
years have elapsed since that sentence was written.   King Eyo
Honesty continued friendly to the mission till he died in 1858.
His two sons were baptized.   The elder, who died in 1861, fell
from his profession, but on his death-bed, he professed great
penitence on account of his sins, and a reliance on the Lord
Jesus Christ.   The younger brother is now in a state of hope-
less idiocy, but up to the time when his mind was thus beclouded,
he showed himself to be serious and sincere.   A good many
natives have been baptized ; and two native churches have been
formed.   Some of those who were received to baptism, have
gone back to heathenism, and others continue steadfast.

All united in testifying their appreciation of the deceased
missionary's worth.

From Dr. Robson's letter of consolation we give the following extracts :—

" It is a sad, sad bereavement—a very great—I had almost
said, an irreparable loss to the mission ; but we dare not say
that.   How much have brothers and sisters lost, in losing such
a brother !   I have been very much impressed with that passage
in the Psalm, in connexion with your dear brother's death :—
' Be still, and know that I am God.   I will be exalted among
the heathen, I will be exalted in the earth.'   This is just one
of the ways in which God will accomplish the great work to
which he had devoted his life—the exalting of His name among
the heathen. . . . With regard to dear William Jameson, we
cannot and dare not sorrow.   With him all is well—the work
achieved—the fight finished—the victory won—the crown conferred !   His works shall follow him. . . . Your brother has
fallen at the post of peril and of glory, and great shall be his
reward in heaven.   The Church mourns, and her harp is on the
willows.   But light will arise in the darkness.   This note imperfectly reflects the state of my heart in reference to the departure of my early, dearly beloved, and incomparable friend.   I
was to open his church in Old Calabar !   Well, that may not

be ; but I hope, through grace, to meet him in that temple where the Great High Priest ministers, and to join him yet in a song of triumph, as we hail the arrival of redeemed sinners from Creek Town and Duke Town ; and who knows but Eyo may yet join us in the anthem ?"

The Board of Missions expressed their sentiments in a minute, in which they recorded the " high estimation in which they held their departed brother, who, both by natural and acquired endowments, and especially by the abundant grace bestowed upon him, was pre-eminently qualified for missionary labours. Possessing a peculiarly warm and affectionate heart, great prudence, deep and fervent piety, and untiring energy and zeal, he lived for his work, and dedicated all his talents to the glorifying of God through the salvation of perishing men."

The Rose Street Missionary Society, who had been identified with him in all his missionary career, gave utterance to their feelings in similar language ; as also the Missionary Society of the students in connexion with the Divinity Hall.

Dr. Somerville, in improving his death in Rose Street Church, thus spoke : — " He was a man who by many attractive excellencies, who, both by natural and acquired endowments, and especially by the abundant grace conferred upon him, was admirably qualified for missionary labour. Possessing a singularly affectionate disposition, and endowed with remarkable humility and disinterestedness, he ever exhibited the gospel as a religion of love, and attached to himself by the strong cords of affection, all that came within his influence. Prudent also in the management of his affairs, peculiarly pious and devoted, much given to the exercise of faith and prayer, he lived for his work, and exerted all his energies to glorify his Divine Master in the salvation of perishing men. His amiable temper, combined with his fidelity, single-heartedness, and untiring zeal, made him not merely successful as a missionary, but most useful as a missionary correspondent. His communications, breathing such a spirit of piety, affection, and spiritual fervour, were often extremely beautiful, very touching, and impressive, and calculated to awaken in those that read them feelings similar to those that glowed in his own fervid bosom."

Mr. Waddell wrote :—" Our brother's universal kindness and affability were calculated to be of great service in correcting prejudice, allaying irritation, and disarming enmity."   Mr. Goldie : " He taught not only by his words of wisdom, but by the holiness of his life ; and won the affections of all with whom he had any intercourse, by his amiable disposition and total forgetfulness of self.   His life was an eminent example of Christian humility."   Mr. Edgerly :—" The eyes of the whole Mission were upon him as our counsellor and friend.   His suasive tact in imparting instruction in the things of God to the unenlightened, I have seldom seen equalled, never excelled."

A wail of sorrow arose in Goshen.   Father Jameson is dead !   Mr. Campbell wrote :—" The mournful intelligence of the universally lamented death of my beloved, and honoured, and now sainted predecessor, was a stunning stroke to us all. You have no idea of the excitement of the people here when the report was circulated, and when it received confirmation. And well, indeed, may they mourn the loss of the prayers of a servant of the Lord, whose equal in devotedness to the work of the Lord, and zeal for the salvation of souls, has been seldom seen in our world."

We fondly hope and earnestly pray that the above record of the life, labours, and death of an earnest missionary, embalmed as he is in the memories and hearts of many who admired and loved him, will not be unacceptable or unprofitable to the Church of God.   " The name of William Jameson is endeared to all our churches—a name that was the symbol of all that is simple in character, lovely in temper, elevated in aim, unwearied in zeal, and enterprising in action.   The sepulchre of this fallen missionary has hallowed the soil of Old Calabar." [1]

May his mantle fall on many of the young men of the churches of Jesus Christ, so that there may be no lack of labourers to go where the Lord calls them, whether to the sultry

[1] Rev. Dr. Eadie, Life of Rev. Wm. Wilson, in "Fathers of the United Presbyterian Church " (p. 130).

and pestilential coast of Guinea, or the central parts of vast Africa; or to the myriad populations farther east. Let no faint-heartedness deprive any one of the honour of having a place in the Lord's army of foreign service. My brother, whose aspirations after this department of the Master's work are apt to be cooled by the fear of hardships, depend upon it that things come easy as you advance; difficulties are not so formidable in the actual contact, as they looked in the prospect; and, like all true-hearted missionaries who ever lived, you will rejoice in the choice which you make, at the call of Heaven, to preach Jesus among the sadly degraded children of heathenism. Seek such a spirit as animated William Jameson; seek to be as devoted, yea, more devoted; as unselfish, yea, more unselfish; as courteous, yea, more courteous, to fellow-labourers; as trustful and zealous, yea, more and more so. Come to the help of the Lord against the mighty. Oh, how constraining a thing is the love of Christ! William Jameson falls in six months. But no one turns coward, and flees from the field. Others descend into the dark mine. Other graves gather around that first one, under the shade of that stately palm. It waves over the dust of Edgerly, one of the first brave band; of Sutherland, whose too short course proved his devotion to the cause; and of two gentle sisters who came but to die,—to pass to glory from the presence of heathenism. And these all, in their home on high, unite with hundreds more whose dust rests in the soil of Ethiopia, in the battle-cry that once fell from the lips of a dying missionary: "Let thousands fall, ere Africa be abandoned." Although these died, yet others have been baptized in their room; and the word of God is still preached to the children of Efik.

We cannot better conclude this Memoir, than by calling the attention of the reader, and especially of missionaries, to two things in which Mr. Jameson excelled.

First, he never allowed any study or pursuit to occupy his time and attention, except what was strictly connected with his work. In this he was like the devoted Judson—the apostle of Burmah. The latter, both from principle and from choice—

impelled at once by a sense of duty, a love for his own special work, and a conviction that the day when one can work is short —would allow the claims neither of literature nor of science to occupy a moment of his precious time. Missionaries are often stigmatized as illiterate and ignorant, if they do not make any contributions to science, by recording phenomena and collecting specimens. Now, this is wrong ; it is unjust. Let science send its own *savans*, as religion sends her missionaries, and as commerce sends her traders. The trader has little time or strength for anything beyond his trade. And how should an earnest missionary have time or strength for anything beyond his high enterprise ? He can admire the works of God around him, and take an intelligent interest in their grander and minuter features ; but his work forbids that he should spend his time and mental or bodily energies in the detailed and special examination which is necessary to make his observations of use to science. We go to preach the gospel to the heathen, and not to serve the interests of commerce, civilisation, or science. The success of our enterprise will benefit these important interests, but our attention must not be distracted by them. It is better to err with a Judson or a Jameson, even in spite of the stigma that may be thoughtlessly put upon us, than be lauded for contributions to the whole circle of the sciences. If missionaries covet distinction in these things, it will be a serious snare to them ; and it is safer to incur even reproach for going to the other extreme. A Judson or a Jameson in heaven, no doubt, rejoices in the grace that enabled him to study that singleness of aim for which he was distinguished ; and those who are now in the work, would do well to follow such examples.

The second thing is Mr. Jameson's firm faith in the success of Christian missions in Africa. His faith rested on what he understood the oracles of God to teach. In these he saw special promises to Ethiopia ; and as he neared the end of his course, his faith seized them with a more vivid realization. His soul thrilled with a scriptural conviction of the certainty of the conversion of Africa. He knew that the seed which he had begun to sow, would be made to yield fruit. He believed that God would regenerate Ham's land,—and that, by means of the gospel of His Son.

Let that church which traces her origin to the stand for God's truth made by two of the ancestors of William Jameson, go on in its career of missionary enterprise. Having put her hand to the plough in the rugged soil of Africa, she can neither halt nor retreat without shame and disaster. Much effort has been expended in Old Calabar. But has there been that effectual fervent prayer which brings the life-giving breath of God upon the slain in the valley of dry bones? The field is full of darkness and full of death. But it is as full of interest and of hope.

> "Our lamps have been quench'd for thy light, Calabar!
> We have sown thee our lives for a harvest in thine ;
> Buried seeds spring to sheaves ; and the night, star by star,
> Hides her train in the dawn, that the day-spring may shine.
>
> We have buried our dead, dear to Christ, in thy land,
> The redemption of Afric believing to see !
> For we bought our Machpelah, a pledge for the land,
> When we laid in thy bosom the first of the three."

EDINBURGH : T. CONSTABLE,
PRINTER TO THE QUEEN, AND TO THE UNIVERSITY.

NEW WORKS AND NEW EDITIONS

PUBLISHED BY

ANDREW ELLIOT, 15, PRINCES STREET, EDINBURGH.

THE SABBATH

VIEWED IN THE LIGHT OF REASON, REVELATION, AND HISTORY;
WITH SKETCHES OF ITS LITERATURE.

By the Rev. James Gilfillan, Stirling.

Crown 8vo, cloth, price 6s.

British and Foreign Evangelical Review.

"This is a work of uncommon excellence; full, judicious, and learned; eminently seasonable, and worthy of the noble subject to which it is devoted. . . . A work rich in multifarious information respecting every aspect and every department of the extensive question of which it treats."

Reformed Presbyterian Magazine.

"This volume belongs to a class too rare in these days of hasty authorship; for no one can open it without discovering that it embodies the fruit of researches and meditations prosecuted during many years. Its value is out of all proportion to its bulk."

Evangelical Repository.

"An earnest vindication of the perpetuity of the Sabbath institution—a subject to which Mr. Gilfillan has evidently consecrated a very large amount of time and energy. His book is brimful of information regarding Sabbatic literature and the history of the Sabbath observance."

British Standard.

"In this work Mr. Gilfillan has done great justice to the arguments for Sabbath observance, and satisfactorily disposed of all possible objections."

Bulwark.

"A perfect treasury of knowledge on the subject of which it treats; and we cannot help saying that it not only places the authority of the Sabbath upon the strongest basis, and illustrates the unspeakable value of that great institution, but proves to what an extent all the battles of spiritual religion and Christian truth have been fought around this old intrenchment of the fourth commandment."

CONSOLATION.

By James W. Alexander, D.D., New York.

Crown 8vo, cloth, price 3s. 6d.

HEART RELIGION:

Or, A LIVING BELIEF IN THE TRUTH.

By Rev. Alexander Leitch,

Author of "Christian Errors Infidel Arguments," "The Unity of the Faith," &c.

In the press, crown 8vo, cloth.

2866 4